Reinventing Pragmatism

Reinventing Pragmatism

American Philosophy at the
End of the Twentieth Century

Joseph Margolis

Cornell University Press

Ithaca and London

First published 2002 by Cornell University Press

Printed in the United States of America

Library of Congress Cataloging-in-Publication Data

Margolis, Joseph, b. 1924
   Reinventing pragmatism : American philosophy at the end of the twentieth century / Joseph Margolis.
      p. cm.
Includes bibliographical references and index.
   ISBN 0-8014-3995-7 (cloth : alk. paper)
   1. Pragmatism.   2. Philosophy, American—20th century.   I. Title.
   B944.P72 M37   2002
   144'.3'0973—dc21

                           2002007457

Cornell University Press strives to use environmentally responsible suppliers and materials to the fullest extent possible in the publishing of its books. Such materials include vegetable-based, low-VOC inks and acid-free papers that are recycled, totally chlorine-free, or partly composed of nonwood fibers. For further information, visit our website at www.cornellpress.cornell.edu

Cloth printing   10 9 8 7 6 5 4 3 2 1

for the new century, for all our best hopes

Contents

Preface

In the last thirty years of the last century, American philosophy came to be focused, unpredictably, beyond any local presumption, on and through a running dispute between two of the best-known contemporary professionals, Hilary Putnam and Richard Rorty. Their quarrel attracted an unprecedented readership, chiefly, I suggest, because everyone who followed their printed disagreements—often seemingly trivial—sensed a deeper contest that spread through the whole of twentieth-century English-language philosophy and, indeed, through a very large part of Western philosophy. The quarrel has not entirely subsided though it is obviously spent and though Putnam and Rorty seem diminished by their exchange: Putnam, by being bested (at least for the time being); Rorty, by a remarkable rise to pop fame, which has obliged all who were drawn to read and listen to judge for themselves what exactly Rorty meant to champion and what the quarrel yielded.

I try in what follows to place that quarrel in the setting in which, as a result of its sheer energy, American pragmatism was snatched from near oblivion, was granted the gift of a second life, and was thereby forced to answer whether the great labor of its "first" life, which spanned the work of Charles Sanders Peirce, William James, and John Dewey, warranted its "second."

The account that follows is largely confined to the story of that second life. I touch from time to time on Dewey's early Idealism and his successful effort to escape those traces that might otherwise adversely color his distinctive realism. It is Dewey's realism, I am persuaded, that informs the best assessment, finally, of what Putnam and Rorty may be said to have accomplished as "pragmatists." But I make no claim to have done justice to the classic figures. I read even Dewey's achievement primarily in terms of the continuing promise of pragmatism even now. And I have certainly not sought to provide a full-bodied account of Dewey's views. That would have taken me in an altogether different direction, one that may well have been difficult to present in a balanced way when so much of what Putnam and Rorty have written have almost nothing to say about Peirce, and what they write about James is on the whole perfunctory. In fact, to have written about Dewey in the detailed way I do about Putnam and Rorty might well have required a very brief treatment of both of them or else a somewhat monotonous comparison. It would have made a very different book.

Both Putnam and Rorty profess to have been much influenced by Dewey, but they have worked in ways opposed to one another and, many would argue, in ways opposed to Dewey himself. It was surely Rorty's dialectical skill and unorthodox analyses that catapulted a minor quarrel that began as a bit of gossip to philosophy's front page. But apart from motives within the American academy (power-mongering, for instance), the quarrel actually does bare the nerve of Western philosophy and raises questions about its honest calling and supposed resources, which, once asked, cannot be ignored. It's said that such questions sometimes make a golden age, and we are hardly "there," of course. But if we could catch a bit of the quarrel's original fire, we might contribute to a silver age. It's not impossible, but it might require a "third" life.

I must, before I begin my tale, thank Raeshon Fils for having once again put a sprawling manuscript into final form—it always comes as a surprise; also, Roger Haydon of Cornell University Press for his very agreeable mix of advice and support; and two unnamed readers for Cornell University Press, whose advice and comments proved to be first-rate.

J.M.

Philadelphia, Pennsylvania
June 2001

Acknowledgments

All of the papers previously published or chapters committed for publication have gone through a number of incarnations. I thank all those who commissioned the originals or agreed to publish them. The prologue, "Reconstruction in Pragmatism," was presented at a meeting of the Society for the Advancement of American Philosophy, Fall 1998, and published in *The Journal of Speculative Philosophy* 13, no. 4 (1999): 221–229; chapter 1 first appeared in German as "Der cartesianische Realismus und die Widergeburt des Pragmatismus," trans. Joachim Schulte, in *Die Renaissance des Pragmatismus,* ed. Mike Sandbothe (Velbrück, 2000); chapter 2, "Richard Rorty: Philosophy by Other Means," appeared in abbreviated form in *Metaphilosophy* 31, no. 5 (2000): 529–546; chapter 3, "Anticipating Dewey's Advantage," was commissioned by William Gavin for a collection *Passing Dewey By?* the publication of which has been delayed; chapter 4, "John Dewey: The Metaphysics of Existence," was presented in the lecture series, "Nature in American Philosophy," School of Philosophy, The Catholic University of America, fall 2000, and is to appear in *Nature in American Philosophy*, ed. Jean De Groot (Catholic University of America Press, 2002).

Reinventing Pragmatism

Prologue: Reconstruction in Pragmatism

I

Pragmatism's history is at the very least improbable. It begins with the immense influence of Charles Sanders Peirce and the instant dissemination of further pragmatist work by William James, John Dewey, possibly Josiah Royce, and, at a remove, George Herbert Mead and F. C. S. Schiller. Now, more distantly, it includes Hilary Putnam, Richard Rorty, and, by various peculiar acquisitions, the later Ludwig Wittgenstein, the pre-*Kehre* Martin Heidegger, the original Ralph Waldo Emerson, W. V. Quine (very marginally), and by dint of sympathy and assertion, Karl-Otto Apel, Jürgen Habermas, and other enthusiastic German philosophers and social theorists.

There could not have been a center to the pragmatist "movement" if there had not been a Peirce; however, Peirce himself was never the recognized center of the movement until it was largely spent, even in the eyes of those who drew (or who said they drew) their original pragmatist inspiration from him. The "center" of pragmatism has proved to be Dewey, and the center perceived very early in Europe (and the United States) was, for a time, James. Even now, at the turn into the new century, Peirce is honored chiefly by the unexplained departures that mark James's alleged usurpation of the pragmatist label for a theory of truth that Peirce found preposterous, as well as Dewey's insouciant eclipse of all of Peirce's painstaking alternatives to Kantian transcendental reason. It is more than plausible to say that both Peirce and Dewey are undoubted pragmatists. But it is exceedingly difficult to give a rounded account that commits them both (or James) to congruent doctrines or inquiries.

Only recently, in fact, did a knowledgeable commentator, Morris Dickstein, neatly twit the misleading impression of the "revival" of pragmatism while introducing the papers of a 1995 conference on the cultural impact of that revival: "If pragmatism began with James's strong misreading of Peirce," Dickstein declares, "it came to life again with Rorty's strong misreading of Dewey, whom [Rorty] described as 'a postmodernist before his time.'"[1] In the same collection, Stanley Cavell reflects on the need for a more disciplined resistance against the cannibalizing idea that "Emerson is to be understood as a protopragmatist and Wittgenstein as, let us say, a neopragmatist."[2]

I find a definite undercurrent of conceptual embarrassment in this hearty "revival," which I think confirms the important fact that pragmatism never had a single doctrinal or even methodological center. It had an undisputed source of great originality and power (Peirce), which it largely ignored save for the pieties of acknowledging a thin (but definite) debt and an even thinner inspiration. It was its diverse and diversely centered originality, the obligatory recovery of Peirce as an ancestral voice (more cited than fathomed), and the remarkable influence and popularity of James and Dewey—first James, then Dewey—in their seemingly radical social, political, and educational views, that explain the initial *frisson* of promise in the recent "revival."

There is, one must admit, a bit of self-advertisement that has started the ball rolling. But there is also a validity in its buccaneering spirit, which is to say, the plausible promotion of an American label for a second hegemonic spurt of a philosophical (*cum* moral/political) energy bent on coming to grips with the issues of our time and inclined to feature recent themes of analytic (and postmodern) thinking.

Pragmatism could not have taken hold again in its original terms. All the dearest themes would have been more than difficult to revive. Peirce could not have shared the muscular transformative energies Dewey and James proclaimed: if theirs is the paradigm, then Peirce surely held a suspect view, one in which human inquiry served a more distant and mysterious, even alien, *telos;* and if Dewey's social and liberal values must be paramount, then we have surely waited too long to revive even Dewey's philosophical charms.

No. The revival proceeds by a canny effort to redefine its force—promotionally, let us say—in a way that more than matches the innocent but still concocted collection of the original pragmatists. For the original label did mean "American" primarily, in the way of a first innovation of Eurocentric aspirations possessing all sorts of heterogeneous parts. That cannot be what is now meant by pragmatism's revival, though it is true that the energies fueling its redefinition are very much "American" and reckless in the American way.

Had not Rorty and Putnam identified themselves as pragmatists *in* the process of reviewing and disputing the professional prospects of realism, relativism, knowledge under the condition of history, public and private responsibility and values, no one would have envisaged a "revival." It *is* a genuine revival for all that, and it is succeeding largely because of that single contingency. Putnam and Rorty literally tell us how to read the pragmatists in order to count themselves as their closest progeny. Without their guidance, the connection might have been as unlikely as Cavell suggests it is with Emerson and Wittgenstein.

The curious thing is that once it was applied, even where it was reasonably disputed, the pragmatist epithet stuck and drew its crowds of enthusiasts *pro* and *con*. It's the brute fact that counts, not any of the languid glosses of the academy. For good or bad—I'd say for good—pragmatism is now engaged in a number of important quarrels that it had never addressed in its original incarnation, but that, with a little ingenuity, can be plausibly reconciled with the older history.

The important point remains: the resolution of the now-principled quarrel—which I tag "the contest between pragmatism and naturalizing," in effect, the turf contested between Putnam and Rorty (Rorty, partly as a spokesman for Donald Davidson)—should not be pursued "archivally," as if the texts of the early pragmatists might decide the newer questions, for that simply cannot be. The game before us is a new one, whatever its *geistlich* or conceptual connection with pragmatism's past. What, finally, Rorty has made possible is the industry of redefining pragmatism again and again— which, in the United States, has become the operative incantation for flagging the important philosophical contests of our day. In the absence of that small device, the revival would have collapsed without a murmur.

Putnam and Rorty are bound to fade, and are fading as I write! They have nearly completed their assumed tasks. They have, eccentrically, brought to our attention—in the context of discussing an army of analytic and continental voices—the single most important philosophical issue at the end of the twentieth century, namely, the conceptual adequacy or inadequacy of analytic "naturalism," which is to say, the various policies and doctrines that have evolved from Quinean and Davidsonian "naturalizing."[3] In this sense, naturalism is the trimmed-down successor of all the grander analytic movements of the twentieth century—now more than a feasible contender despite its obvious taste for remarkably spare conceptual resources, made strong in part by the lucky confluence of the exhaustion of European philosophy and the sheer animal vigor of the American academy.

Putnam and Rorty are, I believe, unable to fashion a viable thesis within the arena they have effectively defined: Putnam, because he has spent all his philosophical powder on a series of failed and increasingly inexplicit forms of realism; Rorty, because his postmodernist and naturalist allegiances are incapable of being reconciled or even separately strengthened without either project damaging its twin. His own enthusiasts tend to be straightforward epistemologists (even if they are not standard naturalizers). They are certainly not postmodernists, though the reversal is hardly remarked by anyone but Rorty himself.[4]

Furthermore, each has invented his own fatal weakness: Putnam, by adhering to a would-be *Grenzbegriff* (limit-concept) under conditions of change and abandonment of privilege that simply disallow *any* robust form of realism of the gauge he favors;[5] Rorty, because his naturalism is no more than a transient form of loyalty to Davidson's executive dicta, and because his postmodern advocacy of ethnocentric solidarity precludes legitimation and cannot ("in principle") be reconciled with naturalism.[6]

Nevertheless, Putnam and Rorty contrive a better gift: first, by clarifying the lesson of their explicit opposition on a grand run of topics that promise to collect the best energies of our age; second, by abiding by their opposed interpretations of the "revived" pragmatism they share; third, by discovering, through their accumulating disputes (together with all those who have read along with them), that their local contests have somehow isolated the overarching question that informs their own best questions—and ours. *At least for the time being!*

The benefit is pure serendipity. The hegemony of analytic practice has been blunted by its own perceived deficiencies, and its late colonizing temperament has forced us to reconsider new ways of joining the better forces of Anglo-American and continental European thought. The intuitive appeal of a revival of pragmatism has always been subliminally colored by the wish to restore a full philosophical dialogue in the Eurocentric world. That seems now to be dawning, partly as a result of certain extreme efforts among analytic philosophers to distance their conceptual resources from continental contamination. We are, it seems, on the edge of a new perception.

The original pragmatist themes have pretty well run their course, and the intentions of the new pragmatists must be respected for what they are. The classic pragmatists plainly harbored doctrines that were deficient, defective, misleading, banal, equivocal, contradictory, and downright false. It is impossible to mention a single defining thesis that any of the original group championed that the others would have been automatically prepared to adopt as a sign of membership. Peirce could not have abided James's theory of truth and very probably would not have understood Dewey's notion of a "problematic situation." James could hardly have reconciled his irrealist and realist tendencies or, for that matter, his more than occasional attraction to subjective representationalism while opposing any principled disjunction between the subjective and the objective. Dewey would have found the Schellingian and Emersonian (idealist) overtones of Peirce's evolutionary "agapasm" incomprehensible in transactional terms—or at least something to avoid like the plague. And none of the other pragmatists, not even Dewey, was prepared to adjust evolutionism (or empirical evolution) along the potentially radical historicizing lines that Mead very tentatively began to explore.[7]

Imagine treating Peirce and Dewey as bosom logicians of the same stripe, or Peirce and James as companion semioticians, or Dewey and James as social and political meliorists of the same activist sort, or Mead and Peirce as puzzling over the social nature of the self in the same psychological terms. No, the linkages are far more attenuated, hospitable perhaps to a common program they never explicitly shared in their near-hundred years of loose family connections, possibly in the way of a "philosophical temperament" (to pirate Putnam's felicitous term,[8] a term offered for another occasion, for a doctrinal contrast that might actually assist us now in identifying what to count as a unifying force for our own time).

It may be the absence of any single explicit philosophical creed that is responsible for pragmatism's fresh prospects and palpable energy. Certainly, one does not have the sense of anything like the failed verificationism of the positivists or the cunning rearguard maneuvers of the transcendentalizing Kantians. Yet, if pragmatism were no more than an inchoate promise, it would by now have settled into the dead sediment of philosophy's past. But it resists its own demise. The strong programs that now command the field (apart from pragmatism) are clearly bent on co-opting pragmatism and may, for that reason, invite a deep correction of the other. If so, then pragmatism may be able to afford more than a genteel rereading of its original texts. That seems in fact to be the case: the opportunistic prod for a revival that would otherwise be no more than arbitrary.

II

As I say, the principal philosophical contest of our day could not possibly exclude the implicit struggle between pragmatism and naturalism (that is, naturalizing). There are perceptible tensions between the two that qualify the impression of a gerrymandered opportunity. Still, one is likely to protest: "But pragmatism is already a naturalism." Of course it is, but not of the "right sort"!

The story is not altogether obvious, partly because the recent upsurge of interest in pragmatism has largely featured the liberal-democratic themes Dewey himself favored, which, however worthwhile, distract us from the decisive issues, and partly because the leading American naturalists of the day (the "naturalizers," in the sense of Quine's important paper "Epistemology

Naturalized"[9]), either already admit their affinity for pragmatism (as Quine does, lightly) or are said to be pragmatists at heart. Rorty even says this of Davidson and himself, though Davidson is hardly keen to be so characterized. For instance, Davidson is unconditionally opposed to pragmatist views of truth and meaning.[10]

The simple truth is that what we understand by "naturalism" changes drastically when we move from the early pragmatists to the very different discipline practiced by Quine, Davidson, and Rorty. The transformation is absolutely fundamental to the history and future of American philosophy, so much so that "naturalizing" in Quine's and Davidson's sense (which are also different from one another) is demonstrably incompatible with the pragmatism of the classic figures. The truth is that the naturalism of the early pragmatists was philosophically innocent, never coupled in any strenuous way with tendentious claims of the sort the recent naturalizers prefer. It is for that reason exactly that the revival of pragmatism draws its energy from the other's philosophical imperialism.

Rorty's role in all this is a busy one. In one sustained stroke, he must (and does) abet Davidson's naturalism; challenge conventional philosophy (including pragmatism) by way of postmodernist doubts about legitimation; reduce pragmatism to postmodernism; and then convey the gymnastic impression that the naturalizers have properly inherited the pragmatist mantle! Rorty achieves all this in his very smooth way,[11] but all of it is doubtful; and, despite the best intentions, the would-be demonstration goes some distance toward identifying what *is* the true thread of philosophical pragmatism and why, at the end of the century, it must confront naturalism irreconcilably. Beyond the local narrative, the contest is a metonym for the deepest disputes of the Eurocentric tradition. That is hardly a negligible part of its appeal.

The difference between the two naturalisms depends on this: among the original pragmatists, naturalism is little more than a refusal to admit nonnatural or supernatural resources in the descriptive or explanatory discourse of any truth-bearing kind. In that sense, naturalism is a conceptual scruple that pragmatism shares with all sorts of heterogeneous doctrines: positivism and Marxism for instance. But naturalism in the now fashionable sense of "naturalizing" is a very carefully contrived philosophical program that supersedes pragmatism's original scruple and advocates certain disputatious and exclusionary doctrines that the other could never accept.

Nearly all naturalists (that is, naturalizers) support the following doctrines: (1) truth-bearing explanation is ultimately causal; (2) causal explanation is constrained by the "causal closure of the physical";[12] (3) all description, analysis, and explanation of mental and cultural phenomena are paraphrasable in accord with doctrines (1)–(2) if admissible at all, or else they conform with some version of supervenientism, that is, with the notion that there cannot be a determinate change at the mental (or cultural) level without a corresponding change at the physical level;[13] and (4) pertinent inquiries, claims, and explanations that fail to meet the conditions of doctrines (1)–(3)—notably, epistemological "explanations"—are senseless or philosophically illegitimate.

Here you begin to glimpse how Rorty combines naturalism and postmodernism and how he supposes his own thesis may be drawn from Dewey and Wittgenstein.[14] But if so, then you surely see how the adherents of a dampened Kantianism or Hegelianism or phenomenology or Marxism or Foucauldianism might consider uniting American and European forces in resisting the new hegemony of Anglo-American "naturalizing." The idea is not impossible, but it is still too inchoate to be directly pursued. It is hard to imagine Dewey and Foucault, for instance, converging in any unforced way, or Dewey converging with Heidegger, for that matter (though Rorty suggests that Heidegger is a pragmatist of sorts).[15]

On the tally given, pragmatism and naturalism are simply irreconcilable, no matter what Rorty says. The counter-doctrine might propose instead that the real world was *"natural" but never "naturalizable."* There you have the dawning sense of the most important and strategic doctrine the classic pragmatists implicitly supported but never had occasion to insist on. The reason may be no more than that the reductionisms and physicalisms and eliminativisms that now populate our landscape were hardly in control of the philosophical field when Peirce, James, and Dewey first shaped their principal contributions. "Natural but not naturalizable" may yet prove to be the best short statement of pragmatism's late discovery of itself. In a fair sense, that is what Putnam and Rorty disputed—and what the entire Eurocentric world has, in modern times, always debated.

The irony is that the spread of naturalizing in English-language analytic philosophy—in metaphysics, epistemology, the philosophy of mind,[16] as well as in the colonizing doctrine the naturalists are bent on exporting to a market not altogether aware of the conclusions and loyalties it means to exact—has now obliged the reviving pragmatists to discipline their own philosophical commitment in a more precise way than ever they cared to do or could have done. Too much, however, is now risked by a continuing nostalgia. So that those who are drawn to the pragmatists' themes—pragmatists or not—owe a considerable debt to the new naturalists: for they would never have recognized themselves if they had not perceived what they now realize they must oppose.

If you scan the well-known overviews of the pragmatist movement, whether early or late, you will hardly find any explicit mention of the contest between pragmatism and naturalizing within the span of twentieth-century American philosophy. I take that to mean that the contest did not impress itself on the original pragmatists at the time of their most inventive work, because (as remarked) the turn toward what is now called naturalizing had not yet congealed in the salient way it has and because pragmatism's promise, *beyond* its original novelty, could never have been reclaimed from a past that did not know the turn that might be needed.

The best, the most usual, the most reasonable reading of pragmatism in the classic sense—as you are bound to find by scanning such unequal accounts as those offered by Charles Morris, Israel Scheffler, John Smith, H. S. Thayer, R. W. Sleeper, Carl Hausman, Murray Murphey, Gerald Meyers, John P. Murphy, and H. O. Mounce[17]—converges on the perceived import of Peirce's various formulations of the so-called "pragmatic maxim," for instance:

> that a conception can have no logical effect or import differing from
> that of a second conception except, so far as, taken in connection
> with other conceptions and intentions, it might conceivably modify
> our practical conduct differently from that second conception.[18]

But, as is well known, quite apart from the technical difficulties Peirce came to see would have to be resolved (for instance, to avoid verificationism and the confusion between the theory of meaning and the theory of truth, or to escape the paradoxes of subjunctive conditionals), this precise formula is peculiarly prone to the effect of something like a Gresham's law of conceptual clarity: the formula has surely dwindled in our time, or given way to something like American solidarity or a respect for the democratic ethos. I spare you the textual evidence bearing on the last option and urge you only to consider if that is what pragmatism comes to philosophically, it is already dead from the neck up.

In any case, recalling the maxim can be nothing but the barest beginning of a recovery, for pragmatism's true center of gravity lies rather in the dialectical contest with naturalizing. (It is worth remarking, however, that Peirce's maxim appears to be distinctly incompatible with Quine's "indeterminacy of translation" thesis—reading both doctrines in broadly behavioral ways. The opposition counts as another piece of evidence of pragmatism's heterogeneity.) Also, of course, Peirce's actual formula is no more than the barest hint of a pragmatist analysis of what Peirce calls a conception—which would have to be more than a semantics. Peirce veered off increasingly in the direction of an infinitely extended inquiry that threatened to be no longer "pragmatist" (for that reason) or particularly concerned with the "here and now" of the original account.

We may, if we wish, treat pragmatism in a bifurcated way, featuring the "idealist" tendencies in Peirce or featuring Dewey's tendency to focus rather on the management of the actual circumstances of life here and now. But the latter theme, which inevitably all but eliminated the vestiges of Dewey's own early induction into the views of the German and British Idealists, now provides the minimal sense of the entire movement. Certainly, Peirce's "long run" is a pragmatist invention that disallows any fixed *telos* or truth or rightness or any reliable invariances in the encountered world; but it is increasingly made to collect the best energies (and aspirations) of human societies in *what cannot be secured here and now;* and that, as we now understand these matters, is either not pragmatism at all or else an alternative utterly irreconcilable with it. That is, in fact, precisely what is meant finally by treating Peirce as a (displaced) German Idealist who glimpses the work of a larger Mind in nature, where Dewey is viewed as a pragmatist shedding as completely and as quickly as he can all vestiges of an early Idealist indoctrination.

Here you begin to fathom the extraordinary "cunning" of philosophical history, for the opportunism of redefining pragmatism beyond its original intuitions regarding the nature of meaning (which, after all, were understandably eclipsed with the collapse of the livelier prospects of positivism, and which, in an odd way, almost vindicated James's misreading of Peirce) has actually prepared the ground for a proper recovery of the deeper unifying "temperament" of the original pragmatists, who were unable to foresee the full strength of their own unity. Their themes rightly centered on their opposition to what is common to Cartesian and Kantian (transcendental) strategies, which, as it happens, is quite similar to what they would have discovered in the naturalizing ventures they would have found impossible to endorse.

So it is that the local quarrels between Putnam and Rorty have, by an unlikely route, quickened pragmatism's "recovery" by putting before us (and its would-be champions) a proper *agon,* a contest of greater importance than they could possibly have guessed. For the pragmatists rightly saw themselves as the beneficiaries of the post-Kantian tradition; and the confrontation the new naturalism has introduced palpably ignores (or dismisses) the work of the entire pragmatist movement, in the return of the naturalizers to what (from a pragmatist perspective) can only count as the impoverished resources of the pre-Kantian age.

Pragmatism is nearly the only English language movement that did not, early in the twentieth century (for instance, under the direction of Bertrand Russell and G. E. Moore), turn against the post-Kantians. Still, to say that the pragmatists did not dismiss the work of the post-Kantians is not to say that they *were* post-Kantians. Peirce may perhaps be fairly treated as a post-Kantian somehow transplanted to America. But Dewey, who favors Hegelian themes, may have more in common with the British Idealists than the post-Kantian German Idealists (apart from Hegel). The fact is that when Russell repudiated the Hegelians, he had the British Idealists more in mind than Hegel.[19] Dewey's own effort was primarily directed toward exorcising any vestige of "Absolute Mind" in his own doctrine, whether of German or British pedigree.

The intent and perceived import of Peirce's maxim, particularly when viewed as common ground between Peirce and Dewey, pretty well comes to the following (though that is not clear from the maxim itself): (1) the rejection of Cartesian and Kantian intuitionism, apodicticity, transcendentalism, and necessitarianism; (2) the social embeddedness of beliefs, perceptions, and judgments in a continuum of similar elements and, hence, their contingent and benignly holist interdependence; (3) the methodological and practical linkage between thought and action, along with the effective determination of meaning and the assessment of truth in terms of distinctions (consequences) grounded in shared experience; and (4) the entirely open-ended, constructive, socially determined process of judging what to count as knowledge and intelligence. In a word, the maxim is a sketch of a meta-philosophical orientation regarding the philosophical analysis of inquiry and not an approximation of any sort to a criterion of meaning (or, bearing James in mind, of truth). That is precisely why the divergence between Peirce and Dewey is so significant.

I cannot deny that my having featured these four themes tends to favor Dewey over Peirce and James: against Peirce, against the former's unfinished synechism (theory of continuity) and teleologism; against James, against the latter's insistence on nativist or necessary truths.[20] I see nothing wrong, however, in constructing an idealized conception of such an obviously heterogeneous movement as pragmatism, provided that we acknowledge that it is a deliberate construction and that we justify it by what we find in it that appears to be philosophically defensible and serves the maxim in whatever disputes are bound to prevail in the twenty-first century.

The fact is—it is a little startling if you think about it—the maxim I've cited makes no mention of the problem of the relationship between the short run and the long run that bedeviled Peirce's version of fallibilism. (Peirce favored the "here and now" in his earliest formulation of pragmatism. In this sense, he favored the "short run." But when he speaks of the correction of belief for the sake of truth, he applies fallibilism to the "long run." Dewey and nearly all later pragmatists confine fallibilism to the short run, even though Peirce had put his finger on an unresolved puzzle.) But it is Peirce's, not Dewey's, version that I've cited, which suggests (I believe) a proper basis for going beyond both Peirce and Dewey, for seizing the new themes Rorty and Putnam put before us, and for going beyond them as well in terms of the "natural but not naturalizable." In any case, read this way, the maxim suggests the sense in which Peirce anticipates James (and Dewey) and the sense in which pragmatism need not be thought to have rejected Peirce's strong intuitions in yielding in Dewey's direction.

Nevertheless, on any reading of Peirce's various formulations of his maxim, the emphasis on grasping what a speaker means is grounded (in however informal a way) in the conceived consequences of what he pertinently believes here and now. That is the central force of Peirce's well-known objection to the abstractness of Descartes's "clear and distinct ideas." It is precisely the perception of that insistence that gives James's "misreading" of Peirce its importance in the history of pragmatism; and it is precisely Peirce's veering off beyond the "here and now" that, retrospectively, signifies his departure from pragmatism's main tendency. To endorse the judgment is more of a decision than a finding—but there are no simple findings here.

Whatever must be abandoned or reconsidered of the older corpus we may as well give up with a good grace: Dewey's reading of his *Logic* for instance, which is hopeless, although the original project was surely more than merely interesting (in a sense akin to Hegel's view of logic); Peirce's synechism, which now seems like a longing to imitate and improve on Kant (despite his opposing Kant's *a priori* necessities); James's blunders (early and late) about the pragmatist conception of truth, as well as the separation of his pragmatism from his radical empiricism (which James himself conceded was justified).

None of this is really essential to the principal thrust of pragmatism as that must now be viewed in the new century: that is, after the intervening history of all the contending currents that took form during the rise of pragmatism or, even more significantly, after it had crested. That is why I make so much of pragmatism's quarrel with naturalizing. The maxim is not entirely useless, but it is too slack; even more important, what it could be made to mean, what it perhaps does mean in a prescient way, cannot be recovered from the effects of the present debasement of its philosophical currency. To claim to see a genuinely promising way of recovering its original force is, I think, all that can be meant by anticipating or endorsing pragmatism's revival against the new naturalizing.

There can be no serious point to a revival that does not take into account the half century of vigorous dispute that has, on any reading, eclipsed its older energies. The newer quarrels are now bound to spell out the promise of the original movement. Put another way: to "revive" pragmatism within the terms of nothing more recent than whatever Dewey wrote in his best moments is to confirm pragmatism's demise, though I have the greatest regard for Dewey's achievement; by contrast, to go beyond Dewey, to address the entire force of the analytic tradition that is best defined by Quine's responses to Rudolf Carnap and Gottlob Frege is to make room for the intervening serendipity of Putnam's and Rorty's quarrels.

III

I have a suggestion (which I have more than hinted at) regarding how a reclaimed pragmatism should conceive its altered project, and I offer a small legitimating narrative to go with it. I cannot tell you what the boundaries of Peirce's maxim should be: I think it hardly matters, so long as our options oppose the tally favoring naturalizing and accord with the second tally offered in the maxim's name. But I do claim that there is a decisive minimal reading of the maxim's import that Peirce touches on (not always perspicuously), which the pragmatists never really pursued—until perhaps Putnam's skirmishes with Rorty.

The key is still the rejection of Cartesianism, which, of course, is more than Descartes's own philosophy. But you must bear in mind that Western philosophy, though it has indeed decisively solved Descartes's problem—I mean the problem posed by Descartes's realism, which, as the history spanning Kant and Hegel confirms, very few rightly grasp—entails the solution to Descartes's dualism as well. The rejection of Cartesianism points to a double irony. For, first of all, all the classic pragmatists were explicitly focused on the defeat of Descartes's impossible realism (on epistemological grounds) and were aware (however unequally) that this defeat entailed the repudiation of Descartes's dualism (or at least the representationalism Descartes and Locke shared). In this way, they recovered in their own idiom the adequate solution buried in Hegel's verbal excesses. But the lesson has never been so completely mastered that the Cartesian specter no longer haunts us. The lesson is almost embarrassingly simple: *if* we speak of the objective world as "absolutely" independent of our inquiries, then we must reject any realism that treats our epistemic competence *in relational terms* (cognizing subject to cognized object). To argue otherwise is to court Cartesian paradoxes in insoluble ways. That is indeed Hegel's lesson (already Fichte's), and that is what Dewey never abandoned in his interminable opposition to all sorts of dualism.

Hence—and this is the second irony—we are now just after the turn into the new century still as busy battling Cartesianism as ever, from the middle of the seventeenth century to the beginning of the nineteenth. I do not mean this in a contrived way. The import of the divergence between the two forms of naturalism is simply that, when properly deciphered, the naturalizers' version *is* an attenuated way of restoring Cartesianism itself. That is the point. Furthermore, by one of those marvels of intellectual history, these same connections are all but acknowledged—in their breach—in Hilary Putnam's latest epiphany, his John Dewey Lectures, where he writes as a self-confessed pragmatist at the end of the century against the Cartesianism he now finds in his own philosophical bosom, which he had for years been fighting in others and thought he had successfully exorcised in himself.

You may treat Cartesianism as a term of art. (I return to it more pointedly in the next chapter: in particular, to its meaning in our own time.) But, on any serious reading, you can hardly deny that the essential philosophical questions that arise from the first appearance of Descartes's principal tracts persist to the very end of the twentieth century. We are evidently still trapped by the two unavoidable paradoxes Descartes has bequeathed us: one, that of his realism, requires a radical disjunction between cognizing subjects and cognized world and pretends to reclaim an objective and neutral grasp of the way the world is apart from our inquiries, a world uncontaminated by the doubtful beliefs and appearances that occupy us in the process; the other, that of the conditions for resolving the first puzzle, *if* we are epistemically confined to inner thoughts and perceptions, even if we suppose them to represent (somehow) the independent world.

Now, certainly, the pragmatists—Peirce and Dewey, preeminently—are the beneficiaries of the solutions first adequately formulated by Hegel (in the *Phenomenology*). For his part, Putnam, who plainly regards himself as a pragmatist and is indeed a pragmatist (attracted in different ways to Peirce, Dewey, and James) confesses that he had unwittingly bought into Cartesian representationalism, though it violated an important lesson he had already gained. It may even be that Putnam was in part seduced by James's flirtation with Lockean representationalism, though James of course officially opposed the idea and Putnam now dissociates himself from James's lapse.[21]

In any case, Putnam rejects his own well-known doctrine of "internal realism"—in the John Dewey Lectures—by which he means to repudiate at least the idea (offered in *Reason, Truth and History*) of construing reality as "mind dependent," a notion he objects to in James, together with the Lockean theme of representationalism, which he somehow joins to internal realism. Here, Putnam relies on John McDowell's escape from Cartesianism as formulated in the latter's John Locke Lectures, which, indeed, offsets the double Cartesianism (the two Cartesian paradoxes) just sketched. But McDowell succeeds only in formal terms, that is, without any explicit account of the conditions of objective knowledge or the conceptual linkage between knowledge and reality.[22]

Pragmatism cannot fail to be suspicious of such a gain: it goes against the spirit of the original maxim. And Putnam has surely given up too much— more at least than he could rightly afford or defend—*if* indeed he means to maintain a pragmatist calling. In any event, once matters are put this way, it is plain enough that the entire quarrel between Putnam and Rorty revolves around the "Cartesian" question. Putnam's defense proves to be untenable; but Rorty's dismissal goes arbitrarily beyond any reasonable application of the conceptual evidence. Pragmatism, of course, is then seen to be revived and defended by a pair of defective maneuvers!

It's not true that Putnam's repudiating representationalism requires *in any way* repudiating his denial of a principled disjunction between the subjective and the objective. The original denial ("internalism"—which is best read as an epithet for accepting the post-Kantian lesson) does not implicate, *ontically*, the mind-dependence of the real world. That is a misreading, which puts Putnam at odds with the pragmatists he so much admires. ("Hegelian idealism," we may say, is *not* an idealism at all, if "idealism" signifies that the natural world is "mind-dependent" in the ontic sense.)

The denial of a principled disjunction between the subjective and the objective is, of course, the most memorable claim in Putnam's Paul Carus Lectures, which Putnam links pretty clearly to the pragmatists' "insistence on the supremacy of the agent point of view."[23] There would be little reason to trot out all these details if they were merely local features of James's and Putnam's idiosyncratic views. But they are much more than that: they are the compelling (and neglected) clues for understanding (*now*) the soundness and sanity of the pragmatists' original program (properly drawn from Peirce and Dewey at least) *and* the effective advantage of pitting the pragmatists against the naturalizers—preeminently, Quine, Davidson, and even Rorty. Although they are all nominally opposed to Cartesianism, you cannot find a compelling explanation (or defense) of just how Putnam, Rorty, Davidson, and McDowell mean to turn the trick. (That is hard to believe.)

In any event, Putnam's newly minted denial of his earlier denial of the subject/object disjunction (if that is indeed what he now denies) risks his joining forces with the Cartesian realists he opposes—hence, also, the naturalizers, whom he tries, quite impossibly, to enlist as pragmatists. You must remember that the pragmatists can make common cause with the post-Kantian "Idealists" and other movements that cleave to the post-Kantian achievement only if they oppose the naturalists and only if doing so has nothing to do with adopting "idealism" as that is ordinarily understood. In short, to oppose idealism (both subjective idealism and post-Kantian Idealism) while remaining committed to the epistemological lesson Kant and Hegel share, we have only to distinguish between ontic and epistemic questions (without allowing them to be separated) and to hold that the inseparability of the subjective and the objective applies to the epistemic and not to the ontic aspects of realism. Inevitably, that changes what we should mean by "realism"—it cannot any longer be Cartesian realism; it must take a constructivist form. But that is what all post-Hegelian realisms must affirm.

Putnam affirms that it would be a "mistake" to suppose that the question "'Which are the real objects [that constitute the world?'—in choosing between alternative 'metaphysics' answering to different interests]" is "a question that makes sense *independently of our choice of concepts.*" Furthermore, no sooner does he say this, than he tries to enlist Davidson, Goodman, and Quine among the friends of "the great pragmatists," though they draw back on that account. Putnam urges that they be less reticent and discounts the evidence that Davidson and Quine are naturalizers, which is to say, effectively, Cartesian realists (though of a very much dampened kind); he goes on to ask: "What can giving up the spectator view in philosophy mean [Dewey's familiar diatribe,[24] which he himself supports in advocating 'internal realism'] if we don't extend the pragmatic approach to the most indispensable 'versions' of ourselves and our world that we possess?"[25]

You may glean here how the contest between the pragmatists and the latest naturalists should be construed. For, of course, Davidson and Quine are cleverly disguised Cartesians (Cartesian realists, that is), though you might not know it. The argument is worth a closer look. (I remind you again that the meaning of "Cartesianism" will depend to some extent on the discussion of the chapter that follows.) But you must bear in mind that Putnam explicitly makes the realist question hostage to our conceptual options—to what, as we shall see, Rorty rejects as extraneous "*tertia*," what, thus far at least, agrees with Cartesianism and naturalizing.

I single out Putnam's views, as well as his philosophical difficulties, because Putnam is the end-of-century pragmatist who has most valiantly attempted to reconcile something close to the pragmatist maxim and a direct engagement with the naturalizers' programmatic turn. I concede that Putnam has blundered not only in linking the rejection of representationalism to rejecting the denial of a principled disjunction between the subjective and the objective, but also in supposing that the original denial entails the "mind-dependence" of the real world. I note also that the naturalizers are committed to opposing that denial and to construing it as tantamount to the idealism they themselves abhor. That is Cartesianism pure and simple, but it is also a non sequitur. It is, indeed, what Quine, Davidson, and Rorty expressly affirm (in their different ways): they all oppose Putnam, and he opposes all of them. *We* are the beneficiaries, because, in reviewing their implicit quarrel, we are led to see what, dialectically, is the only way pragmatism could proceed if it were to recover the force of its original orientation.

Putnam and Rorty are obviously aware of the quickening contest. They are its principal abettors. In fact, in his remarkable "Pragmatism, Davidson and Truth," Rorty explains the sense in which he conflates naturalizing and his own brand of postmodernism—and produces thereby a new "pragmatism." The union hardly succeeds, and it is not really argued for. Furthermore, neither Davidson nor Putnam nor Quine (who is also mentioned) would be willing to characterize his own view in Rorty's way: Davidson and Putnam have in fact publicly distanced themselves from Rorty's resumés. But that's hardly the point of featuring Rorty's maneuver. It's rather that, in noting the way in which the naturalizers turn the pragmatist program against itself, we learn how to redirect pragmatism's best intuitions against the naturalizers—and why. That's not what Rorty wishes to encourage and not what Putnam manages to salvage. But it's the principal lesson of recent Anglo-American philosophy, nevertheless.

I offer two remarks from Rorty's paper that betray the Cartesian and antipragmatist spirit of Davidson's naturalism (a fortiori, Rorty's naturalism). In Rorty's hands, they lead us to conclude that Putnam's internal realism actually violates the *pragmatism* Rorty finds in Davidson's naturalism! The reversal is a gymnastic wonder.

The essay begins this way: "Davidson has said [Rorty reports] that his theory of truth 'provides no entities with which to compare sentences', and thus is a 'correspondence' theory only in 'an unassuming sense.'" Rorty finds the doctrine "reminiscent of pragmatism, a movement which has special-

ized [as he says] in debunking dualisms and in dissolving traditional problems created by these dualisms. The close affiliations of Davidson's work to
Quine's and of Quine's to Dewey's make it tempting to see Davidson as be-
longing to the American pragmatist tradition."[26] This is one of the clever-
est reversals of the facts that I can recall in the recent philosophical literature.
I take my hat off to it. Rorty pays no attention to Davidson's own "dualism"
between semantics and epistemology (in *his* [Davidson's] theory of truth)
or between either (or both) of these and metaphysics (as in his supposed realism).

More to the point, Rorty focuses on the meaning of Davidson's "slogan"
(Rorty's term), "correspondence without confrontation," which, by invoking Davidson's well-known attack on the "dualism of scheme and content,"
leads (on Davidson's view) to defeating "the idea that something like 'mind'
or 'language' can bear some relation such as 'fitting' or 'organizing' to the
world."[27] We are shown a little later that Rorty's paper is directed in good
part against Putnam: it queries a relational tertium quid (something Locke
might have offered) that might be supposed to play an explanatory role in
epistemic contexts.[28]

So we are alerted to a certain collection of facts: (1) Rorty and Davidson
oppose, as naturalizers, Putnam's internal realism (which Putnam repudiates in his John Dewey Lectures), though it had originally seemed to be a
bona fide instance of Deweyan anti-dualism; Putnam's "mistake" is now
made to support Davidson's and Rorty's own dampened Cartesian realism
(that is, "correspondence without confrontation"). (2) The naturalizers move
to entrench the formal idiom of correspondence (without ontic or epistemic
encumbrance) as a natural extension of pragmatism itself, although Davidson correctly believes that pragmatism *is* committed to truth's playing an
explanatory role, possibly even in a proto-positivist sense.[29] And (3) the naturalizers take it as evident that to treat the theory of truth as explanatory *is*
to affirm an indissoluble ontic and epistemic relationship between cognizers and cognized, subjects and objects (hence, to risk affirming idealism):
thus, on a pragmatist reading, mind or language does indeed "organize" the
world in some constituting ("idealist") way.

Arguments of the third sort are specifically directed against Peirce and
James and (more tactfully) Quine and Michael Dummett and, more pointedly, Putnam. Here, now, is the second remark I wished to cite from Rorty's
paper, which very neatly brings the entire contest into full view:

> If truth itself is to be an explanation of something, that explanan-
> dum must be of something which can be caused by truth, but not

caused by the content of true beliefs. The function of the *tertia* which Davidson wishes to banish was precisely to provide a mechanism outside the causal order of the physical world, a mechanism which could have or lack a quasi-causal property with which one might identify truth.[30]

It is for this reason that Rorty draws attention to Putnam's insistence that truth *does* have an *explanatory* function (which we apparently fix by fixing the "assertibility conditions" under which true beliefs prove true).[31] For, of course, *if* truth has an explanatory function—or, better, if our accepting claims and statements as true on the basis of supporting evidence signifies that there must be *some* epistemological explanation of that policy—then there must also be *non-causal* (or, non-naturalizable causal) explanations (intentional explanations, say) included in our account of the way the world is and the way our knowledge of the world is said to fit the world. And if that is so, then naturalizing must be false and could never be tantamount to pragmatism; and pragmatism itself would be rightly committed to insisting on the indissoluble relationship between the epistemic and the ontic—or, between subjects and objects—though not (or not necessarily) in the idealist's way. In any case, *if* truth is a realist construction proposed in accord with one or another meta-philosophical policy, then it is clear that "truth" must have an explanatory function, without needing to reclaim any form of privilege; and if that is so, then Rorty has simply misread the lesson of the history of epistemology—preeminently, Hegel's and Dewey's contribution.

IV

I support the finding and, supporting it, see a strong directive for a strengthened pragmatism. I am not suggesting that we follow Putnam in any of his passing phases: say, in his Cartesian phase as a unity of science theorist or as an internal realist or as a "natural realist" (as he now calls himself, following McDowell's lead).[32] Putnam has hardly settled on a viable realism of his own. But there is no question that, during his internal-realist period, he had his finger on the essential contest.

Bear with me. I have brought the quarrel between Putnam and Davidson and/or Rorty to bear on whether, with regard to the defense of realism, we require "*tertia*" (or interpretive intermediaries) or do not. Effectively, Putnam had said yes in his internal-realist phase, but he has now repudiated his answer. Therefore, though he does not agree with Davidson or Rorty, he appears to have conceded their essential charge: the charge that the admission of a constitutive relationship between mind and language and world (often labeled "idealism," sometimes "anti-realism," but always such as to require a theory of truth in the explanatory mode) *is* fatally flawed at the point of admitting *tertia*. If you consider how far Putnam has retreated and how much he has put at risk, you see that his treatment of truth in terms of "assertibility conditions" (his pragmatism) now hangs in the balance.

Let me clarify matters a little in a terminological way. When Rorty rejects *tertia* (in his own name and Davidson's), he rejects subjective representations ("ideas," in Locke's sense), at least those mediating between cognizing minds and cognized world. But *that* has nothing to do with whether objective knowledge implicates one or another conceptual interpretation of the epistemic relationship between mind and world. (Putnam has championed both doctrines as if they were one and the same.) "*Tertia*" may also be invoked in the second sense, which is to say, as an inseparable (or, perhaps better, *adverbially* qualifying) "third" affecting the epistemic relationship between mind and world, but not the world we posit as independent of our inquiries.

Put more simply, *tertia* may be no more than the conceptual perspective and vantage of interest from which we identify and describe the world: it being the case that we can change our vantage but cannot escape speaking from one perspective or another. In a related sense, the view that *truth* is an unanalyzable surd is itself a corollary of a correspondentist reading of realism (a version of Cartesianism), that is, the mark of a successful correspondence that cannot be expressed by means of any determinate or standard concepts. For, if "truth" is a critical artifact, it cannot be a surd. Conversely, if truth is a surd (as Davidson insists), then it can only implicate an assured form of "direct" realism that need never be legitimated.[33] If, then, correspondentism is repudiated, if the need for interpretive intermediaries is acknowledged, then causal and legitimative questions cannot be conflated and cannot fail to be joined in epistemic contexts, and "truth" itself cannot fail to have an explanatory role. Which is precisely what James and Dewey concluded. But if so, then the naturalizing stance favored by Davidson and Rorty cannot rightly be tagged as a pragmatist position, unless Humpty-Dumpty was right after all. If Davidson and Rorty reject correspondentism in the epistemically operative sense, then how can they convincingly fall back to treating truth as epistemically unanalyzable? There's a paradox here that seems to be insuperable. (Their saying what they do hardly makes it true.)

As a Jamesian pragmatist, Putnam had originally claimed that

"Truth," in an internalist view, is some sort of (idealized) rational acceptability—some sort of ideal coherence of our beliefs with each other and with our experiences as those experiences *are themselves represented in our belief systems*—and *not* correspondence with mind-independent or discourse-independent 'states of affairs'. There is [he affirms] no God's Eye point of view that we can know or usefully imagine. There are only the various points of view of actual persons reflecting various interests and purposes that their descriptions and theories subserve.[34]

The commitment is still essential; but, now, Putnam can offer no suitable defense. Truth is not a correspondentist surd: Putnam means to escape Cartesianism. It marks, rather, the indissoluble link between mind and world that "makes" objective knowledge possible. How, the question nags, can Putnam ensure *that* role from the side of belief alone? Putnam fails us here. But Dewey does not.

Pragmatists, as the inheritors of the post-Kantian resolution of the Cartesian problem, cannot now fail to hold to something like an "internalist" view of truth (that is, by construing truth in terms of the epistemic assignment of truth-values); and Putnam, for his part, hardly tells us how to replace it in his new-found "natural realism." He had, as we have seen, judged himself to be an unwitting Cartesian or Lockean representationalist; and he has now decided (if, indeed, that is what he has decided) to repudiate (by a complete non sequitur, as it turns out) the denial of a principled demarcation between the subjective and the objective. Doing that, he has undercut his own pragmatism and (ironically) retreated to a deeper Cartesianism, or at least risked doing so. To put the point obliquely: to insist on the indissolubility of the subjective and objective aspects of the cognitive process is an entirely different matter from that of the ontic dependence of the world on some sort of constituting mind: the first is the great epistemological discovery of the post-Kantian tradition (Hegel, preeminently); the second is an expression of its attraction to some sort of panpsychism (Schelling, paradigmatically).

I venture to say that any pragmatist solution will concede: (1) conceptual "intermediaries" that are *not* relationally defined, as they are in representationalism, but only as conceptual or *adverbial* qualifications of our cognizing powers; (2) the continued rejection of a principled demarcation between the "subjective" and the "objective"; and (3) second-order epistemological explanations or legitimations that are not expressible in (that is, not restricted to) causal terms. A standard way of putting the point (against the naturalizers) simply says that legitimation requires normative resources and that such resources cannot be equated with whatever is merely causal. (That is exactly McDowell's reminder in *Mind and World*. He's right, of course, but more is needed.)

There's the pivot of the emerging contest, because Davidson and Rorty willingly deny that truth has any explanatory role. Davidson concedes a semantic role, but then severs semantics from epistemology, which no "Hegelian" would willingly support. On the argument Davidson and Rorty offer, if truth had such a role, it would have to be a legitimating role that could not be naturalized; as a result, *they* imply, they would themselves be rightly accused of being Cartesians of the worst kind: "There are no relations of 'being made true,' which hold between beliefs and the world."[35] If that proved true, then *tertia* would be easily precluded. The fact remains— it is perfectly obvious—that we can save the idea of epistemological explanation that is not restricted to the causal and yet is not relational either (in the representationalist's sense). Davidson and Rorty have simply overlooked a perfectly plausible option: *tertia* need not be independent third "things" at all ("ideas," say); they may be no more than interpretive qualifications of our doxastic powers (our capacity to form beliefs) relative to the realist standing of our truth-claims. But that is constructivism.

Davidson concedes a role for evidence, so he is not a postmodernist in Rorty's sense; but he opposes Quine's verificationism for the same reason he opposes Putnam's internal realism: it leads, he says, to "skepticism"—"for clearly a person's sensory stimulations could be just as they are and yet the world outside very different. (Remember the brain in the vat [he adds, that is, Putnam's thought-experiment].)"[36] Davidson rests his entire case on a coherence theory of *beliefs*—*not* truth—which can be explained causally and consistently through affirming that "most of the beliefs in a total set of beliefs are true."[37] Hence, coherence functions as a "test" of truth, without requiring a theory of truth of the offending sort (an epistemological tertium quid of Putnam's or Quine's sort). You may complain fairly enough that that provides no secure ground for supposing that *this* belief or the *next* is actually true: the argument looks like an instance of the fallacy of division, or a confusion between truth and abductive inference (that is, inference to the best explanation).[38] And so it is.

But, more to the point, if, as Quine has obliquely noted (against Davidson), you grant the historical drift and transformation of our beliefs over time—preeminently, our science (without yet invoking Thomas Kuhn, as Davidson might suppose we would)—then Davidson's rejoinder must be seriously defective.[39] If it is, then the pragmatist option (an option akin to Putnam's internalism, spared the latter's crudities) strikes the mind as having been wrongly dismissed. (First-order evidence without second-order epistemology is blind.) Notice, also, that Quine's naturalizing—but not Davidson's—tolerates interpretive (adverbial) "thirds" (not Rortyean *tertia*).

You now have before you the scattered pieces of an argument that can completely reclaim the soundness of the pragmatist undertaking, that is, a fresh strategy dialectically pitted against the dominant naturalizing stance of analytic philosophy that (in Rorty's eyes) believes itself to have strengthened the original pragmatist cause. It remains to put the pieces in place.

I suggest that any reasonable solution will entail the following consistent triad: (1) the physical world is independent of mind, language, inquiry, and subjectivity; (2) whatever determinate entities belong in the ontic sense to the world according to (1) are *not,* or not for that reason, also epistemically independent of mind, language, inquiry, or subjectivity; and (3) metaphysics (or semantics) and epistemology are indissolubly linked, so that inquiries in the one implicate inquiries in the other. Pragmatism has always subscribed to something like this triad; naturalizing cannot and will not; and postmodernism pretends that philosophies that embrace (3) are not worth taking seriously.

This "new" solution, which the pragmatists share with the post-Kantians, disallows a dualism of subjects and objects, a dualism of the subjective and the objective, hence also a dualism between realism and idealism. But if that is so, then Putnam went much too far in rejecting his internal realism when he rejected his representationalism; and Davidson and Rorty go too far in construing arguments akin to the triad just mentioned as entailing the mind-dependent constitution of the independent world or the "relational" treatment of *tertia.* What this leads to, rather, is this: that there can be no viable realism that is not also a *constructivism;* that realism's ontic sense can never be detailed except by way of an indissoluble epistemic encumbrance; and that constructivism is not, or need not be, tantamount to idealism. Dialectically, its deeper implication is that what Davidson concedes by the formula "correspondence without confrontation" already implicates what has just been said in support of a constructive realism. (There is no escape.)

Constructivism means at the very least that questions of knowledge, objectivity, truth, confirmation, and legitimation are constructed in accord with our interpretive conceptual schemes—the interpretive qualification of the indissoluble relationship between cognizer and cognized; and that, though we do not construct the actual world, what we posit (constructively) *as* the independent world *is epistemically dependent* on our mediating conceptual schemes. It is but a step from there to historicizing the entire practice. Here is the clue that links pragmatism and the Hegelian vision.

This captures all that can be relevantly salvaged from Kant's solution of Descartes's problem, which is precisely what the post-Kantians and the pragmatists correctly inferred. It is also what (we may now suppose) twenty-first-century philosophies will finally acknowledge. There's more that can be said about pragmatism's prospects: for example, about the theme of history. But any such recovery would presuppose the effective and final defeat of Cartesian realism. The fact is, we are still struggling with the Cartesian project.

Cartesian Realism and the Revival of Pragmatism

I

Richard Rorty is widely credited with having revived pragmatism's sagging fortunes. And so he has. But it is hardly clear whether what Rorty has revived, beginning with *Consequences of Pragmatism* (1982), *is* indeed the recovery of pragmatism proper. Certainly, he has earned the pragmatist badge through the sheer exuberance, drive, and inventive continuity that he has forged between his own views and that of the classic pragmatists; but the connection seems to owe as much to a kind of squatter's rights and the skillful use of the *obiter dictum* as to any compelling fresh version of a pragmatist argument or canon. Think, for instance, of Rorty's mistaken disjunction between the public and the private, offered as genuinely Deweyan,[1] or Rorty's deliberate deformation of Dewey in Heidegger's direction and Heidegger in Dewey's,[2] or, possibly even more puzzling, the flat-out reversal of the intent of William James's original theory of truth.

Rorty says straight out in the introduction to *Consequences of Pragmatism* that "the essays in this book are attempts to draw consequences from a pragmatist theory about truth. This theory says that truth is not the sort of thing one should expect to have a philosophically interesting theory about."[3] Informed readers will protest: "Whatever you make of the misunderstanding between James and Peirce, James surely believed his theory of truth *was* the most important conceptual plank in the whole of pragmatism." One may also react to that reaction: "Well, Rorty never meant to dismiss James's theory, he hardly thought it was pointless or misguided; he meant rather to salvage its essential lesson!" But if you say that, you must ask yourself whether Rorty's theory about theories of truth, especially James's, *is* sufficiently like James's theory to count as an extension of it—hence, as an extension of pragmatism—or is no more than a clever subversion of James's doctrine. And then we'd be off to the races.

My own sense is that without Rorty's wide-ranging discussion of the classic pragmatists, Dewey chiefly, there would never have been a revival to speak of. After all, pragmatism was moribund by the end of the 1940s. Even so, the sense in which pragmatism has gained a second life may depend more on the free-wheeling dispute that arose between Rorty and Hilary Putnam that began in the 1970s before the publication of *Consequences,* than to any particular thesis of Rorty's. The energy of those running debates effectively defined the significance of the American revival—or, better, defined pragmatism's reinvention, which is now neither Rorty's nor Putnam's creation. Questions about what pragmatism now means cannot possibly be answered in textual terms, but neither are those questions pointless. Both Rorty and Putnam, I concede, exhibit pragmatist loyalties of a sort, but neither can be said to have recovered the force of any particular tenet favored by the original pragmatists.

Rorty and Putnam rather nicely feature (between them) a number of the essential quarrels of our time, which they designate (not altogether plausibly) as a debate about the nerve of pragmatism itself. They also define an opportunistic space in which additional options opposing their own contest and their own opposed doctrines suggest themselves and invite comparisons with pragmatism's past. In any case, the pragmatist revival is the invention of a substantially new confrontation drawn from the saliencies of our own time that claim a measure of congruity with pragmatism's original "spirit"—not, however, by adhering closely to any explicit pragmatist doctrine or program.

To see this is to see how little we may care to invest in terminological quarrels. But it would be a blunder to ignore altogether the question of what now to count as the essential pragmatist issue. There's a great deal of power compressed in controlling the name and, as a consequence, a great deal of influence in affecting the perceived validity of opposing arguments. The trick is to find a strategy that can command a measure of attention collected at an unlikely point of entry that might force an honest reckoning. I suggest that we begin with Rorty's account of his own attempt to present Donald Davidson's theory of truth in a fair light, his candid report about Davidson's opposing his own summary view, and his interpretation of what Davidson's rebuff signifies. I doubt you will find a more perspicuous way of entering the heart of late American philosophy or late pragmatism.

The fact is that James's theory of truth, primitive and flawed though James's handling of the concept was, is of the greatest importance in defining the distinction of classic pragmatism. Rorty's deliberate reversal in Davidson's favor must count as one of the most bold-faced misrepresentations of the plain facts as any that Rorty has foisted onto the profession. One cannot really say that Rorty is mistaken in his reading, since he would not have put the idea forward if he did not intend to disorganize thereby the entire conventional reading of the classic movement as a condition for advancing his own rather daring (and impossible) equivalence between Davidson's naturalizing and his own postmodernism. The picture is complicated indeed. But the recovery of pragmatism "proper" cannot but rest on two extraordinary intuitions, neither of which was ever presented by their originators in an acceptably developed form: the first is surely Peirce's intuition about the meaning of a concept, and the second is James's intuition about the meaning of "truth." In fact, merely to insist on these two constraints—though neither Peirce nor James would ever have accepted them in the sense the other required—would instantly block a good deal of the conceptual confusion Rorty has deliberately spawned as to what we should understand by the revival of pragmatism. It would also be fair to say that Davidson was both annoyed and (philosophically) nonplussed by Rorty's reading of his own opposition to James and Putnam.

Here is part of what Rorty says about Davidson:

> In an article on Donald Davidson [Rorty's "Pragmatism, Davidson and Truth"[4]], I suggested that we interpret Davidson both as a sort of pragmatist and as a sort of minimalist—as someone who, like James, thought that there was less to say about truth than philosophers had believed [in effect, that both were "deflationists" about truth]. . . . I interpreted Davidson as saying that the word "true" has no explanatory use, but merely a disquotational use, a commending use, and what I called a "cautionary" use. . . . In an article of 1990,[5] Davidson partially repudiated my interpretation. [Davidson] said [he was] neither a deflationist nor a disquotationalist. . . . [He] concluded that "[t]he concept of truth has essential connections with the concepts of belief and meaning, but these connections are untouched by Tarski's work,"[6]

which, if it comprised "all of truth's essential features," would be deflationist.

Davidson does indeed insist, contrary to what Rorty says, that truth has a distinct but dependent role in explanation. It's also true, as Rorty correctly reports, that Davidson's theory of the explanation of true belief remains thoroughly causal. The details need not concern us for the time being.[7] But *that* hardly justifies Rorty's concluding that "what Davidson adds to Tarski, when he displays the connections between the concept of truth and those of meaning and belief, has nothing whatever to do with the question of whether, or how, we can tell when a belief is true."[8] (This was meant to vindicate Rorty's saying that Davidson has only "partially repudiated" his interpretation.)

All Davidson actually says is this: that, regarding "certain familiar attempts to characterize truth," "[w]e should not say that truth is correspondence, coherence, warranted assertibility, ideally justified assertibility, what is accepted in the conversation of the right people, what science will end up maintaining, what explains the convergence on single theories in science, or the sources of our ordinary beliefs. To the extent that realism or anti-realism depend[s] on one or another of these views of truth we should [Davidson concludes] refuse to endorse either."[9] Very few would disagree with Davidson's judgment here, but it hardly entails truth's not having any explanatory power (if that is what Davidson means) or not having any conceptual bearing on explanations of the standing of cognitive claims (which is what Rorty means).

Roughly, then, what Davidson really has in mind is that truth read in the correspondentist sense (or in any more attenuated sense that approaches the correspondentist intent) is and must be a surd, that (in that sense) truth never plays a criterial or legitimating role of any kind. To insist that it does would be to endorse "Cartesianism."

Davidson would have been right to oppose James's theory *if* James had been a correspondentist in advancing his own conception. But that is precisely what James was not doing. The way to correct the impression is as follows: merely read James's pragmatist formula as operative within the terms of a constructivism or constructive realism (as explained in the prologue). There is then no reason to deny truth an explanatory role affecting the standing of belief and truth-claim: we need only avoid all epistemic or criterial traffic with correspondentism! Nothing could be simpler.

In fact, Davidson himself *uses* a "correspondence" formula when speaking of truth, but he does not mean it in the correspondent*ist* sense. No more does James. But James does believe that *we* decide what to count as true relative to our interests and involvement with (what we take to be) the way the world is. Hence, when James speaks of truth being "made," he is not (in his best moments) speaking criterially. He is explaining the way in which the constructivist treatment of "true" answers to pragmatism's metaphilosophical orientation regarding truth and reality. In that sense, James cannot avoid ascribing an explanatory role to truth. If you grant that much, then both Davidson's and Rorty's arguments collapse at a stroke. But all that has nothing to do with the nonsense of affirming that figures like Frege, Sellars, Dummett, Davidson, and Heidegger are all pragmatists "in some important sense."[10]

Certainly, it does not bear on James's distinctive claim (unless to reject it) or on what might be made of Davidson's claim read in James's way (which, of course, would violate Davidson's purely causal reading). Even Tarski's account, which Davidson claims to espouse, has more than merely "semantic" force: it's plainly committed to a strong extensionalism *wherever it applies*— hence, it applies in epistemic rather than merely causal terms. Or, wherever Davidson actually invokes Tarski's model without relying on Tarski's own extensional analysis preparatory to truth-value assignment, the appropriation comes to little more than a vacuous version of the correspondence doctrine Davidson opposes. Tarski, of course, made a point of acknowledging the recalcitrance of natural-language sentences vis-à-vis the fruitful application of his conditions of analysis: that cannot be confined to an exercise in formal semantics alone; it is already implicitly epistemological in import.[11] Also, when Davidson adopts Tarski's account as an incomplete first step in providing an analysis of "true," he loses the extensional force of Tarski's "definition" of "true" because he takes "true" to be indefinable, to be a surd.[12] But, of course, that puts the connection between the "pragmatist" side of Davidson's account of truth and Tarski's strongly extensionalist account at insuperable risk. There is nothing left to salvage.

As far as I can see—as far as Davidson succeeds in defending his view— we ought not support any of the doctrines mentioned *if* they are thought to function criterially or in some cognitive or evidentiary way apt for justifying (and therefore explaining) why this or that belief about the ("independent") world is true. Davidson says nothing against the legitimacy of explaining why we *take* this or that belief to be true (on, say, a causal theory of belief and meaning and the conditions for assigning "true" and "false" in cognitive contexts): he "merely" opposes building an indubitably realist or anti-realist force into the ordinary use of "true." I say (again) that Davidson means to oppose what, in accord with his own view, is untenable in Cartesianism and skepticism; but he does so from a vantage that is still palpably Cartesian. (You may rely, here, on your intuitions about "Cartesian" as a term of art. I shall return to define it more explicitly shortly. It is meant as a convenience and an economy and a constant reminder of a compressed history spanning nearly four hundred years.)

On the substantive issue, this is what Davidson intends: we can, by way of the causal theory of belief, explain why we treat particular beliefs as true. But doing that has no legitimative force. I am not convinced that a causal theory of truth could ever work; it would always require an epistemic standing that it could never capture. But certainly it goes beyond what Rorty reports Davidson as holding. Hence, when Rorty suggests that *we* should treat Davidson as a "pragmatist"—in the same way in which he (Rorty) treats James as a pragmatist—he gets both of them wildly wrong. I draw your attention to the improbable fact that, in recent writings, Rorty simply announces the following: "As I shall be using the term 'pragmatism', the paradigmatic pragmatists are John Dewey and Donald Davidson."[13] Dewey, of course, shared (in fact, improved) the main theme of James's theory of truth. There is no other explicit thread in Davidson's account of realism that could support Rorty's attribution, except his opposition to any criterial recovery of Cartesianism. But that would hardly distinguish Davidson from an army of philosophers who would not qualify as pragmatists.

If, intending to avoid any cognitivist reading of correspondentism and representationalism, James had offered his own pragmatist theory of truth to replace such views, he would still have intended to advance his theory in an explanatory way; but, if so, then anyone—Rorty, say—who offered an account of "true" in which truth had no explanatory function at all would have drastically distorted what we should rightly understand to be a revivified pragmatism. For, surely, if Rorty ever lost Davidson's support, he would have no grounds at all for insisting that "true" had no explanatory role to play—or for claiming that he himself was improving pragmatism's lot! At the very least, Rorty would have to explain the conceptual link between belief, meaning, and truth (which, of course, Davidson undertakes to do); whereas Rorty, speaking as a postmodernist, simply holds that there is nothing there to know.

In fact, nothing would remain of James's pragmatism if it were denied that James had advanced a theory of truth that was meant to identify the key considerations in virtue of which beliefs are judged to be true. The fact that James was an innocent in his attempt (in *Pragmatism*) to give suitable form to his intuitions about truth is neither here nor there. What *is* extraordinary is that James should have hit on a fundamental element in pragmatism's theory of inquiry that was plainly within Peirce's grasp, which simply eluded Peirce (the better theorist) because of the latter's more ambitious (post-Kantian) vision. But Rorty cannot dismantle James's theory without dismissing James's standing as a pragmatist or without explaining how his doing so affects his analysis of Dewey. He fails to address these concerns.

What Rorty says in summarizing Davidson is also murky: he equates pragmatism with "naturalism" and construes both in a very thin postmodernist (or "postphilosophical") way. But Davidson is unwilling to tag along, and it's a fair question to ask whether pragmatism can, or should, be viewed as hospitable to the naturalist's claim. I think it should not, as I have argued in the preceding section. At times, the benefits of redefining pragmatism are stretched beyond all plausibility. The principal point of the quarrel about truth is this: to admit the vacuity of the correspondentist account of truth and the unacceptable paradox of the Cartesian account is to grasp how we are driven to a constructivist form of realism if we favor realism at all; to adopt such a view is to require an account of truth that explains (in the normative sense) why particular claims and beliefs are rightly counted as true; to agree to that is to eclipse any merely causal theory of belief, which cannot (causally) distinguish between true and false beliefs; but to admit all that is to defeat naturalizing hands down. Davidson is caught by his unwillingness to treat truth in completely deflationary terms: he is aware that, in resisting Rorty's helping hand, he risks the defeat of his own naturalized reading of realism. But there is no escape.

II

This odd piece of gossip, then, *is* philosophically worthwhile. It defines the most strategic question confronting American philosophy at the end of the twentieth century, hence also the best prospects for a redefinition of pragmatism, if it is to proceed along the lines Rorty favors: the question, namely, of what should we understand by the compatibility or incompatibility of pragmatism and naturalizing—and, further afield, between pragmatism or naturalism and Rorty's brand of postmodernism? As it turns out, the larger question is more than a local matter; rightly interpreted, it is the American version of the most pointed question that now confronts the whole of Western philosophy. The quarrel between Rorty and Putnam is, then, another tribute to the cunning of Reason.

There is a single reference to Rorty in Putnam's influential little book, *Reason, Truth and History,* which appeared a year before Rorty's *Consequences of Pragmatism* and which defined Putnam's "internal realism," now abandoned or put at risk in a way that is not yet entirely legible,[14] an "internal realism" that was, in effect, Putnam's candidate for adjusting pragmatism so that it might meet the most up-to-date puzzles of analytic philosophy. Putnam fastened very pointedly on what he took to be what was risked in the way of pragmatism, realism, analytic philosophy, philosophy in general, as a result of Rorty's postmodernism (which Putnam read as a form of relativism, hence as incoherent).

In the last two paragraphs of *Reason,* Putnam emphasizes that answers to questions about "a more rational *conception* of rationality or a better *conception* of morality" (or even a better *conception* of truth) cannot proceed solipsistically, that such questions invite us instead "to engage in a truly human dialogue; one which combines collectivity with individual responsibility."[15] This may strike you as rather vague. I read it as indicating the sense in which both Putnam and Rorty favor very thin forms of the Hegelian theme that appears in Dewey and James and the later Wittgenstein; also, I read it as anticipating Putnam's acknowledged sympathy for Jürgen Habermas's "dialogic" theme.[16] What the remark is meant to capture—it is the theme of the book's last chapter—is the "entanglement" of questions of objective fact and objective value that lie at the heart of Putnam's pragmatism, in particular, his opposition to absolutism and Cartesianism, his attack on relativism,[17] and, of course, his resistance against naturalizing.

The deeper significance of this vagueness comes out in the final paragraph of the book, which Rorty picked up very promptly and which, as I say, defines the contest between their two interpretations of pragmatism and realism—defines the very revival of pragmatism. Here is what Putnam says:

> Is there a *true* conception of rationality, a *true* morality [or only a "dialogue," as Rorty says]? . . . But how does the assertion that "there is only the dialogue" differ from a self-refuting relativism . . . ? The very fact that we speak of our different conceptions as different conceptions of *rationality* posits a *Grenzbegriff*, a limit-concept of the ideal truth.[18]

This cannot be right and cannot even be defended on the grounds Putnam provides. It was entirely reasonable for Rorty to challenge Putnam's remark about his own remark ("only the dialogue") and Putnam's preoccupation with his would-be *Grenzbegriff*. "I would suggest," Rorty says, "that Putnam here, at the end of the day, slides back into the scientism he rightly condemns in others." "[W]hat is such a posit supposed to do, except to say that from God's point of view the human race is heading in the right direction?"[19] It is hard to make the case that if this kind of objection counts against Putnam, Davidson could possibly be less vulnerable. What is the philosophical rationale for holding that "most of the beliefs in a coherent total set of beliefs are true." It *cannot* be a purely causal argument. In fact, by pressing his causal argument (his naturalizing), Davidson simply confuses a second-order argument meant to displace Cartesian certainty and Cartesian skepticism with a merely first-order empirical argument to the effect that "most of our beliefs . . . are true." (That is a mistake Davidson nowhere repairs.)[20]

You see, of course, how these questions implicate Davidson's rebuff of

Rorty's postmodernism, also the warning's application to Putnam. For Davidson's resistance on the matter of truth entails the verdict that anything like a "limit-concept" would instantly generate Cartesian skepticism (a remark Putnam found puzzling).[21] Putnam and Rorty's running quarrel has become the very paradigm of the evolving effort to redefine pragmatism as well as the evidence that both Putnam and Rorty must fail. It has in fact become a sign of the need for a more plausible reading of pragmatism's recovery.

The story runs as follows. Putnam believes that the loss of the *Grenzbegriff* of truth (or rationality), which would have followed from Rorty's postmodernism ("only the dialogue"), leads directly to an incoherent relativism. Rorty believes that insisting on the *Grenzbegriff* constitutes a form of scientism (or Cartesianism), which Putnam himself had rightly inveighed against. Putnam's objection does, indeed, betray his conflicting views and is ultimately self-defeating (as Rorty realized): "That rationality is defined by an ideal computer program [Putnam muses] is a scientistic theory inspired by the exact sciences; that it is simply defined by the local cultural norms is a scientific theory inspired by anthropology."[22] The first option answers to the extremes of positivism; the second, to the extremes of relativism. Yet, though he means to escape between these two horns, Putnam provides no third option accessible from his vantage. In fact, the only possible option would *require giving up all Grenzbegriffe and adopting a constructive realism instead* (which, I remind you, need not entail, as Davidson wrongly supposed, an unacceptable idealism). In any case, we cannot make sense of a regulative *Grenzbegriff* that has epistemic force that is not also constitutive of knowledge.

We must remind ourselves that Putnam's insistence on his *Grenzbegriff*, whether with respect to science or morality, is palpably out of step with Dewey's characteristic emphasis. *Reason, Truth and History*, which many think is Putnam's most important book-length argument, was never quite a pragmatist manifesto, though Putnam drew his accumulating output more and more in the pragmatist direction very shortly after the book's appearance. It represents, therefore, a divided allegiance from the very start: one essential theme presses in the direction of "internalism," which could never countenance a *Grenzbegriff*, though Putnam insists on one; the other presses in the direction of "externalist" constraints of objectivity (which mean to avoid Cartesianism) by way of internalist resources, which (in terms of the latter) could never be sufficient to the task. Putnam is spread-eagled, therefore, between his older loyalty to Carnap (his scientism) and his newer loyalty to Dewey (his pragmatism). Rorty saw at once that Putnam's *Grenzbegriff* could not but be an externalist intrusion in an internalist account. Ultimately, Putnam fails in both regards—and, in failing, fails to escape the relativist stigma he means to attach to Rorty.

I cannot be certain of Putnam's train of thought. But I would be willing to bet that, after judging Habermas's "pragmatized" version of Karl-Otto Apel's *Grenzbegriff* to be congenial (in rational ethics) and reasonably in accord with the fact/value "entanglement," Putnam was strengthened in his belief that there *should* be a pragmatized *Grenzbegriff* for truth, as well. That is hardly an argument,[23] but it does explain Putnam's having been strongly attracted to James. In fact, pragmatism could not possibly claim to have found a *Grenzbegriff* in practical *or* theoretical reasoning. It would oppose *Grenzbegriffe* in either context: consider Peirce! Apel and Habermas simply fail to grasp the point.[24] Davidson seems to have believed that both Rorty's thesis about truth *and* Putnam's thesis about his *Grenzbegriff* would lead inexorably to skepticism: Rorty's, because it gives up important parts of fundamental philosophy; Putnam's, because it falls back into Cartesianism. Davidson has a point; though, for his part, Putnam is aware that Davidson slights the need to answer the epistemological question that realism poses.

I am not familiar with any sustained analysis of Davidson's version of realism from Putnam's point of view, except for brief remarks like those that appear in Putnam's *Pragmatism* (or what may be inferred from what McDowell offers[25]). But what Davidson says of his own position seems congruent with what Putnam says or might have said of it: "My form of realism [Davidson says] seems to be neither Hilary Putnam's internal realism nor his metaphysical realism. It is not internal realism because internal realism makes truth relative to a scheme, and this is an idea I do not think is intelligible. . . . But my realism is certainly not Putnam's metaphysical realism, for *it* is characterized by being 'radically non-epistemic', which implies that all our best researched and established thoughts and theories may be false."[26]

If I understand this correctly, then Putnam's objection to Davidson (which I must reconstruct from scattered remarks) would go this way: (1) that, although Davidson's realism has "epistemic" import, it lacks an "epistemological" rationale by which to legitimate true beliefs; and (2) that Davidson's adherence to causal explanation entails his failure to admit anything like a *Grenzbegriff* and, as a result, his failure to obviate relativism or (for that matter) arbitrariness. I think thesis (1) is justified but not (2), because Davidson and Rorty are right in thinking that Putnam's maneuver commits him to "Cartesianism" (hence, to skepticism). But if that is so, then the *only* way to secure a realism without paradox must be by means of a frank constructivism (a constructive realism), which of course neither Davidson nor Rorty would countenance.

There are a number of vexing difficulties Putnam raises against Davidson's realism. For one, the causal theory of belief, which, holistically, favors coherentist criteria of reliable belief, cannot help us with the determinate causes of particular true beliefs. (Think, for instance, of analogues of paranoid coherence.) Second, if holism is to be parsed as if by "an omniscient interpreter," then the legitimative problem will return with a vengeance and will require a Cartesian resolution, which Davidson means to avoid. (Think of Putnam's *Grenzbegriff!*) Finally, Putnam adds: "But the real worry is that *sentences cannot be true or false of an external reality if there are no justificatory connections between things we say in language and any aspects of that reality whatsoever.*"[27] All three objections are compelling—and the third is surely a *reductio.* Davidson is a Cartesian, *malgré lui.* The semantics of "true" is inseparable from epistemology.

The upshot of the entire exchange confirms that none of our three discussants—two who are self-styled pragmatists and one who is not a pragmatist at all—could possibly secure his own best doctrines against the objections of one or the other of the other two. Davidson clearly signals that Rorty probably misrepresents both James and Dewey (who is close to James on the matter of truth) and that neither James nor Dewey gets the matter right.[28] Putnam retreats to internal realism to overcome the threat of Cartesian realism but is forced back to Cartesianism by way of his *Grenzbegriff.* Rorty abandons "objectivity" for "ethnocentric solidarity," believing he can secure as much of commonsense realism (and of Davidsonian naturalism) as he wants; but he ends up with an arbitrary and vacant postmodernism. And Davidson finds that, to avoid the untenable options of Cartesianism that keep surfacing at every turn, he must himself abandon the pretense of having secured a defensible realism.[29] Behind the scenes the Jamesian advantage beckons. Pragmatism may yet gain its second inning.

III

Theorists like Davidson are too much wedded to the notion of an objective science that knows the "mind-independent" world more or less directly. They therefore repudiate in advance all alleged interpretive *tertia,* the supposed intervention of conceptual schemes between ourselves and the world, relative to which (they fear) realism might be legitimated at too high a price. They themselves pay a price for relying on the supposedly higher rigors of "naturalism," which Rorty promptly equates with pragmatism (and post-modernism).[30]

Davidson's formula seems straightforward: "Since we can't swear inter-mediaries to truthfulness, we should [he says] allow no intermediaries be-tween our beliefs and their objects in the world. Of course there are causal intermediaries. What we must guard against are epistemic intermediaries."[31] Regarding the connection between realism and truth, a fortiori the question of knowledge, this simply means that "naturalism" is best served by causal explanation. Davidson does not actually affirm that naturalism avoids non-causal theories of any kind. Recall Tarski's theory of truth, in accounting for the realist standing of our sciences. Apart from advising us to avoid inter-pretive "intermediaries" (misleadingly: *tertia,* in Rorty's idiom), Davidson explicitly says that naturalism is constrained by the search for "a *reason* for supposing most of our beliefs are true that is not a form of *evidence.*"

Davidson means this quite literally, that is, in the first-order sense that supposes that the central mass of our aggregated beliefs are (even must be) true—which is surely more than doubtful. He never considers, for instance, the consistency of holding that, in the second-order sense in accord with which we mean to displace Cartesianism, we cannot be "massively" wrong about the world and yet, aggregatively, in our first-order beliefs, we can in-deed be wrong most of the time. The briefest, perhaps the best, clue regard-ing the *second*-order argument that Davidson needs (but never supplies) is Ludwig Wittgenstein's remark, in *Philosophical Investigations*: "If language is to be a means of communication there must be agreement not only in def-initions [or meanings] but also (queer as this may sound) in judgments." Wittgenstein would, of course, deny that he was "doing" philosophy in the canonical way. But what he caught in his handful of words was the inter-locking unity of linguistic fluency, which entails understanding meanings, knowing what one believes, and knowing much that is true about the world—which implicates something very close to the normative conception of rationality that Davidson requires but suppresses.[32] It is also worth re-marking that Wittgenstein's lesson accords very well with Dewey's distinc-tive realism, which I turn to in chapter 4.

The avoidance of "intermediaries" is supposed to preclude any taint of idealism or skepticism, but the argument is muddy. If, on the one hand, we are talking about a world we can actually know—an "intelligible" rather than a "noumenal" world—then merely coming to know the world cannot meaningfully entail the offending doctrine (idealism); for, of course, every realism would instantly become an idealism. In that case, "intermediaries" would make no difference. On the other hand, if we are talking about knowing an "independent" world—a world that, though known, remains unaltered by the effects of its merely being known—then, unless we were entitled to claim privileged access to that world, we could never argue convincingly that "interpretive intermediaries" (or *tertia*) did not affect the realism that we actually espouse. In that case, "intermediaries" of *some* kind (*not* relationally interposed) would be unavoidable.

But, of course, it remains entirely possible to abandon epistemic intermediaries that either force us to conclude that the "real" world is somehow "constituted" by the mind (idealism) or is somehow known only through private mental states (representationalism) whose evidentiary standing entails their being externally related to whatever part of the independent world we claim to know. Davidson seems to be caught in a trap of his own devising. In short, even a causal explanation of realist beliefs would (if it worked) *be* an explanation of James's sort! (I trust it will not confuse matters if I intrude here with the bare reminder that these corrections are little more than a summary of Hegel's argument in the *Phenomenology*. They are also, of course, inevitably, variants of Dewey's corrections.)

For his part, Rorty offers the following summary of what he means by "pragmatism," what he takes Davidson to mean by "naturalism," and why, as a consequence, he concludes that "Davidson and James are both pragmatists":

(1) "True" has no explanatory uses.
(2) We understand all there is to know, about the relation of beliefs to the world when we understand their causal relations with the world; our knowledge of how to apply terms such as "about" and "true of" is fallout from a "naturalistic" account of linguistic behavior.
(3) There are no relations of "being made true" which hold between beliefs and the world.
(4) There is no point to debates between realism and anti-realism, for such debates presuppose the empty and misleading idea of beliefs "being made true."[33]

The most distinctive feature of Rorty's account is its uncompromising commitment to doctrines more extreme than anything Davidson offers. Davidson himself corrects doctrine (1), you remember. Because of its unyielding assurance, doctrine (2) can hardly be read as anything but a Cartesian formulation. And doctrines (3) and (4) oppose *tertia* (not merely relationally identified representational "ideas" but interpretive intermediaries), because *tertia* violate the naturalizing rigors of (1) and (2). It is odd that, as a know-nothing champion of postmodernism, Rorty champions an unusually extreme form of naturalism. But, in doing that, he simply dismisses all the telling questions—as Putnam has shown. More than that, Rorty avoids (without the least effort at explanation or defense) any constructivist account of realism that would fit either Peirce's or James's constraint on meaning or on truth or both, which, together, are the minimal marks of classic pragmatism.

For his part, Putnam is flatly inconsistent: there's no gainsaying that. In advancing his internal realism, he is aware that there cannot be "'a point at which' subjectivity ceases and Objectivity-with-a-capital-O begins."[34] Nevertheless, fearful of the self-refuting relativism he believes he finds in Rorty's "ethnocentric solidarity," he finds himself obliged to invoke his *Grenzbegriff* without explicit Cartesian assurances—which presents an even weaker case than the Cartesian claim. For in cognitive matters there cannot be a regulative norm that is not also constitutively grounded in our evidentiary powers. (That would amount to a privileged plea.) It is impossible, therefore, to validate Putnam's realism any more effectively than Davidson's or Rorty's naturalizing. Alternatively put, Putnam's theory is hopelessly inconsistent with his own "internal realism" and, of course, all three are open to the charge of scientism.

Putnam is searching for an assurance of objective knowledge about an "independent" world on grounds that are blind to the difference between the subjective and the objective, whereas Davidson is searching for an assurance of the objective truth of our beliefs about an "independent" world without regard to any evidentiary considerations applied to those beliefs. I take all three of our discussants to be Cartesian pawns despite their efforts to escape.

I remind you that these quarrels were aired at the end of the twentieth century! They belong by rights to the seventeenth and eighteenth centuries—with very slight adjustments. There is nothing in them that the pre-Kantians could not have envisaged. We have evidently not yet cast off the paralyzing assumptions of the Cartesian vision. In the Anglo-American world, it is of course the classic pragmatists who were the most promising opponents of Cartesianism running from the mid-nineteenth century to the middle of the twentieth. Now, in their "revival," what we find is a considerable muddle: effectively, a very large part of English-language philosophy, whether pragmatist or naturalist (or an amalgam of the two), turns out to be bent on pursuing various ways of converting pragmatism into the sparest form of Cartesianism.

I owe you, therefore, an aside on the pointed use of the epithet "Cartesian." I speak of "Cartesianism," here, in a sense that is not intended to be textually bound to Descartes's realism but inclines as well (by whatever means) toward its characteristic sense of an objective knowledge of reality. In its most conventional form, "Cartesian realism" is correspondentist in some criterially explicit regard, favors cognitive faculties reliably (even essentially) qualified to discern the actual features and structures of independent reality, is context-free and ahistorical, strongly separates human cognizers and cognized world, and is committed to one ideally valid description of the real world.

Any doctrine that favors the objectivist drift of this sort of realism, however it departs from one or another plank of Descartes's original vision, possibly by some form of representationalism (Putnam), or by an undefended assertion of our knowledge of the independent world (Devitt), or the unearned assurance of the central core of our truth-bearing beliefs without facultative privilege (Davidson), or the invariant logic of our realist claims (Dummett), counts in my book as "Cartesian." Kant is a Cartesian in this sense: both because he remains a representationalist and because he insists, in the context of realism, on transcendental privilege.

I take the original doctrine and its twentieth-century innovations to be utterly without defense, completely indifferent to the historical rebuttal offered by the post-Kantian tradition (apotheosized in Hegel), opposed (in American philosophy) to the strongest themes of classic pragmatism, and inherently incapable of resolving its own paradoxes. The epithet serves, therefore, to identify a philosophical defect often not acknowledged to be such. Needless to say, in the American setting, "Cartesianism" is not dualistic, is in fact usually materialistically inclined.

It is important to emphasize that the rejection of "Cartesian realism" is not tantamount to rejecting "realism" altogether, though realism does require redefinition. The minimal Cartesian dogma is that it is cognitively feasible to gain a true account of the way "the world is" apart from any presumed distortion effected by human inquiry. Under that assumption, there is no room for alternative valid realisms, unless they are fragments of a single, inclusive, true account. Hence the plausibility of the disquotational theory of truth; hence, also, the plausibility of insisting on an exceptionless bivalence in the most responsible sciences.

The rejection of Cartesian realism, which reached an adequate and notably powerful form in Hegel, depends entirely on exposing Cartesianism's insuperable paradoxes *and* disallowing all reference to an epistemically inaccessible world and to alleged distortions regarding its true nature. Those paradoxes cannot be resolved: they must be abandoned. Some, therefore, seeing that Hegel terms his alternative conception a "phenomenology," are tempted to conclude that he must have abandoned realism. But it would be entirely fair to point out that Dewey's *Experience and Nature,* which is plainly influenced by Hegel's argument, demonstrates that the main themes of a Hegelian "phenomenology" (turned against Cartesianism) is quite capable of producing a convincing and robust but very different sense of realism. I am inclined to read Hegel as such a realist. It would have to be a constructive (or constructivist) realism, however.

The mark of that concession is the assignment of an explanatory role for truth. That is the essential connection between pragmatism and the post-Kantian tradition, no matter how thinly it may be stretched or how few of Hegel's own formulations remain in play. But to admit constructivism (and truth's explanatory role) is to disallow any disjunction of the classic realism/idealism sort, though it is also to disallow any entailment to the effect that the real world is a construction or an artifact of the mind. Hegel is not an "idealist" in the classic sense, and constructivism is not (need not be) idealism.

Ever since Fichte and Hegel, continental European philosophy has never entirely lost the master thread of its anti-Cartesian metaphysics and epistemology, though it is apparent that the new American naturalism is making substantial inroads into German and French philosophy against the lesson of that discipline. So it is reasonable to suppose the pragmatists' original resolve might be strengthened by daring to experiment selectively with themes drawn from the Hegelian and post-Hegelian tradition: from Marx, say, from Nietzsche, from Dilthey, Heidegger, Horkheimer and Adorno, Gadamer, Wittgenstein, Foucault at least. There is a risk, of course: we must bear in mind that no recent self-styled American pragmatist is more adventurous than Rorty in claiming to join the analytic and the continental; and yet, none is more likely to convert such an effort into a stiffening of Cartesianism itself—or, into a complete postmodernist ("post-philosophical") abdication of the essential philosophical motivation of both pragmatism and naturalism.

Earlier I mentioned one reason theorists working in the pragmatist or naturalist orbit regularly failed to fashion a viable realism that was not a form of Cartesianism: everyone who put his hand to the puzzle construed realism in Cartesian terms. (Witness both Davidson and Rorty.) Yet if the original pragmatists succeeded at anything, they succeeded in shaping realist and near-realist options that eluded any Cartesian weakness of the gauge we find in Putnam, Rorty, and Davidson.

So American philosophy has lost ground twice in its slim history: once, in failing to come to terms, at the end-of-century, with the full achievement of the post-Kantians, who first succeeded in exposing and overcoming all the Cartesian traps (meaning, by that, to span the work of Descartes and Kant, though Kant of course is the decisive, if equivocal, figure in the formation of modern philosophy's anti-Cartesian programs); and, again, in failing to hold fast, within pragmatism's "revival," to the original pragmatists' inventive simplification (almost invisible after Peirce) of the work of the post-Kantians themselves.

It is, of course, true that Cartesian foundationalism and representationalism, as in Locke and Kant, have been largely retired—not entirely and none too soon if, in the European tradition, we bear in mind such figures as Husserl and Apel, and closet Kantians like Heidegger, or, in the American tradition, figures like Roderick Chisholm and Wilfrid Sellars and, more surprisingly, Putnam,[35] or even James and Peirce at times. The history is quite confused, you see: small wonder pragmatism has slipped in the Cartesian direction.

What is still more interesting is that recent American philosophy has produced new Cartesian puzzles of its own: witness our exemplars. There will surely be others to be tracked in the same way: predictably, perhaps more fashionably, those drawn to computationalism, supervenientism, reductionism, eliminativism, extensionalism, and the subtler varieties of the new naturalism. But it is surely a great gain to have discerned the intention of recent analytic philosophy to continue the Cartesian project as if it were the successor or continuator of pragmatism, particularly in the effort to reunite the strongest currents of Anglo-American and European philosophy closest to the post-Kantian.[36]

I see no prospect of usefully recovering Cartesianism in any of its protean forms. It counts as a complete disaster in its effort to sustain a viable realism, the fatal first stroke at the beginning of the modern age that has deflected us for centuries from coherent alternatives to which we must still return.

With hindsight, one may imagine that the alternative to Cartesianism was already incipient in Descartes's day—in, say, Montaigne's skepticism (which was no skepticism at all); for Montaigne did indeed anticipate Descartes's hyperbolic doubt—noted it and rejected it—which must have stiffened Descartes's resolve to affirm his *cogito*.[37] Montaigne is too weak a figure to rely on, of course, but his ruminations run in the right direction and cleave to the humanism of his century at least fifty years before Descartes's windfall.

Descartes's great contribution rests with having oriented the Western world to the primacy of epistemological questions in an effort to confirm an adequate scientific realism. But his own solutions, both the realism and the dualism (which are inseparable), have misled the entire genius of the era that culminates in Kant. So the double failing of late American philosophy takes on a grander meaning in its own thoroughly confused age.

IV

There is only one conclusion to draw—the single most promising finding to be gained from four centuries of speculation. And that is this: (1) every viable realism must be a constructivism (a constructive realism), in the sense that there can be no principled disjunction between epistemological and metaphysical questions, no neutral analysis of the disjunctive contributions to our science drawn from cognizing subjects and cognized objects; (2) the admission of (1) precludes all necessities *de re* and *de cogitatione;* (3) the admission of (1) and (2) disallows any principled disjunction between realism and idealism, as these are defined in the Cartesian tradition—in effect, this confirms the unavoidability of interpretive intermediaries.

I explicitly spell out these consequences redundantly in order to avoid misunderstanding. But you must see that doctrine (1) already entails (2) and (3); for instance, it defeats Kantian constructivism hands-down (the constructivism of the First *Critique*) and provides a space for the constructivism and historicism of the post-Kantian movement (notably, in Hegel), without falling back to idealism. For the *assignment* of what is subjective and objective in realism is itself an artifact internal to reflection in accord with (1)–(3). The entailment does not supply any particular form of realism especially suited to our own temperament—witness Putnam's uneasiness with his own internalism. But that is why the classic pragmatists attract us, if they attract us at all, and that is where the latent Cartesianism of Davidson and company goes entirely astray.

I must, however, enter a caveat here. For though Hegel's constructivism functions in a social way, it is not explicitly a "social constructivism." It is not, for instance, collectivist in origin or import, as tradition and natural language are. It needs to be pressed to go another mile or two: *Geist (spirit, mind),* in Hegel's account, is constructed, interpreted, yet historically productive and influential, more like an artifact corresponding to Rousseau's *volonté de tous* (the will of all, aggregatively) than to his *volonté générale (the general will).* By the time of Marx's writing, the full collective option (which does not and need not entail collective agency) is plainly a ready choice. What is collective in this sense is not at all alien, of course, to Dewey's pragmatism, but it is clearly muted there. The point is of some importance, because, of course, you cannot find a ramified account of the collective aspect of societal life (in the predicative sense) in such diverse figures as Putnam, Rorty, Searle, McDowell, and Brandom. But that means that these and similar figures are not likely to provide a more powerful recovery of either pragmatism or analytic philosophy than the pre-Kantian, Kantian, and the early post-Kantian traditions have already made provision for.

We are, therefore, empowered at the turn of the century to bring philosophy back to lines of speculation that are not self-defeating in the Cartesian way. That is reason enough to redefine pragmatism for our time. In American thought, pragmatism is nearly the only current that has resources enough to validate the philosophical "re-turn." The European tradition houses other currents closer to the original post-Kantian sources. But whether we will finally abandon the old delusion is hard to say, because false doctrines die hard. Furthermore, the charm of the American experiment lies with its promising the most focused version of the contest in promising to combat naturalism. That is no longer a parochial quarrel, but it cannot go forward without gaining a measure of rapprochement with the most congenial European movements (which have for a long time explored the historical and collective aspects of human cognition).

The foregoing may be put more compendiously. If Cartesian realism were valid—not merely about the "mind-independent" world but about assurances that our cognitive powers could discern that that was so—then the preservation of late American philosophy, that is, the naturalism Davidson and Rorty share and Putnam approaches only because he cleaves ambiguously to a more generic Cartesianism, might be honored as a valiant struggle against the bewitchment of the entire post-Kantian dénouement. But the fact remains that it was the post-Kantians, building on Kant's immense advance, who first completely exposed the paradoxes of the Cartesian vision and sketched the minima adequate for its correction.

Furthermore, both the pragmatists and the naturalists of our recent end-of-century draw back from the classic forms of Cartesianism. It seems hardly to have dawned on them that to give up the classic Cartesian resources was to give up the prospect of recovering *any* part of Cartesian realism: witness Davidson and Putnam. But that means that only a constructive realism could possibly be viable.

In a curious way (a way one might overlook), Putnam is aware that his rejecting any principled disjunction between the subjective and the objective makes provision for "constructive" choices within the bounds of realism. But (apparently) he does not see that realism itself must be constructivist all the way down. As we shall see, that is the element that is missing in Putnam's turn to (what he now calls) "natural realism," a fortiori what is missing in McDowell's realism, which Putnam now guides himself by. In Putnam, the constructivist theme leads only to a form of "pluralism" that brooks no chance for a relativist or incommensurabilist or historicist form of realism itself. (I shall come back to this before I end this chapter.)

I must take a moment to explain the multiple equivocations on the term "constructivism" (or "constructive realism"). Both Kant and Hegel are, of course, constructivists; Kant is a transcendental constructivist, Hegel is not. Minimally, constructivism signifies that there is no principled disjunction between metaphysics and epistemology or between cognizing subjects and cognized objects or between appearances (*Erscheinungen*) and the real world. (Call all these variant constructivisms forms of "symbiosis.")

Kant, of course, believes that the "subjective" side of perception and belief *can* be exclusively assigned the pure intuitions of space and time and the categories of the understanding. In that sense, Kant *is* an idealist; for the objective world that we perceive is, on Kant's theory, actually formed, composed, constituted, "made," by the cognizing mind (the transcendental Ego: *not* human cognizers). But Hegel is no idealist; for, apart from whatever formative role is assigned history (which, in "internalist" terms, is said to affect our choice of concepts), constructivism is confined to the minima mentioned just above. Hegel defeats the strong division between the ontic and the epistemic in terms of which the older "idealist" accusation alone makes sense. But there is still a great gulf between the constructed perception of what is given in sensory experience and its historically evolving reinterpretation (according to the *Phenomenology*) and the historicized, collective formation of our perceptual powers in the first place. Without the additional innovation (at least incipient in Hegel), it would be all too easy to fall back into a Kantianized or (even) Platonized Hegel (such as, for instance, we find in John McDowell). If we rest there, we may find that we have not moved very far from the Cartesian options we thought to escape.

There is no reason to deny that there is an independent world, though that is not to say that everything that is real *is* uniformly "mind-independent": certainly, the things of the world of human culture, artworks and machines, for instance—and, I should say, selves—are fully real, exist robustly, but are hardly "mind-independent."[38] Also, even if we admit the independent world, *that* is not to say (agreeing with Davidson) that we *have evidence* for this; nor is it to say (contrary to Davidson) that we have *reason* (rather than evidence) to affirm this, *if*, by that, we mean (as Davidson plainly does) to justify saying that "most of our beliefs are true." Surely, that is the old

Cartesianism under diminished auspices (possibly the obscure equivalent of epistemic *tertia*). If so, then appropriate answers to metaphysical questions about what exists in the independent world cannot be independent of our answers to the matched epistemological questions about our cognitive competence to know *that*—contrary to what Michael Devitt, for one, has tried to demonstrate.[39]

There is no cognitive way to establish *that* our admitted cognitive powers (perception, for instance) ever discern what there is in the "independent" (noumenal) world. To say that we have "reason" to believe that we know the independent world by perceptual means, but have neither evidence nor reason for believing that this particular belief or that is true, is irretrievably vacuous; and to say, with Davidson, that, nevertheless, we do have reason to believe that "most of our beliefs are true" is to put the cart before the horse— to argue in a completely arbitrary way. Surely, only if we know *to be true* (or have reason to believe we know) a large number of determinate (true) beliefs, could we possibly venture to say that "most of our beliefs are true." That alone would hardly enlarge our knowledge of the world. But it would recover the true nerve of Hegel's criticism of Kant: we would be reclaiming two centuries of misplaced history. And we would be acknowledging constructivism's unavoidability—which Davidson manages to disregard.

Still, it *is* reasonable to hold that we know the independent world and know, as by exercising our perceptual powers, that a great many of our beliefs about the world *are* true! But the "reason" that supports us here is thoroughly "constructive," not a privileged reason, not a Kantian reason, not anything that might vindicate a form of Cartesian realism—*or of naturalism*. That is what Davidson misses. Remember: both Davidson and Rorty insist on eliminating "epistemic intermediaries" (*tertia*); they are prepared to give up the classic Cartesian position, but only because they wrongly suppose they can hold on to *this* part of Cartesianism—which they require— *by other means*. That is the proper lesson of Davidson's, Rorty's, and Putnam's diminished realisms. To speak in the constructivist way is to concede the inseparability of metaphysical and epistemological questions, but it is also to refuse any regulative principle of truth or knowledge. Davidson's and Putnam's theories are but the inseparable halves of the same failed undertaking.

Constructivism holds that the objectivity of our beliefs and claims about the world *is itself a constructive posit* that we impose holistically and without privilege of any kind. It proceeds dialectically as a *faute de mieux* maneuver. Nothing hangs on it "except" two very modest but all-important gains: (1) that we must (and may) put away every Cartesian longing; and (2) that, admitting (1), we must conclude that the appraisal of every logic, every semantics, every metaphysics and epistemology, proceeds only within the holism of our constructive posit: it never exits from it.

The supposed disjunction between realism and idealism (or between realism and anti-realism) is made completely pointless by our adopting the most modest version of post-Kantian symbiosis. Constructivism signifies that the realist standing of all our sciences is an artifact of our symbiotized world; that alone subverts the naturalist's economy in disallowing "epistemic intermediaries."

I said a moment ago that I was repeating Hegel's criticism of Kant and the pre-Kantians. It's true enough but hard to discern in the prose of Hegel's *Phenomenology*—and possibly not even adequately formed there. Let me risk a few lines from the *Phenomenology*'s introduction to confirm Hegel's mastery of the Cartesian *aporia* Descartes and Kant share and the purely verbal difficulty of matching what I have been saying and what Hegel himself says. I won't attempt an exegesis—but I *am* recovering Hegel's principal point, if we can find it in Hegel's problematic text:

> One must [Hegel affirms] come to an understanding about cognition, what is regarded either as the instrument to get hold of the Absolute, or as the medium through which one discovers it. A certain uneasiness seems . . . bound to be transformed into the conviction that the whole project of securing for consciousness through cognition what exists in itself is absurd, . . . For, if cognition is the instrument for getting hold of absolute being, it is obvious that the use of an instrument on a thing certainly does not let it be what it is for itself, but rather sets out to reshape and alter it. If [however] cognition is not an instrument of our activity but a . . . passive medium through which the light of truth reaches us, then again we do not receive the truth as it is in itself, but only as it exists through and in this medium.[40]

The bearing—on Descartes, Locke, and Kant, and even Davidson—of what Hegel says here may, I hope, be recovered without too much difficulty. Hegel implies that the entire Cartesian project is impossible *sans phrase*, but he does not say that it is therefore impossible to claim to speak of the independent world! That last is what constructivism secures. We cannot know the independent world as it is "absolutely" independent of cognitive conjecture, but we can construct a reasonable sense of what to characterize as the independent-world-as-it-is-known-(and knowable)-to-us. The correction of *any* particular belief will be an artifact internal to that same holism. We have never surpassed Hegel in *this* regard.

If you allow this small concession to history without yielding to Hegel's grandiose conceptions, you cannot fail to see that Rorty's *Philosophy and the Mirror of Nature* is quite literally a Hegelian critique of a large part of Western philosophy.[41] Fine: that serves to remind us of an essential part of the pragmatists' original inheritance of the post-Kantian discoveries. But it also confirms the disastrous equivocation on interpretive *tertia* (or "intermediaries," in Davidson's idiom) that both Rorty and Davidson espouse. Regarding "intermediaries," Hegel featured and opposed *any epistemic "instrument"* or "medium" that operated *relationally* between cognitively separable consciousness and reality; whereas the "intermediaries" Davidson and Rorty oppose (pointedly, in Davidson's "A Coherence Theory of Truth and Knowledge") *are any "epistemic intermediaries" at all.* That now verges on incoherence.[42] (Nonetheless, Hegel does not go far enough.)

Davidson and Rorty rule out all constructivist intermediaries, even those "intermediaries" that disallow any initial separation between consciousness and reality (the upshot of a symbiotized world). But that *is* Cartesianism without benefit of argument. Doubtless, Davidson's rationale trades on the fact that constructivism would defeat reductive physicalism and extensionalism at one blow, though it need never put at risk the usual rigor or achievement of any of our sciences. Put in the simplest terms, Rorty cannot support both Davidson and Hegel—or Davidson and the pragmatists or Davidson and the historicizing epistemologists.

The entire history now falls easily into place. Michael Devitt, for example, appears as a Cartesian innocent when he confesses at the start of the second edition of *Realism and Truth:* "There is something a little shameful about spending one's time defending something so apparently humdrum as the independent existence of the familiar world"—which he urges in accord with the maxim, "Settle the metaphysical issue before any epistemic or semantic issue."[43] This "cannot" have been written later than the seventeenth or eighteenth century!

Similarly, though he is incomparably more interesting than Devitt, Michael Dummett, for all his "anti-realism" (which Devitt exploits against him), is hardly more than an abler Cartesian when he remarks:

> Although we no longer regard the traditional questions of philosophy as pseudo-questions to which no meaningful answer can be given, we have not returned to the belief that a priori reasoning can afford us substantive knowledge of fundamental features of the

world. Philosophy can take us no further than enabling us to command a clear view of the concepts by means of which we think about the world, and, by so doing, to attain a firmer grasp of the way we represent the world in our thought. It is for this reason and in this sense that philosophy is about the world. Frege said of the laws of logic that they are not laws of nature but laws of the laws of nature. . . . Reality cannot be said to obey a law of logic; it is our thinking about reality that obeys such a law or flouts it.[44]

This, of course, is a kind of Fregean Kantianism[45]—Cartesianism, in effect. Dummett somehow manages to separate (without explanation) semantics from epistemology—a fortiori, semantics from metaphysics—and to give priority to the semantic analysis of our concepts over epistemology and metaphysics. But what are our *concepts,* if they are not the constructed powers of human understanding abstracted from our actual cognitive engagements? To insist otherwise is to advance a kind of Fregean analogue of either Kantian or Husserlian apriorism. Certainly, it is to advance a form of Platonism. It's for this reason that Dummett believes he can afford to yield on excluded middle (but not on bivalence) and therefore gives cognitive priority to logic over metaphysics; whereas, on the constructivist account, logic (Dummett's sort of logic) is itself a form of metaphysics,[46] a metaphysics "by other means."

v

I offer, finally, some remarks drawn from John McDowell's John Locke Lectures (1991), which may be the most promising of these contemporary variations on the Cartesian theme. They are important, beyond their explicit contribution, partly because of Putnam's reliance on McDowell's argument in abandoning his own "internal realism,"[47] partly because they suggest a way of bridging the gap between pragmatism and Cartesianism (by way of Kant), and partly because they do not venture far enough to specify a realism adequate on both metaphysical and epistemological grounds. Putnam believes McDowell's argument enables *him* to recover his pragmatism as a form of "natural realism" (as he now terms it), but the argument is not yet clear.

McDowell's avowed objective is "to consider . . . the way concepts mediate the relation between minds and the world," to which he adds at once: "Representational content cannot be dualistically set over against the conceptual." By these two sentences, McDowell allies himself (with important qualifications) with Kant (*and* Hegel) and against Davidson and that part of

Rorty that agrees with Davidson.[48] McDowell then draws the perfectly sensible inference: *"That things are thus and so* is the conceptual content of an experience, but if the subject of the experience is not misled, that very same thing, *that things are thus and so,* is also a perceptible fact, an aspect of the perceptible world."[49] This marks very clearly McDowell's attraction to the pragmatist recovery of the main accomplishment of the post-Kantian movement, but hardly disallows a Cartesian recovery *of that.* There's the puzzle of McDowell's account.

McDowell opposes the disjunction between our perception and the semantics of our concepts: that certainly signals that he shares common ground with Kant and Hegel; though it obviously is not to share the same ground with Frege, Sellars, Dummett, Davidson, or Brandom. It is itself a purely formal solution of the Cartesian *aporia;* for, whatever McDowell's epistemological intuitions, it requires only (and supplies no more than) a denial of the old separation of cognizer and cognized. (Nothing more is supplied in *Mind and World* that bears on cognitive disputes: for example, under alternative conceptual schemes, under historicized conditions, within epistemologically incommensurable theories, or the like.)

There is no way to gainsay the limitation. What is so astonishing about McDowell's analysis—and Putnam's interest in it—is that *that* single (abstract) theme is nearly the entire gist of what McDowell offers: the rest is more Cartesian than pragmatist. McDowell does draw attention to the deep equivocation on "intermediaries" that I've flagged in Davidson and Rorty; and, as I say, that much supports the judgment that McDowell aligns himself with Kant (*sans* Kant's transcendentalism) as well as with Aristotle and Hegel (very, very lightly), both of whom he reads conformably. But that's all! There's nothing in the way of an epistemologically centered realism (say, "a realism worth fighting for," in Devitt's phrase); or, if there is, what there is is inexplicit and undefended regarding whatever differences separate pragmatism and Cartesianism.

McDowell may be a closet Cartesian of an extremely attenuated "Kantian" or even "Hegelian" sort. This much, however, is clear: if we adopt McDowell's formulation, then the whole of Davidson's objection to "epistemic intermediaries" instantly fails; it is, in fact, rendered irrelevant. That, I concede, is an enormous plus. But, in his defense of realism, McDowell seems to have found it sufficient to retrace *that* argument alone from Kant to Hegel, which is certainly not enough. That is, McDowell fails to consider all that is required of "intermediaries"—bearing on detailed questions of objectivity.

To have stopped where he does (in *Mind and World*) is to fail to distinguish between a Kantian and a Hegelian view of the symbiotized world: a fortiori, to fail to distinguish between a "Cartesian" and a pragmatist account of realism. It's not enough (though it is correct as far as it goes) to say that our *concepts* qualify our perception of the real world: the question is whether the constructivist account of the "real world" proves to be a form of idealism, a Kantianized Cartesianism, or a pragmatist Hegelianism that eludes the snares of the other options. What in effect McDowell very neatly shows is that our "epistemic intermediaries" (our "concepts," in McDowell's idiom) need not be *relationally* defined in the way Putnam found so disastrous for his own internal realism. (Representationalism is now hardly more than a minor aberration: the trick is to spell out the cognitively relevant sources of our concepts. In our age—to put the point in a programmatic way—that can only be done by replacing Kant with Hegel—and strengthening the historicist reading of concepts themselves. McDowell has taken only the first step.)

I agree entirely with McDowell here; but I go on to say that the "*tertia*" Rorty dismisses, in agreement with Davidson (obviously a misnomer for the epistemic resources of any constructive realism), mediate *adverbially* in epistemic contexts (as a consequence of the historicized construction of selves and concepts). But the way in which conceptual or interpretive intermediaries are assumed to function is altogether different in Kant and Hegel: there is, for instance, no recognition in Kant (or in Aristotle, for that matter) of the possibility (the Hegelian and, I would add, the pragmatist possibility) that our interpretive competence is itself a hybrid artifact of our historical culture, not in any way part of an assured and relatively changeless, commensurable, "natural," even essential faculty of reason. Also, as already partly noted, although Hegel acknowledges the historical and cultural context in which human "consciousness" functions, he does not actually analyze the artifactual formation of our cognitive powers in terms of internalizing the collective resources of our historical culture. Hence, McDowell could not rightly find in Hegel's notion of "*Bildung*," which he co-opts, the effective clue by which to avoid the "Platonism" he is attracted to.

As I read him, McDowell does not broach this and related matters as inseparable parts of the realist question he himself pursues. History or *Bildung* provides (in McDowell's account) for a "selection" from our very concepts, but it does not signify the constructed nature of our concepts themselves. (There's an unanswered question there about the meaning and conditions of conceptual "selection" that yields, in McDowell's hands, along the lines of what he himself calls "natural Platonism.")

I have not found in any of McDowell's more recent publications, for instance in the Woodbridge Lectures (1997) or the papers on Wittgenstein,[50] reason to modify my finding. In the Woodbridge Lectures, McDowell pretty well assimilates Hegel to Kant;[51] and the excellent papers on Wittgenstein, being essentially *explications,* disclose very little that bears directly on a "constructivist" view of language and thought that might actually decide the matter between the Kantian (and Aristotelian) cast of *Mind and World* and a robustly historicized account (Hegelian, on my reading, though not entirely Hegel's) of our categories and concepts. It is, of course, the historicized treatment of social life that obliges us to consider certain strenuous epistemological and realist puzzles that never surface in *Mind and World*—relativism, incommensurabilism, and even historicism itself. Putnam and McDowell simply stop short of sketching the main lines of the "natural realism" they seem to share. Here, we begin to glimpse pragmatism's potential "third" life.

It is very difficult to elicit more from McDowell that bears on the fate and prospects of realism. McDowell wishes to avoid Kant's appeal to the "supersensible" (or transcendental), which claims a conceptual source completely "separable" from sensory "receptivity." (I have dubbed that a "Cartesian" feature in Kant, which, on McDowell's reading, correctly accounts for Kant's "idealism."[52]) McDowell is bent on securing a thoroughly "natural" (I would say, an Aristotelian) reading of "empirical thinking" that depends on man's acquiring a "second nature" as a result of *Bildung* (the original acquisition of cultural powers), which finds alternative treatments in Aristotle and Hegel but not in the original Kant.[53] Here, McDowell opposes epistemological dualisms and any reliance on the "supersensible": the transcendental, the supernatural, the "rampant Platonist."[54] He hardly ventures an account of what *he* finally means by our "natural" endowment; or, what he does offer is a Kantianized or Aristotelian Hegel.

So McDowell brings us to the very edge of the quarrel between a fresh pragmatist treatment of the realist issue and a "naturalistic" treatment. The following is nearly all McDowell says on the matter:

we can regard the culture a human being is initiated into as a going concern; there is no particular reason why we should need to uncover or speculate about its history, let alone the origins of culture as such. Human infants are mere animals, distinctive only in their potential, and nothing occult happens to a human being in ordinary upbringing. If we locate a variety of Platonisms in the context of an account of *Bildung* [that is, a "natural Platonism" like Aristotle's, a sense of natural, culturally featured predicative regularities] that insists on those facts, we thereby ensure that it is not a rampant Platonism [that is, that posits a separable world of Forms, an occult domain].[55]

What McDowell says here is not unwelcome. McDowell positions himself in a no-man's land between pragmatism and a "natural Platonism," though he clearly favors the latter. In any case, he cannot reconcile the two. By "Platonism," McDowell means (I surmise) an accessible source of objective predicates that run true and more or less uniformly through the species; by "natural," I take him to mean that the conceptual competence answering to our predicative efforts belongs primarily to our biology but may, in some measure, manifest differences in saliency as a result of our encultured "second nature" (our *Bildung*). It's the open-ended and historically variable (constructed) nature of (what Rorty misleadingly calls) *tertia* that generates the contemporary realist quarrel between the naturalizers and the pragmatists. That is what McDowell fails to address. (And that is what we find in Dewey!)

I should add, here, that I find three very different treatments of *tertia* (or, better, intermediaries): the first, the one Davidson and Rorty dismiss (quite rightly), the one featured so disastrously in Putnam's "internal realism,"[56] which assigns "epistemic intermediaries" a relational (a Cartesian or Lockean) representationalist role; the second, the one McDowell favors in the passage just cited, which signifies that mind and world are indeed "mediated" (adverbially, as I suggest) by "concepts" that belong to our biological endowment but are selected or featured by our *Bildung* (our "ordinary upbringing"); and a third, the one I recommend (against McDowell's "Cartesian"—or Kantian or Aristotelian—proclivities), which treats our interpretive intermediaries as both "adverbial" (rather than "relational") and as "hybrid" (rather than merely "natural" in the biological sense), that is, as historicized, variable, artifactual, and open to the puzzle of reconciling realism and, say, relativism or incommensurabilism. On my view, to admit conceptual *tertia* (or, better, adverbial intermediaries) is to make our realism constructivist from the start and throughout; there is no fallback objectivism to take for granted. I intend this, of course, as an up-to-date reading of Dewey. In the sense intended, it strengthens Hegel's account along constructivist lines that Hegel himself does not explicitly pursue.

McDowell begins *Mind and World* with too slim a project. "The overall topic I am going to consider in these lectures," he advises, "is the way concepts mediate the relation between minds and the world." He favors a Kantian complication at once and warns:

The more we play up the connection between reason and freedom [which is to account for the accessibility of 'meaning', the natural way in which our second-natured concepts are already engaged in intelligible experience], the more we risk losing our grip on how exercises of concepts can constitute warranted judgments about the world. What we wanted to conceive as exercises of concepts threaten to degenerate into moves in a self-contained game.[57]

Put thus, McDowell's effort is essentially a rearguard, but thoroughly recuperative, move. The telltale signs appear in his speaking of "warranted judgments about the world" and of locating a "variety of [natural] Platonisms in the context of . . . *Bildung.*"

The matter is important enough to press a little more insistently. Two qualifications should serve. For one, when McDowell speaks of "second nature" (which is how he brings Hegel and Aristotle together in reinterpreting Kant), he speaks of the "acquisition of a second nature, which [he says] involves responsiveness to meaning." That is what (that is all) he has in mind in speaking of a "normal upbringing": it is meant to defeat (and does defeat) any purely reductive naturalism ("bald naturalism") in which, say, the autonomy and intelligence of a human agent can be explained entirely in biological terms.[58] *That* much is certainly fair: it's what McDowell gains from Kant. But it does not quite touch on the *metaphysics* of our cognitive powers vis-à-vis realism. Or, rather, it assumes the validity of a "naturalistic" account of our conceptual sources and reconciles their mastery with human freedom. Second, when he speaks of the distinction between "sensory experience" and its being intelligible, McDowell is concerned to avoid the empiricist option of the "non-conceptual" representationality of mere sensation (along the lines developed by Gareth Evans). McDowell's entirely sensible account runs as follows: "To say that an experience is not blind is to say that it is intelligible to its subject as purporting to be awareness of a feature of objective reality: as a seeming glimpse of the world."[59] Yes, of course. But that goes no further than the second sense of "*tertia.*" Hegel himself is less than perspicuous here in his account in the *Phenomenology* of the relationship between sensation and perception in the process of reinterpreting (with accumulating experience) what to understand as an objective account of our *Erscheinungen.*

It is in this sense that a pragmatism poised at the turn of the new century could easily recover in a single stroke pragmatism's original promise and "second" energy: by redefining realism in a way that could not have been perceived in its first incarnation and by rereading with care the anti-Cartesian strategies developed by the European progeny of the post-Kantian world (the Marxists, the early Frankfurt-Critical movement, the Hegelian-ized Kantians, the historicists, the Heideggerian hermeneuts, the European pragmatists, the existential phenomenologists, the Nietzscheans, the post-structuralists, genealogists, sociologists of knowledge), who never suffered the conceptual break with the post-Kantian world that Anglo-American philosophy imposed on itself.

Tertia, construed in my third sense, do play an ineliminable epistemic role (contrary to Davidson and Rorty); do apply adverbially, not relation-ally (in agreement with McDowell); *and* are culturally and historically formed and transformed (in the historicizing sense Hegel introduces but does not fully explore and Dewey implicitly favors and McDowell fails to address). But if that is so, then the recovery of realism—in particular, prag-matism's recovery of realism—harbors more troubling questions than the ones broached by Putnam, Davidson, Rorty, or McDowell.

2

Richard Rorty: Philosophy by Other Means

American philosophy, I have been claiming, is passing through a remarkable deformation championed in its forward direction as a liberating turn by Richard Rorty, its principal architect and engine. But it *is* a deformation, however cleverly Rorty deflects us at various conceptual transitions where we must quickly decide what to make of his mounting arguments. All the while he invites us to abandon older scruples and to take up the newer ones he invents ad hoc.

I refer here to the deformation of "mainstream" American philosophy, meaning by that the running practice of debating, extending, adjusting, advancing beyond, and confining discussion to the published views of a small clutch of commanding figures at leading American universities, plus certain favored continuators distributed around the country, a generation or half a generation behind, who may be counted on in some measure to advance the orienting themes of the originating voices without excessive scatter.

There's no mystery there. American analytic philosophy has been regularized largely through the magisterial talents of W. V. Quine, chiefly in terms of Quine's publications in the interval from the early 1950s to at least 1960 (with the appearance of *From a Logical Point of View* and *Word and Object*)[1] by which Quine succeeded in separating off a distinctly American voice from the entire European analytic tradition.

Given Rorty's loyalties and enthusiasms, the "founding" figures were made to include Donald Davidson and Wilfrid Sellars; less so, Nelson Goodman, whose *The Structure of Appearance* and *Fact, Fiction, and Forecast* would ordinarily have assured his inclusion in close association with Quine, were it not for *Ways of Worldmaking*, which caused something of a rift between Quine and Goodman (largely on the philosophical side because of Goodman's rejection of "one world," as well as his noticeably labile treatment of "many real worlds" lacking assured boundaries).[2]

In fact, in the opinion of many, Goodman was far more "Jamesian" than any other American philosopher: hence, he should have been particularly attractive to Rorty (as he was, of course, to Hilary Putnam). The many-worlds theme might have been neatly fitted to Rorty's own program, of course, but it has proved rather intractable.

Davidson was very naturally included, certainly by dint of his earlier "Quinean"-like publications, *Essays on Actions and Events, Inquiries into Truth and Interpretation,* and related papers that run from the 1960s to a little beyond the publication of the collections themselves.[3] But he was included not because he is a pragmatist: he is certainly no pragmatist on the essential issues. His is in fact the analytic voice Rorty most admires and is invariably closest to. Neither Davidson nor Sellars is an entirely convincing exemplar: Davidson, because of his account of truth in the realist context, which leads back in the Cartesian direction and against the pragmatists; and Sellars, because, at bottom, he is very nearly the most unyielding eliminativist (eliminative materialist) America has ever spawned—hence, he is intractably opposed to the Hegelian and pragmatist themes Rorty wishes to feature, though it may seem otherwise.[4]

Rorty began his own work conventionally enough. In a way he was (perhaps still is) even more extreme than Davidson on the question of materialism, which his "postmodernism" obscures: he was, for instance, an eliminativist on the mind/body problem when Davidson wrote as a nonreductive materialist. Davidson's views began to change somewhat imperceptibly, partly against certain problematic concessions on Quine's part that appear already in *Word and Object* but that take increasingly explicit form in the divergence between Quine and Davidson on what to understand by "naturalism"—or, better, "naturalizing" (as that notion is now tagged). Naturalizing (as we have seen) is very different from the pragmatist conception of naturalism, which is in effect Dewey's, and which Rorty professes to follow, even though he openly champions Davidson's doctrine. More accurately put, Rorty tends to shave Dewey's and Davidson's naturalisms so that they converge and, converging, yield to his own "postmodernist" direction, hence abandoning all pretense favoring the effectiveness of any philosophical arguments *pro* or *con.*

You can make out easily enough the point of the difference between Davidson and Quine—that is, Davidson's more unyielding view of epistemology in particular—if you compare Quine's "Epistemology Naturalized" and Davidson's "A Coherence Theory of Truth and Knowledge."[5] Quine's convictions are somewhat divided on the naturalism side: are therefore very possibly inconsistent. But the chief difference between the two (a sizeable one) depends on the fact that, since it advocates in the frankest way an epistemologically construed holism, Quine's naturalizing cannot deny a constitutive role to competing conceptual schemes (interpretive intermediaries or *tertia*) that, ineliminably, orient our truth-claims and their confirmation. Quine calls these diverging perspectives "analytical hypotheses"[6] and has no intention of abandoning them.[7] Quine is more sanguine, therefore, than Davidson about the theory of truth, more tolerant of complications affecting extensionalist analyses of natural language (though he is sanguine enough); more tellingly, he is prepared to acknowledge the philosophical effect of the changing history of science itself. It is for these reasons that Quine is viewed as a pragmatist of sorts, though, at best, a problematic ally by Davidson's and Rorty's lights.

The curious thing is that during the period in which Davidson diverges most from Quine along the lines of a leaner orthodoxy, Rorty gymnastically reconciles Davidson's theory of truth[8] with William James's, makes Davidson over into a kind of Jamesian (if not a Deweyan) pragmatist—a maneuver Davidson steadfastly refuses to allow.[9] (This is a matter on which Rorty only partly relents.[10])

As we have seen, Rorty actually endorses a sparer, more doctrinaire version of naturalizing than does Davidson. His maneuver is a strange one, because he somehow supposes that by his promoting Davidson's effort (the gist of the "Coherence" paper) to bring analytic naturalism to its leanest and most defensible form—in short, to establish a new canon by which to supersede Quine's example—Davidson would somehow advance Rorty's "postmodernist" "reform" of the whole of philosophy. In this way, Rorty resists admitting that Davidson is *not* yielding in the postmodernist direction, though he never applies the epithet explicitly to Davidson. The point is that Davidson believes *he* is slimming canonical philosophy down to its bare essentials (even if against Quine), and Rorty believes *he* is abandoning canonical philosophy altogether in favor of a postmodernist or post-philosophical "redescription" of all the usual contested distinctions. Their proposals may look very similar at times, but they are worlds apart.

Davidson's formula does not quite fit the telltale oddities of his own treatment of truth in the coherence and correspondence accounts of the "Coherence" paper, which probably owes something to Rorty's "influence." In any case, not long after its original appearance (1986), in some remarks titled "Afterthoughts, 1987" (appended to a reprinting of the "Coherence" paper in a volume collecting responses to Rorty's own philosophical views[11]), Davidson admitted the "blunder" (his own word) in having advanced his conjectures about coherence and correspondence *as* an actual "theory of truth."

Yet, in admitting only that, without benefit of a replacement equal in power to what he willingly gave up, Davidson appears to have yielded very far indeed in Rorty's direction: so much so, that the "naturalizing" stance of the "Coherence" paper is now placed in serious jeopardy. Because, of course, *no* program of such unyielding determinacy could possibly be sustained, except by fiat, on the spare grounds Davidson allows us to invoke—all in the name of avoiding a "skepticism" matching the usual claims of epistemological privilege that might otherwise have had to be called into play. To put the point as clearly as possible, this means that Davidson holds fast to his Cartesian orientation but now without the supporting "reasons" of the "Coherence Theory" paper; which is to say, his naturalizing program risks having no supporting rationale at all. "Officially," Rorty need not be concerned in the same way, since *his* postmodernism is meant to obviate the very need for legitimation.

Rorty is in the ascendant, therefore, vis-à-vis Davidson (though unobtrusively), chiefly by way of overstating how much he and Davidson agree and then relenting (or delaying a little) while Davidson takes back his disadvantageous moves, for instance, on truth. There's a bit of a philosophical minuet there. But Rorty is clearly bent on uniting pragmatism and analytic philosophy *and* on taking the new union in a direction neither movement would have willingly endorsed. That is the clue to the deformation I've been suggesting. The analytic movement has gone fallow, and the pragmatist movement has been revived largely through Rorty's own efforts.

The only other American philosopher who has made an influential effort of a sort that bears comparing—Rorty's strongest competitor in the matter of uniting pragmatism and analytic philosophy—is, of course, Hilary Putnam. But Putnam, who is the central figure of the "second generation" to which Rorty belongs, favored a more explicit continuity with the "undistorted," the more conventional, philosophical claims and practices of the two movements. The fact is that with the publication of his John Dewey Lectures (1994), Putnam's "internal realism," his alternative metaphysics and epistemology, collapsed of its own weight and is now in need of considerable, even fundamental, repair.

Bear in mind that in tracking Rorty's "pragmatism" we must allow for its extraordinary ability to masquerade as a strict naturalism or, by a sudden turn, as a dismissive postmodernism more or less impatient with standard philosophical fare. The pertinent lesson is a double one: first, that Rorty is prepared to exploit (by way of conceptual camouflage) any philosophical mode of argumentation that suits his temporary need to undermine an opposing philosophy; second, that, more consequentially, he means to challenge every would-be philosophical argument that proceeds along metaphysical or epistemological lines. The intended transformation in discursive practices *is* precisely what Rorty means by "pragmatism" or "postmodernism" or "metaphilosophy." But the question nags, nevertheless: Is there a justification to be had for the "redescription" of any disputed field of inquiry or is the matter entirely arbitrary and never more than rhetorical? Viewed in these terms, the deformation of pragmatism is entirely consistent with Rorty's evolving "practice." But what, we may ask, is its purpose and rationale? What does the deformation or the "practice" rule in or out—and why?

Allow these questions to simmer a little, while I fill out the cast of characters I've promised.

II

Rorty adds Wilfrid Sellars to his list of "founding" figures in order to define, first, what *he* means by the revival of pragmatism *and,* second, to work out a reconciliation between pragmatism and the leading figures of the analytic movement. Thus he says, in writing as recently as 1998 in a way that catches up his tangled involvement with Davidson and broadly hints at the correct shape of his philosophical program:

> One of the benefits of getting rid of the notion of the intrinsic nature of reality is that you get rid of the notion that quarks and human rights differ in "ontological status." This . . . helps reject the suggestion that natural science should serve as a paradigm for the rest of culture, . . . [N]obody should think that Davidson stabbed analytic philosophy in the back by refusing to take the distinction between realism and antirealism seriously, or that Sellars did so by refusing to take seriously the distinction between knowledge by acquaintance and knowledge by description.[12]

This proceeds persuasively enough, until you stop to think that Sellars is, after all, one of the most extreme eliminativists (scientific realists) America has ever produced! Sellars could hardly be said to have subscribed to Rorty's "getting rid of the intrinsic nature of reality." Turn back, for example, to Sellars's "Philosophy and the Scientific Image of Man" and "The Language of Theories," which are surely among his best-known papers.[13] The retrieval of Sellars from the gathering neglect of the guild illustrates very nicely Rorty's sense of inventing the community to which he wishes to belong—in effect, to which he might exhibit a measure of "ethnocentric solidarity." But you cannot seriously suppose that what I've just cited from Rorty gets Sellars right, if for no other reason than that it *was* Sellars, precisely, who insisted on the irreconcilable difference between the "scientific image" and the "manifest image" by which (in Rorty's words) "quarks and human rights are [only] uselessly said to differ in 'ontological status.'" These are deliberate provocations, plainly irreconcilable with both Dewey's pragmatism and Sellars's ulterior program.

You begin to see how, in shaping his list of American philosophical senators, Rorty tends to favor one particular nerve in the thought of each, which *he* needs for his own philosophical mosaic, in virtue of which he elevates one or another figure to the status he assigns them, more or less disregarding *their* own way of integrating their themes into *their* philosophical "systems." As already noted, Rorty deliberately deforms Davidson's account of truth so that it may be characterized as Jamesian (that is, as pragmatist), although, at the same time, he deforms James's theory so that it appears hospitable to something akin to Davidson's own refusal to treat the theory of truth as explanatory of knowledge.[14]

These are not ordinary "selections" of the standard doctrines of either Sellars or Davidson. They are deliberate distortions—for a purpose that is still not altogether clear—that separate, as if they were free-standing, themes that, in their usual context, cannot take the meaning assigned. This not only reveals an essential part of the postmodernist strategy; it poses the deep risk of Rorty's effort to draw the leading champions of analytic philosophy in his wake. It is by no means obvious that he can succeed beyond that instant fame of his that begins to compare with the tulip craze.

All this explains the reason for Davidson's utter dismissal of James's theory and marks the sticking point of his naturalizing strategy—which Rorty endorses on the mistaken assumption that what he says of both Davidson and James improves the views of each. It is more to the point that the deformation fits with his relentless (completely unsupported) move to repudiate the idea that the theory of truth has any explanatory role of its own. He does not bother to notice that Davidson's semantic account of truth requires (as Davidson admits) *some* systematic connection with meaning and belief. For what Davidson objects to in non-naturalized explanations would never bring him to endorse the summary doctrine Rorty espouses—espouses in apparent loyalty to Davidson himself. Davidson could not possibly reject the offending explanations for Rorty's reasons![15] (He is too conventional a philosopher.) There is no simple explanation of these distortions. They are not, as I say, ordinary mistakes; they are also neither clever nor likely to be persuasive. On the contrary, they put Rorty's readers on their guard. They suggest the need to keep a separate record of Rorty's often divergent readings of the same figures or the same texts.

By means of a related maneuver, Rorty reclaims Sellars as one of his orienting stalwarts, largely because he reads Sellars as having produced a compelling argument against "the Myth of the Given" (thereby defeating empiricism) and, in that spirit, as having shown us a way to eliminate "mind" in its familiar substantive sense. This is why Rorty writes an introduction to Sellars's important essay, "Empiricism and the Philosophy of Mind" (reissued as a separate volume), which, let me emphasize again, originally appeared in the same volume as the eliminativist essays already mentioned. It is in this way part of a new manifesto. Sellars, Rorty says, "may have been the first philosopher to insist that we see 'mind' as a sort of hypostatization of language. He argued that the intentionality of beliefs is a reflection of the intentionality of sentences, rather than conversely."[16] This again is deliberately skewed in the sense already supplied.

In pressing Sellars's candidacy (which has not caught on in quite the way Rorty would have wished), Rorty ignores the plain fact that *Sellars* presses the point of the "Empiricism" paper Rorty cites in the service of a convinced metaphysics of the most unyielding kind. Sellars actually says (in "The Language of Theories"): "According to the view I am proposing, correspondence rules [in an account of a realist view of the language of scientific explanation] would appear in the material mode as statements to the effect that the objects of the observational framework *do not really exist— there really are no such things.* They envisage the abandonment of a sense and its denotation."[17] Can Rorty actually embrace or defend such a view? Can he have meant to defend it?

It's only in a "Rortyan" reading of "similar" undertakings that Rorty himself is able to bring Sellars and Quine together (because both attack and defeat foundationalism, even if by different means). Which permits Rorty to absorb, again by deformation, Gilbert Ryle's attack on the Cartesian myth and Wittgenstein's attack on the private-language argument. All of this miraculously supports Rorty's repudiation of the very enterprise of metaphysics. But nothing could be farther from the truth, as far as the philosophers mentioned are concerned. There's no evidence, for instance, that Wittgenstein would ever have shared anything of Ryle's notion of the myth of the mind: he simply never addressed the matter in Ryle's way (though it does seem that he had very deep suspicions about the sources from which Ryle drew the detailed view he did).

Similarly, when he declares: "As a Sellarsian psychological nominalist,

who believes all awareness is a linguistic affair . . ."—which he offers in the
process of responding to a disagreement with Charles Taylor—Rorty deliberately ignores the fact that he is misinforming us *about Sellars.* For he
(Rorty) obviously means to press the point that "we have no use for the
[metaphysical] distinction between the 'intrinsic' and the 'relational' features of things" (in particular, the "intrinsic" theory of mind and the "relational" theory of mind) because "we have no use" for metaphysics altogether;
whereas, Sellars (as already remarked) wishes only to deny all substantive
standing to what is called mind.[18] Sellars *is* an eliminativist, a bona fide
metaphysician; whereas Rorty dismisses every variety of metaphysics he can
find.

The fatal weakness in Sellars's argument—very possibly in Rorty's (and,
it may be added, in Robert Brandom's "Rortyan" treatment of Sellars)—lies
with the metaphysical standing of language itself: it would be very difficult,
if not impossible, to treat selves eliminatively (as Sellars does) *and* yet allow
the continued objective standing of truth (and language) in the scientific realist's sense. You cannot find in Rorty or Sellars any explanation of how to
admit language without admitting the realist standing of mind. It's all very
well for Rorty to admire Sellars for having seen "'mind' as a sort of hypostatization of language." But what would either say about the claim that the
realist standing of *language* implicates the realist standing of mind? What is
the basis for prioritizing one over the other? Both are silent on the question.

Rorty goes on to say: "There is no point to asking in which of these cases
there is 'a fact of the matter' or 'truth of the matter,' though there may be a
point in asking whether any useful purpose is served by spending much time
in debate."[19] It is quite impossible to read what Rorty says here without supposing that he is invoking Quine's "view" (in the context of the "indeterminacy of translation" passages) to the effect that "there is no fact of the matter."
That is the constant implication Rorty insinuates by such phrases as, "whether
any useful purpose is served. . . ." The "useful purpose" is invariably some
epistemological or metaphysical vestige from the traditional practices he is
about to dismantle. In all of this, you need to bear in mind that Rorty is "applying" Quine in favor of his postmodernism and against Putnam's more
conventional formulation of a pragmatist account of metaphysical and epistemological matters. But Quine himself cannot be easily reconciled with
Davidson, let alone Sellars.

Rorty takes Quine's argument to mean that *there is no fact of the matter—
period!* Hence, that (say) "the philosophical notion of reference is one we can
well do without . . . as ontology is also."[20] But, alas, Quine has himself flagged
Rorty's mistaken reading, which of course might (if it had been valid) have

led Quine to apply Rorty's strategy in the same way Rorty would lead Davidson astray. Quine is admirably explicit:

> In ascribing to me the "claim that there is no 'matter of fact' involved
> in attributions of meaning to utterances, beliefs to people, and aspi-
> rations to cultures," Rorty [Quine says] overstates my negativity.
> How words and sentences are used, in what circumstances and in
> what relations to one another, is very much a matter of fact, and
> moreover I cheerfully call its study a study of meaning. My reserva-
> tions concern rather the ascription of a distinctive meaning or cog-
> nitive content to each separate sentence, as something shared by the
> sentence and its correct translations. I hold that two conflicting
> manuals of translation can do equal justice to the semantic facts,
> while distributing the meaning load differently sentence by
> sentence.[21]

III

Locating these "deformations," as I call them, is a matter of professional
honor. But they are more than deformations. They bear on the sense and
force of Rorty's entire strategy; also, given Rorty's growing influence, they
now threaten to affect the fortunes of the whole of American philosophy.

Rorty's strategy divides along two lines. First, as we have begun to see, he
advances standard objections against selected efforts to defend "mainstream" analytic positions, so as to call into doubt the very legitimacy of all
such efforts. Then, he moves on to propose, piecemeal, opportunistic com-
pacts with possible opponents mobilized against still others who have been
noticeably weakened and whom both he and his temporary allies oppose
(for whatever reason).

Rorty literally recruits allies of mixed and different convictions—muf-
fling philosophical differences for a time, offering a friendly détente or
two, facilitating by other than philosophical means the effective subversion of hitherto valid sources of canonical resistance. Rorty's "coopera-
tion" with Davidson defines the mode of operation here. He seeks out
figures of strategic importance or power, usually at a tier of professional
strength that is less than secure, philosophers committed to one or another key doctrine that, on a very inventive reading, accords (or "could"
be made to accord) with Rorty's own "postmodernist" or "pragmatist" replacement. That is, if only these figures would accept the free offer of
an irenic (a philosophically unencumbered) rereading of their own doctrines!

The first sub-strategy tends to be philosophically well-disciplined; the second is noticeably slippery and opportunistic. The principal target of the first turns out to have been Hilary Putnam all along. Putnam grasped at an early moment the essential nerve of Rorty's purpose and program. He challenged both on grounds that proved too weak or too inflexible to stem Rorty's heterodox maneuvers. Putnam's arguments appeared irrelevant. He was unable to close the gates against them. And thus he lost an excellent advantage—and even, in a way, his own position. As we have seen, Putnam triggered the dispute with Rorty, with the cryptic challenge of the closing lines of *Reason, Truth and History,*[22] which charged Rorty's 1979 presidential address before the American Philosophical Association with being implicitly "relativistic."[23] But the attack backfired badly.

In the introduction to the first volume of his *Philosophical Papers* (1991), Rorty still views Putnam rather favorably—consigns him to his second bin rather than his first. Specifically, he speaks of an "antirepresentationalism common to Putnam and Davidson": the phrasing is meant to signal one of Rorty's temporary concordats—a maneuver proceeding along the lines of the second sub-strategy but armed with arguments drawn from the first. The arguments are never really supplied. No matter! Rorty adjusts Putnam's theory to his own advantage: "This point [namely,] that there is no independent test of the accuracy of correspondence is [Rorty affirms for the moment] the heart of Putnam's argument: that notions like 'reference'—semantical notions which relate language to non-language—are internal to our overall view of the world."[24]

Rorty intends these remarks to function "therapeutically," that is, to eliminate all such inquiries as completely pointless. That could hardly have been Putnam's intention. Putnam means only to identify an inadequate but still-corrigible ingredient in a legitimate philosophical undertaking. But Rorty has already put his finger on Putnam's deeper vulnerability: he has only to spring the trap.

By the time he writes his attack on Putnam—"Hilary Putnam and the Relativist Menace" (1993)[25]—Rorty turns the relativist charge explicitly against Putnam and draws attention to the flaw in Putnam's "internal realism": namely, his completely unguarded reliance on the would-be *Grenzbegriff,* the regulative principle of truth and rationality (meant to ensure his "antirepresentationalism"), which makes its sole appearance on the last page of *Reason, Truth and History.* Putnam had introduced the *Grenzbegriff* to strengthen a plausible realism suited to the admitted achievements of the physical sciences (under "internalist" conditions) *and* to disallow the "relativist" menace of Rorty's presidential address. But the gambit does little more than highlight Putnam's own failure to sustain his double purpose.

Rorty was instantly aware of that misstep and rightly seized the advantage. He claimed he had long ago abandoned the philosophically fraudulent enterprise of shoring up "realism" and, since he also held that "relativism" arises as a conceptual worry only within the realist/anti-realist orbit, he himself was home free—not a proper target for Putnam's well-intentioned appeal to the *Grenzbegriff* (which Putnam somehow insinuated was ineluctable).[26] But that, of course, is not enough to vindicate Rorty's stand— *his* "postmodernism"/"pragmatism"—which still looks like little more than a thumbing of his nose at those who continue to play at metaphysics and epistemology (or, indeed, at textual accuracy).

His treatment of Putnam certainly changes: he first treats Putnam as an ally on the matter of "antirepresentationalism," and then as an overly ripe defender of entrenched positions on realism that he (Rorty) is in the process of dismantling *sine die*. If you see all this, you see how it explains the rationale by which Rorty segregates "opponents" like Thomas Nagel, John Searle, Michael Dummett, Bernard Williams, David Lewis, David Papineau (gathered up with the later Putnam) within the tentacles of the first sub-strategy; and Daniel Dennett, Charles Taylor, Thomas Kuhn, Ruth Millikan, Nancy Fraser (collected, more or less non-confrontationally, with Davidson) in advancing the second sub-strategy.

But, you are bound to ask, how important are the "deformations" you allege? Are they perhaps occasional errors (if they really are) that have no serious bearing on Rorty's effort to change the course of American philosophy? Isn't it true that Rorty's mistakes about Davidson and Quine—I am prepared to argue that they are mistakes—are no more fundamental as to *how*, ultimately, philosophy should be practiced than Rorty's exposé of Putnam's use of the *Grenzbegriff* or Davidson's "blunder" in shaping a coherence-and-correspondence theory of truth?

If that were indeed the entire matter, there would be an end to it. But there *is* more, much more, and it requires a bit of labor. Have patience, please.

Let me offer an instructive specimen: the exchange (in effect) between Rorty and Nancy Fraser on the advocacy of feminism and Rorty's free advice about why feminists should present themselves as "pragmatists."[27] The difference between them runs deeper than may appear. I offer the example to gain some traction on the "deformation" issue—which I shall then locate, more perspicuously, in Rorty's other papers. There seems to be no easier way to proceed.

In any case, I have two points to make: the first, that Rorty's proposal (almost a "marriage proposal," Fraser humorously suggests[28]) is never advanced on "philosophical" grounds but only in the way of a friendly conspiracy touching on the possibility of shared power and patronage; the second, that there is, nevertheless, in Rorty's unsolicited offer of support, a palpable lacuna that Fraser picks up. Fraser objects to Rorty's attempting to deflect the feminists from their own scruple regarding political legitimation. They are likelier to succeed, Rorty opines, if they would only restrict themselves (as "pragmatists" or "postmodernists") to perfecting their "prophetic" message! That is, if they would give up their dreams of public power and fall back to their excellent private utopias. ("Prophecy" is "private," in Rorty's lexicon.)

Rorty unerringly deprecates the usual feminist cry to "create" woman now, to effectuate whatever forms of solidarity might help achieve the social transformations the feminists pursue. In tendering his advice, Rorty fails to see (perhaps he does see after all), first, that the feminists (well, Fraser certainly) are not prepared to disjoin political power and philosophical legitimation or to dismiss legitimation as a matter of no consequence to the first; and, second, that the feminists see no need to "create" woman *ex nihilo*, for their considerable history belies Rorty's implicit charge of arbitrariness. They are well beyond the upstart charm of postmodernism!

Rorty favors little more than an opportunistic rhetoric—no activism at all:

> Here is where pragmatist philosophy might be useful to feminist politics [he ventures]. For pragmatism redescribes both intellectual and moral progress by substituting metaphors of evolutionary development for metaphors of progressively less distorted perception. . . . We drop the notion of beliefs being made true by reality, as well as the distinction between intrinsic and accidental features of things. So we drop questions about (in Nelson Goodman's phrase) The Way the World Is. We thereby drop the ideas of the Nature of Humanity and of The Moral Law, considered as objects which inquiry is trying to represent accurately, or as objects which make true moral judgments. So we have to give up the comforting belief that competing groups will always be able to reason together on the basis of plausible and neutral premises.[29]

Fraser believes there are indeed suppler arguments than Rorty's, arguments that may even resolve the incommensurabilities between standard essentialisms and universalisms and appeals to Reason and whatever the feminists now perceive to be required for political justice. In fact, Rorty takes no notice of these arguments which he dismisses at the same time he neglects to credit the *philosophical* gains Dewey originally believed he had earned convincingly, namely, those he draws from his analysis of a "problematic situation." Rorty presses a deliberate distortion of Dewey's well-known remark to the effect that "the worse or evil is a rejected good";[30] *he means* that *Dewey means* the remark to be taken in the sense in which pragmatism is no longer committed to metaphysics and epistemology and moral reasoning: the sense in which there is never "a fact of the matter."

"Pragmatists like myself," Rorty confides, "think that the Deweyan account of moral truth and moral progress comports better with the prophetic tone in contemporary feminism than do universalism and realism."[31] (You need to remark the sly association of the "Deweyan account of moral truth and moral progress" with the "prophetic," which Rorty attributes to the feminists. In one stroke, therefore, Rorty warns us not to interpret either in the way of providing a defense for "public" policies: the issue is confined to the sphere of the "private.") But that cannot be convincing if there is (as there is) a viable third possibility. You have only to read Dewey with care to see that he was never a Rortyan or a postmodernist in Rorty's sense, and never yielded in his mature work to anything close to Rorty's doctrines. (I pursue the issue briefly in chapters 3 and 4.)

The feminists had already arrived at much the same conclusion before Rorty offered his advice. They have been waiting for Rorty to catch up, not to lead them by the nose for their own good. Why should Rorty have supposed that anyone who was philosophically and politically alert would ever have played into a quietism Dewey had already shown us how to defeat?

You have to feel the weight of Rorty's clever words—"redescribes," "substituting," "drop," "give up" (in the passage cited)—that forces the issue of a rapprochement between pragmatism and feminism to appear to be less than a political recommendation and never philosophically informed. Fraser has Rorty dead right here—that is, his "failure of nerve" (her term). Here is a piece of her argument:

> I would like to suggest an alternative way of characterizing the feminist project. . . . For my disagreement with [Rorty] is a disagreement within pragmatism. I, too, reject moral realism and universalism in favor of the historical view that feminists are engaged in creating new moral identities and sensibilities. . . . And I, too, see the remaking of language as central to this enterprise. [I would] put a more sociological, institutional and collective spin on these ideas and

[would] divest [Rorty's] account of its individualistic, aestheticizing, and depoliticizing residue. . . . Whereas Rorty has made the significant but still incomplete move "From Irony to Prophecy," I mean to go the rest of the way "From Prophecy to Feminist Politics."[32]

The full import of Fraser's criticism may escape you, since what Fraser draws attention to is, first, Rorty's characteristic deformation of Dewey in separating private "irony" from "ethnocentric solidarity" (or, better, his denying public standing to many of Dewey's well-known public interests) and assuring us that this is indeed the right way to read Dewey;[33] and, second, her urging, against Rorty, that philosophy (in the pragmatists' as well as the feminists' view) *is* fully public and therefore bears directly on the legitimation of political norms. "Prophecy," Fraser astutely notes, falls short of politics in Rorty's idiom: hence his "dichotomous view of cultural and discursive space." Politics is public and prophecy, like poetry, "private." But the feminists, like the pragmatists (preeminently, Dewey), reject the division. Rorty offers nothing in the way of a rationale—only a conceptual gap he never bridges.

IV

This, however, is only the preamble, hardly the full argument itself. For that we need a new setting, one in which a classic philosophical problem might be said to be dissolved by "redescriptions" that never implicate a philosophical choice, that is, never rest on specifically philosophical evidence (whatever such evidence might prove to be). The obvious example—which Rorty rightly invokes—is Wittgenstein's "redescriptions" (in the *Investigations*). But there are all sorts of puzzles that besiege us if, for instance, we try to dissolve the mind/body problem or even the puzzle of the "reality" of an apparently inner episode of experienced pain. Rorty is to be congratulated for the courage of risking questions of these sorts in advancing an upstart policy. His subtle, remarkably candid, often ingenious maneuvers to put the entire mind/body puzzle to rest (within the resources of his "postmodernist" program), afford the best opportunity for assessing the true prospects of his proposal. I doubt there is a better setting than the one provided by the paper, "Daniel Dennett on Intrinsicality" (1993).[34]

Before addressing it, however, I draw your attention to the fact that Wittgenstein never sought to "explain away," deny, or disallow first person avowals of pain or reports of other sensations, even where he dissolves "the private-language argument." This is not always remembered. Therefore, Wittgenstein's practice cannot be equated with Rorty's "metaphilosophy," though both profess a "therapeutic" purpose. (Wittgenstein was in fact engaged in a philosophical argument in his theory!)

With that in mind, I suggest that avowals or "first person reports" of experienced pain are (without prejudice to any philosophical puzzles) as stubborn a body of initial "data" as can possibly be mustered on the matter of analyzing the mind. Indeed, that fact alone vindicates the philosophical pertinence of the "redescriptions" both Dennett and Rorty favor in order to dismantle the "Cartesian Theater" (Dennett's phrase): philosophically (in the canonical sense) as Dennett sees matters; "metaphilosophically" (in the postmodernist sense) as Rorty urges.[35]

If we add the sense in which he would have us read them, Dennett's challenge may be put in two sentences: (1) "There is no observer inside the brain." (2) "The Cartesian Theater is a metaphorical picture of how conscious experience must sit in the brain."[36] These are clearly very different claims. "I will explain," he adds, "the various phenomena that comprise what we call consciousness, showing how they are all physical effects of the brain's activities, how these activities evolved, and how they give rise to illusions about their own powers and properties."[37]

Rorty judges Dennett's strategy to be right-minded but philosophically defective; he therefore mixes argument and postmodernist coaxing. For his part, Dennett proceeds to reconcile our "folk" account (first person avowals) with what he claims (tendentiously) are the materialist requirements imposed by the successes of the physical sciences. In the end, Dennett "resists" Rorty's blandishments: first, because, as he says, "I am not convinced that what is true about consciousness is true about everything"; and, second, because "I'm actually still quite conservative in my adoption of Standard Scientific Epistemology and Metaphysics."[38] (The only caveat to enter here, against Dennett, is that it is altogether too optimistic for Dennett to argue that *Science* requires the rejection of first person reports or avowals of inner experience. But I would not say that Dennett's overzealous representation— a palpable distortion—makes him out to be a postmodernist of Rorty's stripe!)

Let me cite a passage, therefore, from Rorty's paper that catches up his view of Dennett's philosophical argument against "anti-holists" like Thomas Nagel and John Searle, who, for their part, believe we *can* "scrutinize the phenomena closely"—pain, for instance. I shall not defend Nagel or Searle, since they argue in a way that is hardly responsive to their objectors' objections. The "data" of our avowals remain as persistent as before—untouched in fact, though Rorty seems to believe otherwise. So does Dennett, of course, but Dennett's argument is straightforward, even if not compelling.

Rorty's argument is, I suggest, a howler of a new sort—a metaphilosophical or postmodernist howler—that pretends to settle the contest between the "holists" and the "anti-holists"—on the very eligibility of mental
"scrutiny"—*by way of "redescriptions" that are said to have no philosophical
pretensions!* Here is the passage:

> For holists like Dennett, suggesting that we can "scrutinize the phe-
> nomena clearly" is itself question-begging. . . . Holists like Wittgen-
> stein, Ryle, and Dennett—people who specialize in replacing
> intrinsic features with relational features—recognize their obliga-
> tion to explain everything anybody has ever talked about. In that
> sense the attribution of consciousness to other people can be viewed
> not as the result of an inference from behavioral evidence (as Nagel
> views it) but simply as a reformulation of that evidence.[39]

What Rorty offers in the way of an analysis is unnecessarily muddled. It
may be true that neither Nagel nor Searle is the best authority on the mental "scrutiny" of pains and the like. For it is entirely possible that errors may
creep into first person avowals (dental-chair reports, cold that feels like heat,
misdescriptions and mistaken identifications). It is also unnecessary to insist (as perhaps Nagel does) on a fixed and inflexible distinction between
"intrinsic" and "relational features"; internal scrutiny (if allowed) need not
be dualistic and need not deny the relational embedding of what is avowed
in its physical setting (as indeed dental-chair avowals show). So it cannot be
compelling to suppose the internal data can be swept away by merely introducing "relational" redescriptions that seem plausible to some. That is a
knock-down blunder on Rorty's part, which begins to expose what may yet
be (what I think is) the Achilles' heel of Rorty's "pragmatism" (or postmodernism).

I must add a few more lines, because Rorty claims to see something seriously amiss in Dennett's argument. He turns—in the spirit I've characterized as the "second sub-strategy"—to recruit Dennett to his postmodernist
team. (You will have noticed that he has already collected Wittgenstein and
Gilbert Ryle under the same auspices he offers Dennett.) But he is obliged
to correct Dennett's holism as "un-Quinean":

> Holists . . . cannot allow themselves the distinction between descrip-
> tion and fact that this suggestion presupposes. They cannot allow
> questions like: is the organism's actual and possible behavior one
> fact and its consciousness another or are they the same fact? For

[they] try to do what Wittgenstein told us not to attempt: to go between language and its object. Holists can allow only questions like:
should our best causal account of how things work include the relations of X to Y or merely an account of the relations of X to Y-talk.[40]

This is as forthright a bit of postmodernist instruction as we are likely to
find. But can it work? It seems caught in a trap of its own invention: a complication it cannot ignore but also cannot resolve. For if you think about it
you will surely see that "our best causal account" will require a working contrast between distinguishable *denotata* and mere *relata*—hence, between
the "intrinsic" and "relational" features of what, for causal purposes at least
(but not invariantly), are to be counted among the first. For instance, does
the fact that my having a toothache causes me to wince signify that this is a
distinct event that cannot be eliminated by merely redescribing in "relational" terms what may have transpired? If I'm right in this, then: (1) Rorty
is and must be practicing philosophy "without a license" when he is practicing his "metaphilosophy"; and (2) his recommended ("postmodernist")
strategy must be inherently self-defeating wherever it has a payoff as substantive as the one just proposed. That's worth considering.

You see, of course, that in the example given the ulterior issue (for Rorty)
is *never* quite whether there *are* phenomenal data or not. For, on Rorty's
view, no such question can ever be decided apart from deciding the allegedly
deeper (*non*-philosophical) question of whether we are prepared to change
our descriptions so that the former question simply dissolves before our
eyes! And yet, the "deeper" question begins to nag—insinuates a whole raft
of new constraints on what might otherwise have been applied to normal
philosophical disputes. (The "intrinsic"/"relational" option cuts both ways.)

Recall Rorty's argument and language. Rorty supposes that if we grasp
the "rules" correctly, then Nagel and Searle will be defeated in an instant,
without ever risking a single philosophical skirmish! But what are the *rules*?
Well, they are disarmingly introduced by addressing us as "we holists." It
seems they are embedded in a set of dicta that always warn "us holists" about
what we "cannot allow." Is that perhaps the beginning of a rogue philosophy? You might have thought Rorty would never invoke such fixities; but he
apparently finds that certain necessities flow from agreeing to be guided
(say) by Quine's holism or Davidson's holism or Dennett's holism or even
the scruple of postmodernism!

Please remember that we have already discovered that Quine has no difficulty at all in reconciling (in effect, against Rorty's interpretation) his own

holism ("the indeterminacy of translation" thesis) and the sensible demarcation of distinct *denotata* suitable for empirical and philosophical debate. Also, Dennett's use of causal arguments in sorting out what to count as "intrinsic" and what to count as "relational" is part of a straightforward materialism and not a postmodernism at all; that is, Dennett would never argue from abstract "holist" rules (of Rorty's kind), since he apparently believes the empirical evidence pretty well decides the philosophical question. In short, Dennett believes that the evidence shows that there are no phenomena to be examined in the "Cartesian theater," and Rorty believes that the question whether there are or are no discernible such phenomena is itself no more than the upshot of a non-philosophical choice of idiom.

Davidson's holism has barely been mentioned—the attack on the so-called "scheme"/"content" dogma, which is meant to be applied to such different figures as Kuhn, Quine, and Putnam, though it is hard to see how *any* such holism could be made to decide *any* substantive question (empirical or philosophical) that did *not* implicate a complete disjunction between "scheme" and "content." If so, then Rorty must be making up the "rules" as he goes along; and, in any case, he could never show that a reasonable interpretation of such rules would favor "metaphilosophy" over "philosophy." (I return briefly to the topic of Davidson's holism in chapter 5.)

You must bear in mind that the metaphysics and epistemology of the "Cartesian theater" may remain as unacceptable as you please; but *that,* the anti-holists may reasonably argue, has nothing to do with the "pre"-philosophical admission or scrutiny of the sensory data. Nagel and Searle undoubtedly overstate their claims, but so do Dennett and Rorty. There is an empirical mystery there. But there is no ineluctable Cartesian dualism implicated in admitting the "initial data." If there was such a dualism, it would be very unlikely that we could ever really defeat it! And there is no assured rule by which to decide the matter. Certainly, no postmodernist rule.

We have only a stalemate to show for our labor, but it's a stalemate that confirms that Rorty's argument (also Dennett's) cannot go forward free of all metaphysical and epistemological encumbrances. There is nothing objectionable in that, unless it is the presumption that evidentiary privilege rightly favors one side over the other (Dennett) or that we are free to change our "descriptions" of the mental, here and now, without any philosophical penalty whatsoever (Rorty). The difference between the two is this: Dennett does not see that his own argument is too weak for the conclusion he wants. (Rorty sees that much, of course.) Yet Rorty also believes (as Dennett does not) that we can surmount the philosophical impasse by sheer redescriptive fiat, even though the maneuver ends by favoring one metaphysics over the other.

There is more that could be said. But this is surely enough for a *reductio*.

v

At a deeper level of analysis, we realize that at stake is the very idea of a defensible philosophical practice that, in spite of the obvious weaknesses of canonical strategies, *is* able to pit opposing intuitions against one another in a reasonably fair and productive way. What is especially worth remarking is that the dispute between (say) Nagel and Dennett and (on a reading favorable to Rorty) between Rorty and either Nagel or Dennett is not merely a dispute between opposed or incompatible convictions but between opposed and incommensurable ones. That is an issue of the greatest possible importance, an issue that arises in a peculiarly insistent way in the deepest puzzles of the philosophy of mind.

As far as I know, the incommensurabilist question is never really acknowledged by the principal masters of the field: that is, that the mind/body problem and the evidentiary status of first person avowals cannot go forward without resolving incommensurable claims that either exclude the relevance of the other's cognitive sources in a wide range of contexts, or disagree profoundly about the evidentiary weight of the sources of each. These are not matters that can be easily swept away by either objectivist or postmodernist premises. Also, you cannot fail to notice that the relativist and incommensurabilist puzzles must, if viable (as I believe they are), affect the realist question itself.

I have, in effect, just demonstrated (obliquely, I admit) that the question regarding the reconcilability of relativism or incommensurabilism and both pragmatism and naturalizing is a reasonable and unavoidable question. In a way, we owe the perception of the argument to Rorty's postmodernist maneuvers—but in such a way that, acknowledging its force, we are led to see postmodernism's own inability to meet the very issue it raises against canonical philosophy. So it provides no advantage here, unless arbitrariness counts as one.

Nagel and Dennett suppose they are advancing philosophically pertinent arguments against one another's claims. Rorty supposes he can decide the matter between them (always in Dennett's favor) by "redescriptive" means that need never examine the epistemological intuitions of either (or of any one else)! But none of this is persuasive. All three fail to consider the matter of appraising opposed legitimations of cognitive competence drawn from the same societal practices, but drawn incommensurably. Our theorists cannot fail to be aware that their most persistent disputes cannot (as we now understand matters) be subsumed under canonical terms apt for their common resolution. The issue is not open to "normal" science or philosophy, but it is a perfectly ordinary, even strategic, concern. (I return to the matter in chapter 5.)

These considerations afford some reason to believe the resolutions Dennett and Rorty separately propose cannot possibly count as "neutral" or "objective"—or decisive—in any simple way. A proper resolution would require novel and more comprehensive strategies of analysis and legitimation that *might in time* convincingly replace those policies that now are judged compelling by their respective advocates—that have actually produced the present stalemate.

Since the resolution of the evidentiary question cannot but depend on how best to construe the continuity of past and future practice (think of the eventual acceptance of Galileo's upstart notion that local motion need not be locally perceptible), philosophical legitimation (if admitted at all) would have to incorporate improvisations supported under the conditions of evolving practice and evolving norms of legitimation. If the puzzles of the philosophy of mind afford fair specimens of scientific and philosophical dispute, then there is every reason to believe that views like Dennett's, Nagel's, and Rorty's seriously misrepresent the difficulty and distinction of philosophical practice itself. There simply is no closure there. But that is not to say that our legitimative assessments are either arbitrary or pointless.

Rorty, of course, says nothing about these complications. Indeed, he rides roughshod over them. But they mark a needed space between fixed canons and the arbitrariness of rejecting legitimative questions altogether. Rorty apparently believes that Thomas Kuhn must have been leaning in his (Rorty's) direction when he characterized shifts in scientific paradigms as ultimately relying on one or another form of non-rational "conversion."[41] But even the resolution of the Priestley/Lavoisier impasse was not achieved without grasping the reasonableness of overriding the perceived incommensurability in Lavoisier's favor—even if *not* in terms of the exclusionary "normal" practices of either Priestley or Lavoisier at any particular moment in their dispute, and certainly *not* in terms of any mere "conversion." Here Kuhn fails Rorty massively, for Kuhn's discovery baffled him, and he never practiced a postmodernism of Rorty's stripe.

More to the point is that Rorty's postmodernist proposals regarding "redescription" appear to presuppose the absence of pertinent incompatibilities, incommensurabilities, divergent sources of evidence, and the like; for if they did not invoke incommensurabilities, they would still need to explain to us what the justifying reasons were by which they could simply "change the topic" as they pleased. In the first instance, they would not even be post-modernists; in the second, they would be caught in the bramble of inescapable philosophical questions.

There are other conceptual resources at hand besides those Rorty recommends—difficult to formulate because we are so easily deflected by the habits of past practice, however much that practice may be judged to be inadequate at any given time. The truth is that the carpentered arguments of one particular partisan or another are effectively assessed on the occasion on which they are advanced; whereas, the reasoning needed to decide the legitimative question, particularly regarding incommensurabilities, requires the full play of extended time and change—time enough to assess the conceptual changes that are set in motion by our instant arguments. We hardly have a grip on the "logic" of such thinking, and Rorty fails to raise the issue at all; it would completely undercut postmodernism's *faute de mieux* mentality.

If, with Rorty, we were prepared to repudiate for cause all the pretensions of philosophical privilege (universalism, essentialism, and the rest) and to turn instead (on Rorty's advice) to promote only those conceptual "redescriptions" we believed would advance our present cause and interest, then there would still be no compelling reason to believe—certainly Rorty offers none—that philosophical legitimation should finally be abandoned. Postmodernism has no leverage here. Impasses like the one regarding the evidentiary standing of interior scrutiny continue to rely on second-order conjectures perceived *by all* to be more responsible than any of Rorty's drastic alternatives.

Once Rorty repudiates universalism and privilege, he apparently believes he has defeated every version of the legitimative question. He urges us, therefore, to be guided solely by considerations of causal effectiveness. (That may strike you as an unlikely reading.) But there is no philosopher whom Rorty has tried to recruit to the side of his agile "redescription" of the other's doctrine (Quine, Davidson, Fraser, Dennett—confining attention to those already mentioned) who has not fashioned a rationale he or she deems less arbitrary than Rorty's and more resistant to dismissal than the traditional canons Rorty repeatedly trashes.

Had Dewey lived, for instance, to answer Rorty's "post-philosophical" reading of his *Experience and Nature,* he would undoubtedly have opposed Rorty's dismissal of the book's metaphysical and epistemological labors. You cannot find in Dewey any tendency to reclaim the failed essentialism and privilege Rorty rejects and may even have learned to reject by reading Dewey.

Moreover, you cannot find in Dewey any tendency to embrace Rorty's rejection of canonical questions. (I am of course speaking "of the writings of [the man Rorty names as] my principal philosophical hero, John Dewey."[42]) Rorty nowhere explains, because he sees no need to explain, why, if we abandon the old forms of fixity and privilege, we will find no genuine alternative to adopt but the "postmodern" options he himself offers. But even the "redescriptive" strategy makes no sense among the epistemically incommensurable alternatives Rorty isolates in pitting Nagel and Dennett against one another; and Rorty's logic would make it impossible to champion any fluxive philosophy.

Philosophy has ignored these complications much too long. What, by sheer chance, Rorty forces on our attention is a sense of the unexpected depth at which incommensurable policies may compete. The difficulty of ever resolving such puzzles accounts, I imagine, for much of the initial plausibility of Rorty's "pragmatist" solutions and the grand relief at having found so simple a surgery. Many of Rorty's specimen problems do indeed occupy a no-man's land between incompatible and incommensurable positions.

It's there, of course, that Rorty believes he has found a friendly earth for a "metaphilosophical" rhetoric plausible enough to stalemate (and replace) every would-be philosophical canon—without the least need to review the powers of any fresh options that claim to depart from the old canons he (Rorty) never tires of mocking; that is, the failed canons that insist on universalism, essentialism, cognitive privilege, transcendental reason, *de re* necessities, Cartesian realism, and the like. But the fact is, the deep puzzlement that incommensurability generates (certainly, the puzzle of the internal scrutiny of the mind), the absence of conceptual anarchy in the historical flux of social life, incompatible judgments that reflect the profoundest differences of scrupulous research and reflection, have already eclipsed the short-run advantages of postmodernist redescription. Or, if they have not, then Rorty has misdescribed his strategy.

Rorty never ventures any *philosophical* improvement, and he never satisfies us as to why philosophy's door is closed. The truth is that we find ourselves in a new age in which new forms of philosophical dispute and resolution arise under conditions that concede historical diversity and change—even the historicity of argument, the absence of changeless epistemic principles, the realization that our disputes may harbor epistemological incommensurabilities that canonical strategies could never countenance. In fact, by a pretty irony that takes advantage of Rorty's own "argument" to the effect that *he* is no relativist (*since* relativism arises only in the context of canonical realist/

anti-realist disputes, which, as already reported, he abandons without a murmur), *we* may now say that *his* "post-philosophical" or postmodernist insistence on "redescriptive" maneuvers cannot yet be shown to bear on *philosophical practices that supersede the canon he* (quite belatedly) *rejects.* If relativism is "internal" to the old canons, then so is post-philosophy! Put another way, Rorty has a happy gift for identifying important questions that the established canons and older practices of philosophy cannot resolve. Noticing the fact, Rorty urges his postmodernist economies too quickly, where the better policy might have been to begin to shape new philosophical strategies to eclipse or supplement those already in place. (The redemptive labor is, I suggest, a charge for the new century.)

The plausibility of Rorty's unbridled rejection of every form of philosophical discipline actually feeds on the illusion that if the argumentative resources of "universalism," "essentialism," "realism," and the like fail (as they plainly do), then philosophy cannot be recovered as a proper mode of argument. But that is itself a very strong philosophical claim, possibly the ulterior claim of postmodernism itself. Philosophy, therefore, may owe Rorty's provocation a considerable debt, if postmodernism obliges us to investigate just how the admission of flux, historicity, the loss of modal necessity and cognitive privilege, the unavoidability of construing every viable realism in constructivist terms, epistemological incommensurabilities, and similar complications may yet recommend very different competences from those the older canons have always featured.

Rorty, after all, has had a marvelously free hand driving a truckload of anarchic policies through the old canon's Maginot defenses. We need a very different model of analysis, one that in favoring changeable and diverse paradigms favors plausibility rather than exclusionary truth. There simply are no final and changeless philosophical demonstrations. Frankly, the shift in strategy was already signaled, two hundred years ago, in Hegel's *Phenomenology.* At the very least, it was confirmed in Dewey's *Experience and Nature.* There's a gap there of at least seventy years (spanning Dewey and Rorty) that Rorty's admirable energy cannot possibly explain.

VI

Meanwhile, we should seize the occasion to dismantle Rorty's odd mixture of philosophical and non-philosophical constraints, the ones he offers, for instance, in the name of "holism." His maneuvers are almost always variants of the same general strategy which I have already defined: he identifies a number of holist policies that, when viewed in the abstract, can hardly be faulted but must be made convincing *case by case.* (Think, for instance, of

how we assess charges of self-contradiction.) Then, having persuaded himself that essentialism, universalism, and the rest are no longer compelling,
he hurries to the unearned conclusion that nearly any rhetorical application
of the "rules" he champions will be perceptibly better than any "philosophical" alternative! There's a grand leap there that Rorty is unlikely to admit.

Here, for instance, is a characteristic Rortyan "manifesto" that confirms
what would otherwise be viewed as an unblinking dismissal of argument itself. You may read it as "deforming" Kuhn's admission of a worry *he* cannot
resolve. Rorty alludes to Kuhn's difficulties in justifying fundamental paradigm shifts: he makes a virtue of what Kuhn identifies as a problem he must
address. Kuhn held profoundly conservative views about the realism of
science: he was well aware that the admitted "arbitrariness" of paradigm
changes threw his entire account into complete disorder. Rorty, however,
never looks back:

> The world [Rorty says] does not speak. Only we do. The world can,
> once we have programmed ourselves with a language, cause us to
> hold beliefs. . . . The moral is not that objective criteria for choice
> of vocabulary are to be replaced with subjective criteria, reason with
> will or feeling. . . . [N]otions of criteria and choice . . . are [simply]
> no longer [pertinent]. . . . Europe did not *decide* to accept the idiom
> of Romantic poetry, or of socialist politics, or of Galilean mecha-
> nisms. . . . [It] gradually lost the habit of using certain words and
> gradually acquired the habit of using others.[43]

Two things need to be said about this ingenious piece of opportunism—
always bearing in mind Kuhn's conservative retreat as opposed to Rorty's ex-
ploitation of a freely confessed stalemate. *On the one hand*, Kuhn's incommensurability problem shows that we must think of argument as *stretching
over a span of history* in such a way that relevant data may *evolve* so as to en-
able us to *reduce* the arbitrariness with which we act to "decide" the validity
of a paradigm shift. This will be ad hoc to some extent, serendipitous, provisional, but never merely a matter of non-rational "conversion."

Galileo, for instance, could not have made his case in his own day,
although a reasonable case was eventually made in historical time. The reason, however, this admission is *not* compelling against the incommensurabilist is, precisely, that the adjudication of pertinently competing claims is
itself consensually (but not, otherwise, evidentiarily) meant to mediate *between* incommensurable alternatives. It is not that, in some appropriately
extended interval of time, ordinary evidence always proves conclusive. It is

rather that the effectiveness of what we regard, in time, *as* evidence is itself qualified by our concern to overcome incommensurable choices. (Epistemologists like Davidson turn a blind eye to such historicized considerations, but they are the bread and butter of theorists like Kuhn and Feyerabend.) Certainly, considerations of these sorts more than confirm the sheer opportunities of Rorty's use of the causal theory of belief (in the naturalizer's sense) and the arbitrariness of his advice to feminists like Fraser and eliminativists like Dennett. He seems unwilling to abide by his enunciated policies when quicker strategies seem to promise more immediate gains.

Here the evidence goes completely against Rorty and his reading of Kuhn. Philosophical arguments are hardly confined to *reductio, petitio, non sequitur,* and the like: there must be room enough for the appraisal of arguments that *gather force historically.* Rorty's post-philosophy favors the same sort of instantaneous argument that the Cartesian and Kantian modes had already entrenched. But to dismiss the one is to dismiss the other. (Kuhn, I would say, ventures no more than a personal confession of failure.)

On the other hand, no one doubts that there are historical forces that alter and adjust our would-be "paradigms" in accord with our sense of the changing questions we can and cannot answer, or believe we "must" answer somewhere. The very idea of the need *to change* our paradigms along potentially incommensurable lines is inseparable from our sense of our argumentative competence and the impasses we are bound to confront. The sense in which history effects "changes" from one language game to another (which Rorty emphasizes) *does not,* as Rorty seems to think, subvert the relevance of philosophical argument and "choice" *tout court.* No, it obliges us rather to redefine the conditions under which a new and more responsive rationale may be constructed. Historicity engenders *and* resolves epistemic incommensurability, but not by canonical means. There you have a good part of the significance of the largely ignored fact that English-language epistemology and philosophy of science (including pragmatism) has hardly acknowledged history's own puzzles. There, also, you may anticipate the import of urging pragmatism to recover the full lesson of the Hegelian vision it has in part embraced.

The fact that at some time t we may be reduced to making guesses (like Galileo's gamble about unperceived motion)[44] *does not mean* that shifting from one paradigm to another shows that "the notions of criteria and choice . . . are no longer in point." Not at all. It shows the opposite to be true! Historical transformation registers a narrative unity that (as Hegel might have said) must be blind to the very agents who directly effect it. At t', however, when *they* formulate their version of that history, they will have considered how *our* argumentative policy may or must be adjusted. I see nothing in Rorty's story that would support his opposed conclusion. (Remember: on the pragmatist conception, there is no principled disjunction between theoretical and practical reason.)

Here you may begin to see how a revived pragmatism, attentive to the puzzles that have arisen between the two periods of its career, is undoubtedly better placed to accommodate the suppleness that those intervening puzzles demand than any of the canons of our day—a fortiori, better placed than the arbitrariness of Rorty's postmodernist proposal and his unwillingness to attempt a better resolution.

Therefore, let me, in closing this part of the argument offer a metonymic clue to the full argument by which we may combat Rorty's use of his largest "holist" strategies. Those strategies *are* unquestionably philosophical devices: principally, the resources of Davidson's exposé of the so-called "scheme/content dogma"[45] and Quine's "indeterminacy of translation" thesis which is abetted by the exposé of the analytic/synthetic "dogma."[46] These are enlarged by Rorty to include Davidson's "naturalizing" policy (which Rorty willingly adopts, in fact, applies in an even more extreme way than Davidson does);[47] and, of course, also includes the more amorphous "holism" of Wittgenstein's "therapeutic" philosophy grounded in the human *Lebensform*.

In the paper on Dennett's attack on "intrinsicality," for instance, all of these resources are mysteriously drawn into battle together. Rorty refers enthusiastically to himself and those he would collect as "we post-Quinean and post-*Philosophical Investigations* holists."[48] He particularly mentions the "full-strength holism" that results from applying Davidson's two strategies (already noted) to the "internal scrutiny" question.[49] Davidson had pointedly affirmed (well before Dennett) that in the effort to cast psychology as a science, it often turns out (untenably) that "a sound footing, whether for knowledge or for psychology, requires something inner in the sense of being non-relational."[50]

This is certainly a clever warning, but it is not at all clear what it rules in or out. It is cited by Rorty to explain the sense in which (though the details are missing) he himself rejects "intrinsicality"—that is, reads Dennett's rejection of that doctrine in his own "metaphilosophical" fashion, believes he is literally applying Davidson's scheme/content argument to the intrinsicality issue, and (through it all) brings his entire labor into easy accord with Wittgenstein's philosophical "therapy" and Dewey's opposition to "dualisms" of every sort.

You must read very carefully, therefore, those passages that lead up to conclusions like the following—in which Rorty finesses the differences between himself and Dennett—in order to fix the force and validity of his own dismissal of *any particular philosophical claim*—which he characterizes as "the high metaphilosophical ground" and which in the name of holism he urges us not to give up:

> There is no perduring, intrinsic character of a human self—no "real me," no me *en soi*, for myself to grasp . . . no intrinsic character of *any* object to grasp. So Nagel's ambition of transcendence is not the tough-minded commitment to intellectual honesty he thinks it, but rather a tender-minded yearning for an impossible stability and order. . . .[51]

You must remember that Rorty's purpose (in the paper) is to *strengthen* Dennett's complete rejection of the admissibility of first person internal scrutiny (regarding sensations, thoughts, feelings, and the like)—the entire menagerie of the "Cartesian theater." But if you look carefully at the argument, you will see that it is: (1) a philosophical argument, *malgré* Rorty; (2) utterly irrelevant on the matter of cognitive sources; (3) too sweeping for Dennett (or perhaps for any of us) to adopt; (4) not a legible or valid application of Davidson's exposé of the supposed scheme/content distinction; (5) not an obvious application of any of the other forms of "holism" Rorty claims to adopt, including Wittgenstein's and Dewey's; and, most important, (6) a maneuver whose seeming validity depends on failing to pay attention to the conditions under which the holist strategies are rightly first applied by their originators (where they are applicable at all).

You must ask yourself whether, when Rorty denies that there is any "real me" (or any "intrinsic character of *any* object"), he means that there are no "realist" constraints at all on verbal "redescription" except whatever we happen to favor in terms of the forms of social solidarity that attract us. But to say there are none is surely a philosophical claim that demands an argument; and to admit that there are pertinent constraints is to concede philosophy's relevance at the start. If you think about Rorty's analysis more carefully, you will see that he has insinuated into the mix the paradox of Cartesian realism in order to gain his postmodernist purpose.

But everyone knowledgeable about the Cartesian paradox rejects the doctrine that generates it; *and* the recovery of a constructive realism assigns a stronger standing (than that of mere "social solidarity") to the "real things" of the world, that is, a standing that cannot be responsibly altered by mere "redescription." There's a profound lacuna at the base of Rorty's doctrine— the same lacuna that bedevils canonical analytic philosophy. You must ask yourself what Rorty means by "the high metaphilosophical ground." Can, for instance, the ontological fate of selves be disjoined from the fate of physical objects—in either direction?

The decisive complaint (against Rorty's argument) is that he apparently believes that *if* the "redescription" of the would-be objects of any discourse can be altered, even retired, without yielding to the usual constraints of "realism" and "essentialism," *then* an extension of the same practice can also alter, or retire, the seeming cognitive sources by which changes of the first sort might be thought to be justified. You probably will urge: "But surely Rorty admits *some* constraints against the obvious dangers of this policy?" He does indeed mention one condition, which he formulates in different ways. In the Dennett paper, it runs as follows: "The only general truth we know, and the only one we need to know about the relation between the objects and the descriptions is that the object X is what most of the beliefs expressed in statements using the term 'X' are true of. . . . objects change as our descriptions of them change."[52]

This certainly sounds like idealism, which would explain in part why Dennett will have nothing to do with Rorty's recommendation. Rorty admits the worry, though he claims (rather mysteriously) that "To retain the idealists' holism while junking their metaphysics, all we need do is renounce the ambition of transcendence" (by which he appears to mean non-relational intrinsicality *à la* Nagel).[53] But this misses the double danger: *first*, that if we can alter or retire our would-be cognitive sources under the same "rule," then, in time, we should be able to satisfy the same rule in nearly any gerrymandered way we please—notice, for example, that Rorty and Dennett are already prepared to retire "interior scrutiny"; *second*, that it cannot be true that if the would-be policy about redescribing objects makes sense, we cannot put the same question to the very sources by which the first policy was supported (which might then lead to a clever regress we would have no way of resisting).

You can see how easily Rorty supposes that to deny the "non-relational" ("intrinsic") standing of the cognitive resource of "interior scrutiny" is tantamount to rejecting the legitimacy of any such resource—in the name of remaining loyal to Davidson's treatment of the scheme/content distinction. But that is surely to misapply Davidson's distinction, as well as to fail to see that there must be reasonable constraints on *what* we first admit into the space of philosophical, scientific, or practical argument, which, therefore, directly bears on the licensing of *any* redescriptive strategy of the sort Rorty recommends.

The least controversial rendering (that I know) of what this "prior" constraint would come to is captured by Peirce's notion of *Secondness*[54]—of the causal resistance of the world (never fully articulated in fixed categories), which both Dewey and James implicitly adopt and which Rorty gives us every reason to suppose he also adopts. But if he does, then he is mistaken about the adequacy of the rule he says we need. If, say, Nagel is hell-bent on defending dualism or the incontestable privilege of the deliverances of internal scrutiny, so be it. There's no ineluctable reason why avowals of pain, sensation, fugitive thoughts, hallucinations, feelings, and the like should not be "relational" in any of the various logical senses that would not disqualify their reportorial eligibility. They need not be "representational" in any sense completely separable from whatever we are willing to say is "representational" in our verbal reports about the physical world (without contracting the disorders of pre-Kantian representationalism). Of course, they need not be indisputable either.

In short, the validation of would-be "redescriptions" presupposes certain cognitive resources, and the confirmation of such resources (whatever they may prove to be) hardly poses the same question that arises about validating particular redescriptions of acknowledged cognitive powers or "real things." Furthermore, along these same lines, *some* scruple regarding Secondness would, though it cannot guarantee truth or objectivity, be a welcome sign of philosophical responsibility.

You must think of "Secondness" as a reminder of the profound—the insuperable—informality of first- and second-order discourse about what is "real." Peirce's notion is not meant as a criterion but only as collecting the sense of our most persistent shared intuitions about whatever we encounter that we find difficult to dismiss as unreal: our not being able to stand in the space that another occupies in a crowded elevator for instance! We can always override such intuitions—but never lightly and never without convincing cause.

Rorty is careless here, conflating the vulnerable criteria of academic philosophy and the robust honesty of entering the philosophical lists in the first place: Secondness belongs to the second, not (justifiably) to the first, the scrupulous refusal to ignore what other players report (more or less prephilosophically) as real. In my own opinion, this *is* the ultimate difference between Rorty's "pragmatism" and Dewey's. It gives the lie to postmodernism and post-philosophy. It betrays (as we have seen) the arbitrariness of Rorty's advice to Dennett and (as we shall see in chapter 5) it shows the way to reclaiming the viability at least of such heterodox doctrines as that of incommensurabilism.

Peirce's intuitions about Secondness are analogous to James's intuitions about truth: they are in touch with pre-philosophical convictions and metaphilosophical recommendations, and neither functions criterially. Rorty's postmodernism might have functioned in a comparable way, but Rorty is too much bent on dislocating philosophy as quickly and as thoroughly as he can.

Rorty construes "metaphilosophical" intervention as entirely verbal or "rhetorical." He nowhere admits any doubts about the complete plasticity of language games. Hence, he has no use for Secondness—though, to be sure, Secondness cannot be an independent criterion of any sort. It is, nevertheless, an important mark of the difference between pragmatism and Rorty's postmodernism, for Secondness reminds us of the unyielding realism of Dewey's original intention, viewed in post-Hegelian terms. At the very least, the theme of Secondness would challenge Rorty's "post-philosophical" (purely verbal) maneuver in the same spirit in which Peter Geach once introduced the pejorative epithet "Cambridge changes," which, according to Geach, produced magical changes of a substantive sort in intentional contexts by a mere change of verbal description. The analogy is entirely straightforward. Metaphilosophy, I would say, is attentive to longer spans of time and history than *some* philosophical puzzles require in order to be resolved; others simply do not depend on evolving history, even where they examine the conceptual artifacts of one historical age or another.

To be sure, there is no end to the problem. But you must see that Rorty begins and ends in a philosophical quarrel that he will not acknowledge; and that, failing there, he collects advantages he nowhere earns.

3

Anticipating Dewey's Advantage

I have been assuming that the leading pragmatists of the day are Hilary Putnam and Richard Rorty; however, I judge their innovations to be almost
completely played out by now, without their having offered any improved
arguments in pragmatism's favor. In that sense, they have, both together,
prepared the ground for an improved pragmatism by isolating the most
up-to-date ways of viewing "meaning," "truth," "realism," "knowledge,"
"philosophical argument," and the like. But they have not answered their
own questions. Undoubtedly, a revived pragmatism must contend with the
strongest currents of late twentieth-century philosophy if it is to make its
way competitively. But Rorty's and Putnam's business remains noticeably
unfinished: our guides have brought us to the water's edge.

No one would deny that Putnam and Rorty have—almost single-hand-
edly—identified the main issues pragmatism must confront if it is to sustain its newfound vigor. But they themselves have not fulfilled the strong
expectations prompted by their debate and influence. By their own admission, they are Deweyan in orientation. But their innovations are distinctly
less compelling than Dewey's at his most original. That has yet to be shown.

They have obliged pragmatism to revisit a whole raft of questions, latent
in Dewey's best work, cast now as an explicit confrontation. These include
at least the following: is the analysis of knowledge, reality, right conduct conceptually or practically pointless or futile, now that the canons of invariance,
cognitive privilege, necessity, essence, indubitability, and neutrality have
been shown to be no longer compelling? Or, can there be a productive and
meaningful recovery under the conditions of flux and historicity, when limited to provisional and divergent constructions and/or bound to our changing interests and societal practices? If the answer to the second question is
yes, then what kind of rigor and competence can still be assigned the work
of philosophical analysis? What answers can be given to the classic questions
of realism, objectivity, explanatory adequacy, truth, normativity, subjectivity, minds and selves, and legitimation? Did Putnam and Rorty simply miss

or misunderstand pragmatism's or philosophy's larger prospects? What more telling undertaking might be recommended, now that we have (*if* we have) the evidence of the short life of their own proposals?

Putnam candidly admits the collapse of his official pragmatism (approximately identified as "internal realism") and Rorty deliberately casts the entire Deweyan critique in the postmodernist mode, which produces its own kind of conceptual cul-de-sac. By a twist of fate, Putnam and Rorty, absorbed in the primary contest of their very different projects, bring a plausible charge of relativism against one another, only to learn that the charge sticks like tar to the accuser as well. Neither seems able to cope with it. The upshot is strange and wonderful, for the distraction proves far more important than the local plans of either: Putnam's, to formulate a viable scientific realism which (he realizes) ought to yield in a Deweyan direction; Rorty's, to displace completely the grand canon of Western metaphysics and epistemology, which (as it turns out) cannot find a rhetoric more fundamental or more convincing than Dewey's, in order to turn against Dewey's own acceptance of the continued pertinence of the questions postmodernism would dismiss.

By these unintended reversals, Putnam and Rorty press pragmatism (through Dewey) to examine more closely the heterodox options American philosophy largely ignores and that they themselves perfunctorily dismiss— for instance, along relativistic, historicist, and constructivist lines. The fact is that these possibilities were never really central to the work of the classic figures, but they assume an entirely new significance against the impending exhaustion of pragmatism's second life. By their own slack resistance, Putnam and Rorty have obliged the philosophical guild to reexamine every seemingly safely marginalized option it had always refused to countenance. (Here, you may recall, in a clinical sense, the reception of figures like Thomas Kuhn and Paul Feyerabend.) The simple reason is that both Rorty and Putnam have judged one another to be arch-relativists, while repudiating, each in his own way, any reliance on cognitive privilege or ontic or epistemic necessities—which, of course, removes any immunity from that same charge. They therefore led pragmatism to begin to review the most radical conceptual options it could imagine, if it was ever to recover the courage of its second life. That, I suggest, is the burden imposed on twentieth-century philosophy by the original post-Kantian lesson, which neither Rorty nor Putnam has rightly addressed.

Pragmatism may be the only currently viable American philosophical movement that is at all favorably disposed to exploring these possibilities, though Putnam and Rorty have given them short shrift. Nevertheless, once we abandon the failed Cartesian canons, in the wake of Peirce's and Dewey's work, we cannot ignore the need to examine the altered limits of conceptual tolerance under the unexamined conditions of flux and historicity. I review the matter here, with an eye to recovering what Dewey affords, by way of first fixing what Putnam and Rorty fail to provide. In the following chapter, I review Dewey's contribution in his own terms. But, as the gathering story already confirms, I do not attempt a full account of Dewey's philosophy or of that of the classic pragmatists as a group. That would require an entirely different tale.

I

Once more, it is Richard Rorty, who after having expansively addressed the philosophical awkwardnesses of feminism in a lecture (reviewed in the preceding chapter) then equated pragmatism with his own brand of postmodernism.(All of this busy work occurred after Rorty heroically revived the prospects of pragmatism two decades earlier.)[1] Rorty's advice to the feminists proved (as we've seen) to be a sly maneuver—half-right but misleading in its provocation—fortified by skimming off and deforming some unguarded remarks offered by Dewey, whom he professed to follow. His invitation to the feminists would, on an innocent reading, have suggested that absorbing the feminist claim "into *our* [the pragmatists'] view of moral progress" meant reconciling the two by acceptable philosophical means. But, of course, for Rorty it meant nothing of the kind!

This is the same man who opened his well-known manifesto, "The Contingency of Language," a few years before making his gesture, with the following remark, which draws on what is already familiar in James and Dewey: "Almost two hundred years ago, the idea that truth was made rather than found began to take hold of the imagination of Europe."[2] You must bear in mind that what Rorty refers to cannot fail to include the constructivist (*not* idealist) treatment of the realist question (if not realism itself) as fashioned by Hegel in the *Phenomenology* that makes its way by sparer and sparer means moving from Peirce to James to Dewey. But to admit the derivation would preclude altogether the postmodernist reading of the same remark. Rorty, you remember, is dead set against the idea that claims are "made true." Which is to say, he cannot be a pragmatist in any innocent sense!

Rorty runs two very different issues together here. The idea that truth is "made" rather than "found" is a shorthand dismissal of correspondentism and allied versions of realism that belong to the pre-Kantian world or to recent philosophies that imagine they can recover some form of objectivism or Cartesianism or a God's-Eye point of view. But the idea that truth is "made" rather than "found" is also a shorthand expression for admitting the conceptual impossibility of disjoining the epistemological and metaphysical faces of realism, a corollary of the Kantian and post-Kantian resolution of the (otherwise) insoluble *aporiai* of pre-Kantian realism, which pragmatism shares. On the one hand, Rorty opposes "made" truth, opposing what he calls *tertia*—in accord with Davidson's naturalism, which is itself effectively a late variant of Cartesianism. (I have already aired the question in the Prologue, including the sense in which Rorty affirms that Davidson "wishes to banish [*tertia*]".) On the other hand, Rorty opposes "made" truth in the same sense in which he opposes "found" truth, that is, in the sense in which as a postmodernist he wishes to dismiss all literal minded realisms, all second-order disputes about the true nature of truth.

What is decisive here—for those who are not postmodernists—is simply that Kant *is* a (transcendental) idealist (as he admits, as we have seen), *though* (or *because*) he is also a constructivist; whereas Hegel is *not* an idealist (in the Kantian sense) precisely *because*, though he *is* a constructivist (refusing to disjoin metaphysics and epistemology), he rejects all forms of transcendentalism. The matter is muddled, because Rorty runs the two issues together. Through it all, we must remain clear sighted enough to realize that pragmatism without James's conception of truth ("made" truth) would be no pragmatism at all. It's the conceptual linkage with post-Kantian "Idealism" (some versions being truly idealist—some versions not) that is decisive in the pragmatist story.

Regarding the classic pragmatists, the clue Rorty points to appeared in its leanest and most compelling form in two flawed volumes of Dewey's, *Experience and Nature* and *Logic: The Theory of Inquiry*. These volumes plainly required a stronger pragmatism than Dewey actually pursued. Hence, when in the same essay Rorty tips his hand to his own postmodernist use of Dewey, we are alerted (candidly enough) to what *he* means by a "strong" philosopher (that is, a philosopher "strong" enough to compare with Harold Bloom's "strong poet"). He means himself! That is, he means to "misread" Dewey wherever it suits his post-philosophical purpose—as in giving advice to the feminists and in supporting the naturalizers. So he says, beguilingly enough, "Conforming to my own precepts, I am not going to offer arguments against the vocabulary I want to replace. Instead I am going to try to make the vocabulary I favor look attractive by showing how it may be used to describe a variety of topics."[3] Of course! What Rorty has in mind is convincing his readers (without benefit of supporting argument) that the doctrine that what is true is "made" true—read in the constructivist sense that runs from the post-Kantians to the pragmatists—*is not* a philosophically viable or productive claim at all!

Here you have a lovely postmodernist maneuver in the modest guise of being an extension of Dewey's pragmatism. It elevates a hint into an entire method. Although Dewey would "agree" with Rorty in opposing the straightest canonical forms of "universalism" and "realism," he would have insisted that there *are* philosophically compelling reasons (still needed) for dismissing such doctrines. He would have seen no point at all in recommending their replacement without benefit of argument, and he would have affirmed that the legitimating arguments needed would not have conflicted with fair objections against the canon. Dewey would have envisioned a *third* option between the old philosophical fixities and Rorty's reckless postmodernism. Dewey never supposed his own recovery of realism was philosophically arbitrary or quixotic. He *had* his reasons, which, quite frankly, Rorty deforms in his postmodernist way.

If we take Rorty at his word—and why should we not?—then the advice he tenders the feminists belongs to the same lesson he offers in the manifesto. He thereby loses the recuperative intent of Dewey's entire doctrine; for, as a "postmodernist" (or "post-philosopher"), he means to sweep away the legitimacy and legitimating competence of philosophy itself vis-à-vis the sciences and the work of moral and political reflection.

This might have counted as Rorty's intended improvement of pragmatism. But you cannot find in Rorty's writings an actual argument to the effect that if we abandon "universalism" and "realism"—effectively, "Cartesianism" or "objectivism" or "absolutism" or "the God's-eye view"—we *will* assuredly find that there is no pertinent difference between (say) philosophy and poetry (or between argument and rhetoric) or between pragmatism and postmodernism! It is true that Rorty reminds us of the hopelessness of the seventeenth- and eighteenth-century philosophies Kant and Hegel so masterfully exposed—almost in preparation for the advent of pragmatism. The reminder is still a welcome one, since so much of twentieth-century philosophy has retreated to the paradoxes of Cartesianism and so much of Anglo-American philosophy has forgotten its Hegel.[4] But the reminder conveys a more sanguine view of philosophy than Rorty would care to support.

Rorty, of course, will have none of it. By his "strong" postmodernist reading ("misprision," in Bloom's idiom[5]), he means that philosophy cannot continue in the manner practiced by the strong figures of the past, even if "universalism" and "realism" are abandoned, as they must be. I agree we should abandon modal necessities, apodicticities, essentialisms, teleologisms, universalisms, exceptionless invariances, First Philosophies, the incontestable verities of a higher Reason: there are good arguments to that effect. But I cannot see how it follows from conceding all this that philosophical analysis and legitimation have no further role to play. Dewey would surely have protested. Rorty's identification of pragmatism and postmodernism still seems completely willful.

II

Rorty's strong dilemma—his challenge to contemporary philosophy: choose Cartesianism (or "realism" or objectivism) or choose postmodernism—is too simple and hardly a motivated choice. On pragmatist and Hegelian grounds, the first option is a dead letter. At the very least, it cannot be resurrected without suitably answering the objections of Kant and Hegel. Hardly anyone believes that this can be done. The second is arbitrary, by deliberate default. It also risks being incoherent wherever we concede that questions of truth and evidence, however pertinent in the general run of first-order inquiries, are not really intelligible unless their legitimation is also intelligible. On this reading, when Rorty says—"I am not going to offer arguments . . ."—speaking in his postmodernist voice but not as a standard pragmatist, what he says cannot fail to be irrelevant, possibly incoherent as well: he is *not* waiving (for the moment) the defense of his conceptions of truth, knowledge, reality, norms, and natures; he is affirming (or insinuating by default) that it no longer makes sense to make any such effort! He never tells us why. But whatever else we may say of Dewey, it seems impossible to deny that Dewey's entire effort was committed to recovering a robust sense of metaphysics, epistemology, and moral and political philosophy under the conditions of flux and historicity; whereas, Rorty plainly believes that once we reject the privilege and substantive necessities of canonical philosophy, philosophy itself will be seen to be impossible. There could not be a more fundamental disconnection.

Many fail to see the Achilles' heel of Rorty's ingenuities. There is, he apparently believes, no genuine philosophy that does not make "universalist" or "essentialist" claims; but he also believes there are no viable such philosophies to consider! None could ever be convincingly defended and no other options are before us. Yet the argument is missing.

Responding to this stalemate, it is very much to Richard Bernstein's credit (Bernstein has been tracking Rorty for years) never to have been tempted by Rorty's postmodernism. Bernstein repeatedly criticizes Rorty's "postmodern" turn: "for Rorty [he says], contingency, historicism, and nominalism 'go all the way down.'" Charged with "self-referential inconsistency," Bernstein adds, Rorty "evades"—recommends *evading*—"the accusation of self-defeating relativism."[6] What Bernstein says in his second remark (against Rorty) is true enough and important; what he says in the first is not altogether perspicuous. We must divide the question; we must take care to consider (against Bernstein himself, against Rorty and Putnam, as well) the bearing of the fact that doctrines like relativism, historicism, incommensurabilism—which are very different from nominalism and contingency, because they (but neither nominalism nor bare contingency)—challenge the legitimacy of our evidentiary sources and may be coherently and viably formulated in doing so. At the very least, their defense should be separated from the defense of postmodernism, since they (but not postmodernism) require a legitimative rationale. In any case, Bernstein's is an objection (requiring courage) offered by one friend against another.

Bernstein correctly remarks that pragmatism "anticipated" the positive critique embedded in what (*per* Jean-François Lyotard) has come to be called "the postmodern condition":[7] going beyond Lyotard's report, pragmatism has been pointedly "concerned with the question of how to *respond* to [postmodernism's] challenges."[8] This is a strong (though incomplete) diagnosis, which collects Bernstein's papers from the end of the 80s—although his book (*The New Constellation*) was published as late as 1992. It identifies an important lacuna in the analytic narrative.

The trouble with Bernstein's treatment of the pragmatist "response" is that the best he can offer is a form of *pluralism* that he neither justifies nor shows us how to justify, for instance, by (say) separating pluralism from relativism in a principled way. This assumes against Bernstein as much as against Rorty and Putnam that relativism is every bit as coherent as pluralism. Bernstein's proffer is completely unsupported, though hardly for postmodernist reasons. It is perhaps no more than a telling piece of evidence of the profound impasse the whole of Western philosophy had come to at the end of the twentieth century.

On that reading, the impasse Rorty obliged pragmatism to address in the 1990s is itself a legible emblem of the larger impasse of the whole of Western philosophy. You begin to see the importance of strengthening pragmatism's hand beyond its original concerns. You must bear in mind that Rorty and Putnam *are*, however puzzlingly, pluralists of a sort (of very different sorts) *and* that each, even more insistently than Bernstein (but no more convincingly), rejects relativism and fends off any and all efforts to tag himself a relativist. (None of them, let it be noted, gives relativism a proper hearing.)

There's an irony there. Bernstein is right to remark that, for Rorty, "contingency, historicism, and nominalism 'go all the way down'"; however, he fails to see the full import of this part of Rorty's thesis. Contingency and historicism *do* indeed "go all the way down"—I won't bother with nominalism, for it's irrelevant here and, when viewed as an epistemological thesis, untenable as well. But since Rorty embraces radical contingency and historicism, I say he cannot escape relativism; and since he also insists he is not a relativist, he has no other option but to declare himself a postmodernist, that is, a conceptual anarchist in philosophical matters who can in good conscience deny the need to answer the original charge. (It does not appear on the postmodernist's radar screen!)

I take the maneuver to be incoherent on the following grounds: first-order inquiries cannot abandon questions of truth and evidence; such questions make no sense without our ability to legitimate our epistemic practices; and the distinction between first-order and legitimative (second-order) matters is itself a second-order matter.[9] (This triad helps to explain what is missing in Rorty's disjunction between the universalisms and realisms he abjures and the postmodernism he would have us adopt.) Besides, what is the point of declaring that one is a nominalist or a historicist or an opponent of invariant or necessary regularities, or a postmodernist for that matter, if saying so is *not* a *claim* of any sort?

Dewey also embraces radical contingency; he might have adopted historicism, which Mead hardly broaches, but he does not do so (though, you realize, Dewey was drawn to Hegel's historicism). What he admits, however, does implicate *some* concession in relativism's favor, which he nowhere explicitly pursues. For his part, Bernstein, who expressly opposes relativism—in fact, offers a form of "pluralism" (not otherwise specified) as the missing third option between objectivism and relativism[10]—risks falling in with the "objectivists," since he opposes a contingency that goes "all the way down"; *or* risks opposing Dewey (whom he claims to follow), *or* risks being unable to distinguish between his own thesis and Rorty's (which he takes to be self-refuting). In effect, Bernstein stalemates his own solution.

What I am signaling here is just *how* the dispute between Putnam and Rorty, the insertion of Bernstein's inchoate third option, and Dewey's adherence to radical contingency, oblige us to consider whether and to what extent pragmatism entails, or is reconcilable with, one or another form of relativism and how that affects, for instance, the quarrels about truth and realism. But you cannot fail to notice, in a company of thinkers drawn to the flux and the denial of modal invariances, the absence of any sustained interest—from Dewey to Rorty—regarding relativism's challenge. That has a distinctly clinical ring. For, once you admit flux or apply it to epistemology (which, effectively, is part of the historicist thesis), you cannot evade the frontal challenges of relativism and incommensurabilism. That is precisely what the different conservatisms of Putnam, Rorty, and Davidson fail to master. Dewey seems more innocent here, though he is still a disappointment.

Bernstein is the unwitting litmus of the entire affair. If you look carefully at his *The New Constellation*, you will find that it is even less confident about the prospects of pluralism than Bernstein's earlier and more important *Beyond Objectivism and Relativism* (1983). In the earlier book, reading Rorty and Putnam as pragmatists (with caveats in Rorty's case and no discussion of Putnam's alternative in the *Beyond Objectivism* book), Bernstein appears to be preparing the ground for something akin to Putnam's conception of pluralism as a third option between the unacceptable extremes (objectivism and relativism). The narrative is not altogether easy to follow, so please bear with me, given that I shall have to hop from one source to another to put the account across clearly.

III

Reason, Truth and History (1981) is the classic locus of Putnam's "internal realism"; it is Putnam's most sustained statement of what, *later,* came to be regarded (on his allowance) as his own version of pragmatism, though at the beginning of the 80s it was still formulated as a strong (perhaps the strongest) version of (a kind of scientific) realism that he found he could still support. In this book, Putnam announced that his "aim" was "to break the strangle hold . . . a number of dichotomies appear to have [imposed] on the thinking of . . . philosophers and laymen [alike]. Chief among these [he notes] is the dichotomy between objective and subjective views of truth and reason."[11]

He plainly thought of the division between the objectivists and the subjectivists as a division between Anglo-American analytic and continental philosophies, but he also associated Thomas Kuhn and Paul Feyerabend (whom Bernstein considers) together with Michel Foucault (and the French poststructuralists in general) in terms of the subjectivist or relativist alternative. In "Two Philosophical Perspectives," the central essay of the *Reason, Truth and History* volume, Putnam went a step further to contrast "metaphysical realism" and "the *internalist* perspective" (or, simply, what he called "internal realism"). In effect, he offered a glimpse of his third option between metaphysical realism (or "absolutism" or "Cartesianism") and relativism.

On the first perspective, "the world [says Putnam] consists of some fixed totality of mind-independent objects. There is exactly one true and complete description of 'the way the world is'. Truth involves some sort of correspondence relation between words or thought-signs and external things and sets of things." This effectively captures what Bernstein understands by the term "objectivism"—a doctrine he of course opposes. (It also captures the meaning of "Cartesianism.")

On the other perspective, the most important consideration proves to be this: "*What objects does the world consist of?* is a question that it only makes sense to ask *within* a theory or description. Many 'internalist' philosophers, though not all [Putnam observes] hold further that there is more than one 'true' theory or description of the world. 'Truth', in an internalist view, is some sort of (idealized) rational acceptability—some sort of ideal coherence of our beliefs with each other and with our experience *as these experiences are themselves represented in our belief system*—and not correspondence with mind-independent or discourse-independent 'states of affairs.'"[12] The thesis is broadly Kantian in Putnam's hands; more Hegelian in Bernstein's. Ultimately, it proves to take a pragmatist form in both, though Putnam eventually treats this same thesis as open to an unacceptable idealist reading.

Let me, for ease of reference, collect the dialectical linkages of the running argument, both of what has already been aired and of what is to come. There is always too much scatter in assembling the separate thoughts of commentators on what another (myself, on this occasion) takes to be the points and counterpoints of a single dispute. I draw together, here, no more than the separate findings that (I believe) the debate turns on, that are easily slighted in the telling.

I recommend you bear in mind the following, therefore: (1) that Putnam's "internal realist" doctrine was not originally meant to capture his "pragmatism"—the use of the label was forced on him by fair-minded commentators, and he has allowed the slippage as a reasonable reading;[13] (2) that Putnam has now abandoned the ("pragmatist") internalism developed from the position just cited, largely on the grounds of having been fatally seduced by William James's "idealism" and subjective representationalism[14]—although it is not yet clear what, apart from his recovering a strong sense of realism ("natural realism," as he now names the thesis, under the influence of John McDowell), actually constitutes his present position; (3) that Putnam had been (and still is) a *pluralist* in the sense already remarked; (4) that he realized he had to defend *the realist sense of his pluralism* against Rorty's charge of relativism, by introducing at the very end of the book—fatally, it now seems—the arbitrary notion of a necessary (or rationally compelling) *Grenzbegriff* of truth and reason that would offset the possibility that *his own pluralism was in effect a closet relativism;*[15] (5) that Rorty took this weakness in Putnam's attempted defense to confirm his own postmodernist critique;[16] (6) that Donald Davidson may have been drawn to improvise his own counterpart "realist" reading of the correspondence and coherence theories of truth—perhaps not yet under Rorty's full influence—explicitly directed (at least in part) against what he took to be Putnam's untenable alternative;[17] (7) that Davidson has now acknowledged, in commenting on Rorty's own philosophy (which he is unwilling to accept in its postmodernist form), the "blunder" (his own word) of his own attempt to join correspondence and coherence in the form of a *theory* of truth—in particular, Davidson has distanced himself from Rorty's inaccurate attribution (and untenable advocacy) of the postmodernist treatment of truth;[18] (8) that Rorty has now relented (somewhat unreliably) under Davidson's criticism, but still means to recover the validity of his own postmodernist account of truth—which appears to be an odd mélange of his postmodernism and Davidson's "naturalizing" (the stance of "A Coherence Theory of Truth and Knowledge"[19]); (9) that Rorty's deliberate "misprision" of the views of other philosophers has begun to unravel—most notably, among recent respondents (that is, among respondents who are still alive), most notably Quine (at the time of writing);[20] and (10) that there are protests by many hands against Rorty in the name of ensuring an accurate interpretation of Dewey, Wittgenstein, and Heidegger on one or another of the topics before us! I have aired most of these themes before, but they needed to be effectively collected to prepare the ground for the next step.

IV

Apart from the relative force of Putnam's and Bernstein's respective analyses, their positions on the extreme options both lay out are very similar. In *Reason, Truth and History,* Putnam rejects as completely untenable the strong—"Cartesian" or "objectivist" or "God's-Eye"—disjunction between the "objective" and the "subjective." At the time of writing, Putnam was not entirely clear about the full implications of his own view. More recently, in the Gifford Lectures (1990), published as *Renewing Philosophy* (1992), Putnam featured the choice between "the absolute conception of the world" (which he associated, for expository reasons, with the view of Bernard Williams) and what he now characterizes more explicitly as "relativism" (a doctrine he associates, in the English-language tradition, with Williams again, and, more revealingly, with Rorty and French philosophy, for example with Jacques Derrida).

He notes, for instance, that "My own philosophical evolution has been from a view like Bernard Williams's to a view much more like John Dewey's," by which he means to mark the acceptable middle ground between absolutism and relativism and to distance his own pragmatism from Rorty's. He means to feature Dewey's pluralism: that is, the rejection of "a final theory," an insistence on the inseparability of theoretical and practical reason, and an acknowledgement of the essential epistemic inseparability of the subjective and the objective (by means of which, for instance, idealism may be effectively evaded).

In fact, Putnam says: "In this book [*Renewing Philosophy*] I want to explain and, to the extent possible in the space available, to justify this change in my philosophical attitude."[21] Hence, by the beginning of the 1990s, Putnam is clearly aware that his own version of scientific realism has had to yield in the direction of a pragmatized realism (*à la* Dewey), *which invites the relativist charge he wishes to evade.* He now offers a tripartite choice between "absolutism," "relativism," and a Deweyan-like pluralism—which comes very close to the general lines of Bernstein's contrast between objectivism and relativism and the preference of a pluralism (between the two) that (in Bernstein) owes as much to Kuhn, Jürgen Habermas, Hans-Georg Gadamer, and Hannah Arendt as it does to Dewey.

The important difference between Bernstein's and Putnam's accounts, quite frankly, is that Bernstein's is primarily a reporter's summary, whereas Putnam's is based on an original attempt to solve the puzzle they share: Bernstein cannot really claim to offer a solution (beyond a sketch of what would be needed if it could be secured); and Putnam has now made the attempt, which has, in his own opinion, failed.[22]

Putnam would probably claim to have succeeded in recovering a defensible "realism" nevertheless—largely through John McDowell's rejection of an "interface" between cognizer and cognized.[23] But the fact remains that McDowell has nothing to say beyond countering Putnam's unnecessary Cartesian demons or Davidson's excessively spare version of realism; in particular, he has nothing to say about the detailed epistemological issues a pragmatist would need to explore. (Putnam needs to look elsewhere.) In effect, there is no satisfactory attempt in McDowell, Putnam, Bernstein, Rorty, or Davidson to meet the threat of relativism or historicism! But, of course, under constructivist conditions, eschewing privilege, every viable realism must yield some in the pragmatist direction—and, yielding there, must address the "relativist menace."

It's here, then, that we may expect to recover the thread of the earlier contrast between Putnam and Rorty. For Rorty is a pluralist of the postmodernist stripe—which, I suggest, signifies that his notion cannot fail to devolve into a form of relativism if viewed in terms of a legitimating rationale (which of course Rorty refuses). By contrast, Putnam (in the context of

Renewing Philosophy) is a pluralist of the pragmatist or Deweyan sort—which I claim, signifies that his pluralism also devolves into a form of relativism. (This always supposes that relativism can be formulated in a coherent and defensible way.) Putnam, Rorty, Bernstein, and Davidson judge this to be impossible, of course. But none of them offers a compelling argument. The fact is that none of the principal discussants has ever conducted a genuinely open canvass of relativism's possibilities *or,* for that matter, of whether any tenable realism (in effect, constructivist views that would include Dewey's, Putnam's, possibly Rorty's, Bernstein's, but not Davidson's) *could* responsibly avoid the relativist option.[24]

I believe we cannot convincingly preclude relativism as a viable constructivism, *and* no known version of a constructive realism (short of transcendentalism) has ever succeeded in excluding it.[25] In short, there is no way to avoid the question whether and to what extent Dewey's realism is or is not compatible with one or another form of constructivism, relativism, incommensurabilism, historicism, or similar possibilities.[26] There, at least, you have a glimpse of pragmatism's likely future. (It may discourage some!)

v

The discussion of relativism between Rorty and Putnam is a curious affair. Each is a decisive critic of the other: each, to my mind, shows compellingly that the other *is* a relativist (of an unacceptable sort) and each is caught in a formal or pragmatic paradox. The strange thing is that neither ever demonstrates that a viable relativism is impossible—or, indeed, that a reasonable extension of Deweyan realism is not already committed to a relativistic treatment of realism! In truth, the analysis of what relativism must entail is extraordinarily primitive in both Rorty and Putnam and never moves beyond the self-inflicted paradox of Plato's *Theaetetus.*[27] The point is that we must bring the diagnosis of late pragmatism and pragmatism's untapped prospects more clearly into line with one another, if we are ever to benefit from the unexpected second life that the running exchange between Rorty and Putnam has now made possible.

Already in *Experience and Nature* (1929) Dewey had demonstrated the coherence of a constructive realism committed to the flux. That is clearly the earliest site of a viable realism in English-language philosophy that is at once the equal of the strongest forms of realism the analytic tradition can boast and the only version that invites a closer study of what a fluxive constructivism might either entail or accommodate.

For their part, Putnam and Rorty are understandably obsessed with the relativism issue. *Renewing Philosophy* confirms how central the question had become for Putnam, and the reason is plain. Putnam had set himself the task of formulating a viable realism that escaped the paradoxes of the "Cartesian" vision of the "One True Theory." He treated the matter autobiographically, as if to exorcise his early commitment to the absolutist pretensions of a scientific realism within the unity of science program. He pursued the matter down to the point where it became clear that his own best prospects required adopting something close to Dewey's realist reading of pragmatism, which happened to converge rather nicely with McDowell's correction of his (Putnam's) own first preference of a Jamesian model.

In the meantime, Rorty sensed the fatal weakness of Putnam's internal realism as early as *Reason, Truth and History*—in Putnam's false step intended to combat the relativism implicit in Rorty's postmodernism, which now began to threaten Putnam's own ability to withstand Rorty's attack on all bona fide efforts to support a proper realism. That attack was linked, in Putnam's mind, to the self-referential paradoxes of Protagorean relativism. Under the circumstances, precisely because he would not (or could not) yield to relativism or historicism or (indeed) incommensurabilism, Putnam defined relativism more and more tendentiously and adjusted his own position as a kind of shadow version of Cartesian realism, under the protection of McDowell's "correction."

Rorty couldn't care less about these niceties, since, from his point of view, relativism *was* incoherent all along (more or less for the reasons Putnam provides). Moreover, postmodernism is not (he insists) a form of relativism at all, since it abandons (as, in a way, relativism does not) all canonical attempts to validate realism itself. This is precisely what Rorty hoped to tempt Putnam into accepting, when he affirmed that "pragmatists should be ethnocentrists rather than relativists."[28] The fact remains that Rorty does venture an argument of sorts to justify his resisting the encumbering of postmodernism with a relativistic charge, but he does not explain whether or why the effort is needed. (I am, for the moment, deliberately allowing the relativist option to remain undefined: first of all, because of the extreme laxness with which Putnam and Rorty explore the question, and, second, in order not to intrude my own preference in a way that might appear to require a form of special pleading. But I shall come to its definition shortly.)

Rorty rests his case rather cleverly on Putnam's having construed truth in terms of "idealized rational acceptability," which, separated from correspondentist presumptions (which both Putnam and Rorty—and, also, Davidson—take to be "absurd" or illicit[29]), undermines Putnam's attempts to vindicate a reasonably full-blown realism. That is one way of putting the failure of the *Grenzbegriff* maneuver.

But, of course, contrary to what Rorty suggests, postmodernism *is* parasitic on the absolutist model of realism which it rejects, since it is the collapse of every *such* program that "forces" or "invites" us to adopt the postmodernist stance. That is precisely what Putnam means by treating Rorty as an arch-relativist.[30] But what if there *were* a third option between absolutism and postmodernism, and what if that option *were* a form of pragmatism (or pragmatist realism), which, in accord with Dewey's advocacy of radical contingency, entailed or was continuous with, or could accommodate, one or another form of relativism (shown independently to be coherent)? We would then, by a single stroke, have defeated Rorty, Putnam, Bernstein, Davidson, and McDowell! I myself have no doubt at all that relativism can be defended. Putnam believes (but has yet to show) that there *are* ways of securing a viable realism that yields nothing to postmodernism. But the evidence remains that he is caught between his *Grenzbegriff* (a vestige of his scientific realism *or* scientism) and relativism (which he insists is incoherent). In that case, Putnam cannot escape.

Rorty's question is the right one. What could possibly vindicate "idealized rational acceptability," if we cannot rely on privilege or correspondence, *except* "ethnocentric solidarity"? The question goes back to Rorty's important "Solidarity or Objectivity?" (1984) which he himself says was a response to Putnam's relativist charge against his own postmodernism—in the closing pages of *Reason, Truth and History* (which involve of course the *Grenzbegriff* maneuver).[31]

In a curious way, the different forms of philosophical failure evinced in Putnam's and Rorty's pragmatisms are neatly matched: in Putnam, by refusing to distinguish between a responsible relativism and an irresponsible postmodernism; in Rorty, by construing relativism as a hopeless maneuver legible only against the backdrop of canonical philosophy, which (Rorty claims) is not true of postmodernism. Both views may be struck down by simply acknowledging that Deweyan pragmatism *is* indeed a constructive form of realism hospitable to relativism! That still needs to be spelled out in a textual way, though the clue is already strong and clear. It is in fact a clue missed by Putnam and ignored by Rorty. I shall look at it more carefully in the next two chapters, but an orienting word may be welcome here.

Dewey's realism is "Darwinian," in the deliberately minimized sense (which, in effect, Dewey shares with Peirce and James) in which the realism of our best cognitions is said to be grounded in the actual conditions—the *non*cognitive conditions—of animal life. (Peirce says, even more adventurously, "protoplasmic" life, which Karl Popper also affirms, speaking as a non-pragmatist profoundly influenced by Peirce.[32])

It would not be too much to say that Putnam fails in his realist efforts precisely because he misses the force and economy of Dewey's leading idea: he is obliged to fall back to Cartesian resources. He makes no philosophical use of the Darwinian theme. But he could not possibly have missed Dewey's maneuver if he had consulted the *Logic, Experience and Nature,* or *The Quest for Certainty.* Rorty's failure, as I say, is largely due to the arbitrariness with which he reviews the realist question: I've flagged it (in chapter 2) in terms of Peirce's notion of Secondness. Rorty is a Darwinian of sorts, but he uses the theme (if indeed he applies it at all) to gain the dismissal of philosophy itself. In effect, Rorty uses Darwinian ideas in the same scientistic spirit he deplores in Putnam. There you have the essential difference between Dewey, on the one hand, and Putnam and Rorty, on the other.

You may glimpse something of Rorty's deliberately slow paced, almost imperceptible retrieval (*from* his own postmodernist avowals) of *philosophical argument* (that is, legitimative, second-order argument) in the opening essay of his recent *Philosophy and Social Hope,* which addresses relativism once again:

> We should not let ourselves be described as subjectivists, and perhaps calling ourselves "social constructivists" is too misleading. . . . We anti-Platonists cannot permit ourselves to be called "relativists," . . .
>
> Our opponents like to suggest that to abandon [the] vocabulary [of Plato and Aristotle] is to abandon rationality. . . . But [we] irrationalists . . . simply refuse to talk in . . . the Platonic way. . . . [Our] efforts at persuasion must take the form of gradual inculcation of new ways of speaking, rather than of straightforward argument within old ways of speaking.[33]

I draw three findings from all this: first, Rorty is surely inching his way toward formulating a "new" form of philosophical argument, opposed to "the Platonic way," that *might* legitimate the position he now advances in his own postmodernist voice; second, he has invented out of whole cloth (without accompanying argument), and apparently *from* the resources of postmodernism, an entirely new vision that might, in time, support philosophical "argument"—but that ignores the plain fact that Dewey *had* constructed such a conception (as have many others within the "Hegelian" clan) but never found himself drawn to anything like Rorty's postmodernism; and, third, the new adjustment belies the "advice" (and the rationale for that advice, already remarked) which Rorty had offered the feminists, who, well beyond his own postmodernism, saw precisely how a constructivist view of politics could be fashioned and saw how (at least implicitly) such a politics would be inseparable from a constructivist view of realism.

In the passage just cited, you cannot fail to see that although Rorty holds that the very formulation of relativism presupposes (agonistically) the language of the "Platonists," he neglects to admit that the same is true of postmodernism. The entire argument collapses, therefore, like a house of cards. It does so simply because it pretends to be introducing a "reasonable" form of "persuasion" (without philosophical argument), where we lack any clear idea, *beyond Dewey*, as to what the important problems *are* in terms of which the facilitating mode of argument may actually be specified. Not to put too fine a point on it, the trouble is that what, according to Rorty, is not within our grasp *is* comfortably caught in Dewey's! (I examine the evidence in the next chapter.)

VI

Putnam and Rorty have excellent arguments against one another. Each is able to show that the other's program is profoundly defective, and each regards the damning evidence as sufficient to confirm that the other is a relativist. These arguments are, however, a little lame, as lame, in fact, as the sense of relativism they share. For neither is open to the possibility that relativism may take a coherent form, may avoid the self-referential paradox of (say) the charge brought against Protagoras in Plato's *Theaetetus*. Neither considers the possibility that relativism may enhance the conceptual resources of the pragmatism they claim to share. There is a perseverating quality there, since both profess to have abandoned all *a priori* fixities and prejudices. (Neither, however, tells us what that entails.)

What Rorty means by the charge (against Putnam) is that Putnam fails in the defense of his "internal realism," except of course by means of the *deus ex machina* of his *Grenzbegriff*, which reliably rules out the threat of relativism at the start. What Putnam means by the charge (against Rorty) is that Rorty offers no justification for his refusal to provide reasons in support of the adequacy or pertinence of "ethnocentric solidarity" (which, otherwise, seems to mean no more than that "anything goes"). Both charges are reasonably compelling. Each, therefore, is able to score points against the other; but neither—the one as a pragmatic realist, the other as a pragmatic postmodernist—vindicates his own doctrine or even bothers to consider whether it may indeed require some reconciliation between relativism and something akin to Dewey's conjunction of pragmatism and realism.

The matter is more important than either seems to realize, since what they share, in describing themselves as Deweyan pragmatists, is Dewey's constructivist approach to truth and reality. In assessing the prospects of Dewey's attenuated summary of the Hegelian critique of Kant and Descartes—applied now to the salient puzzles of late twentieth-century philosophy—we find ourselves obliged to consider the implications of any constructive realism shorn of all the forms of epistemic privilege and pitted against the pretensions of scientific realism and other strong attempts to recover something akin to Cartesian realism.

If (1) Putnam cannot recover a realism stronger than Dewey's, if (2) McDowell (say) does not recognize the need to broach the deeper epistemic questions that Dewey had already formulated (in particular, the sense in which theoretical reason is itself a form of practical reason emerging within "problematic situations") and, beyond Dewey, subject to historical drift, if (3) no contemporary realism has been able to bypass Dewey's "Hegelian" (or "Darwinized" Hegelian) solution (sketched in *Experience and Nature*[34]) or something like it, and if (4) Rorty cannot make his postmodernist subversion of realist inquiry appear intellectually credible, then we must ask ourselves whether a viable extension of Dewey's position might not need to concede an inning to one or another relativist option. The irony is that this seemingly slim question might never have arisen, had it not been for Putnam and Rorty's running dispute. For we see that even if we abandon their particular projects, pragmatism would still be obliged to confront the matter of avoiding the Cartesian-like recovery of realism favored in late analytic philosophy.

Take a closer look at the failure—and the meaning of the failure—of Putnam's and Rorty's actual undertakings. The most telling clues are within our grasp. They may be drawn from Putnam's and Rorty's own texts by way of featuring what each neglects. Each fails to perceive the deep lacuna within his own doctrine, which, once exposed, confirms that not only pragmatism but any viable realism along constructivist lines can hardly disallow one or another moderate form of relativism. How far the concession may be pressed is not the central issue here. We cannot recover the question of the compatibility of realism, pragmatism, and relativism in purely textual terms, because Dewey does not broach the question, and Putnam and Rorty mangle it and render it unmanageable. And yet, since Dewey in *Experience and Nature* expressly attempts to reconcile realism with a pragmatist account of the flux in human affairs, it is impossible that the issue can still be avoided *or,* on pragmatist assumptions, answered unfavorably.

If, then, relativism may take a coherent form, it may be brought to bear on the question of a viable realism; and then, admitting Putnam and Rorty's

quarrel, we would be forced to address the compatibility of realism and relativism. That would mark a decisive turn in an ancient contest. For the history of the dispute, notably in the interval spanning Hegel and Dewey, has
already reconciled realism with a number of important preparatory concessions that lead directly to the relativism issue: (1) with the abandonment
of cognitive privilege, (2) with the denial of the necessary invariance of what
is real, (3) with the insuperable symbiosis of the subjective and the objective, (4) with the new resources of constructivism and the artifactual standing of our discursive categories, and (5) with the historicizing of cognition
and the human condition itself.

If, in addition, we conceded something akin to Dewey's analysis of a
"problematic situation"—favoring *savoir-faire* (practical know-how yielding an acceptable measure of success) over *savoir* (non-distorting cognitive
faculties addressed to the real world) and drawing the realist import of our
cognitive powers from precognitive (animal) impasses (Dewey's Darwinian
theme)—we would have to concede in short order the reconcilability of realism and relativism. That would signify the most extraordinary declension
of the entire realist idea.

My own prognosis is that we *are* led to all this by tracing the path from
Descartes to Kant to Hegel to Dewey and, now, more opportunistically,
through Putnam and Rorty. If more is needed, and I am sure more can be
elicited, then by admitting the Hegelian theme of the historicity of thought,
which the pragmatists largely neglected (even Dewey and Mead), we should
have to concede that realism *was* reconcilable with historicism at least. In
any event, we begin to see how far pragmatism may be coherently extended:
we see how easily Putnam and Rorty may be eclipsed, how much they remain tethered to vestiges of the absolutist arguments they profess to have
discarded. Putnam's *Grenzbegriff*, Rorty's "solidarity," both behave suspi-
ciously like the last defenses of a calling they would deny.

For, the argument might go on: neither pragmatism nor analytic philosophy can continue to justify ignoring the question of reconciling realism
with the historically transient aspects of cognitive competence. Both have
retreated from the pretensions of privilege and the would-be modal invariances of thought and reality—willingly, on the pragmatist side; more defen-
sively, on the analytic. But if that is so, then we can hardly deny that the
reconcilability of realism and relativism and realism and incommensurabilism must at least be aired. It is not so much a matter of vindicating relativism
as it is of stating clearly just what realism can or must allow *epistemologically*.
You have only to recall Davidson's attack on Kuhn and Feyerabend (misplaced, in my opinion) to guess at the lengths to which analytic philosophers

(including Putnam and Rorty) are prepared to go to stalemate the reckoning.[35]

I shall risk a wild conjecture here. My nose tells me that Rorty is too clever to remain a "postmodernist" forever. That pose cannot be more than a self-marginalizing move, once the apparent advantages of trashing the canon have been gained. (They seem to have been gained by now! Or nearly.) Seen that way, Rorty's close connection with the work of his former student, Robert Brandom, suggests very soberly to me that Rorty may regard Brandom's recent efforts to recover philosophical semantics and epistemology as at least a trial balloon for his own eventual return to more standard fare—a move facilitated, as with Brandom, by way of a fresh union of certain themes in Wilfrid Sellars and in pragmatism (in Rorty's case, *via* Dewey).[36] But, having ventured that much, it seems even more obvious that, if he has not abandoned philosophy altogether, Putnam will eventually produce a strengthened form of his own "natural realism." That would mean that the most original efforts of both Rorty and Putnam were very close to being played out, though they may well turn in a new direction.

I cannot undertake, here, the demonstration that relativism *can* be coherently formulated so as to be brought to bear on the realist issue. (I have done so elsewhere—many times. I will come back to it in the final chapter.) But, for the sake of closure, I now say that Rorty's "ethnocentric solidarity" *is* an inchoate form of relativism, which he may yet confess if he reconsiders the recovery of philosophical argument. In any case, there is no way in which one's ethnic home can be relevantly identified in a way that would preclude relativism; and Rorty himself has urged that we should pick and choose our home "society" as we please.

By contrast, once Putnam denies any principled disjunction between the subjective and the objective, which Rorty is prepared to endorse as well, whatever realist proposals we thereafter favor could never vindicate anything as strong as Putnam's *Grenzbegriff.* But if we lacked such a regulative principle, then if Putnam continued to oppose objectivism (or absolutism), he would not be able to distinguish in principle between his position and a moderate relativism.

Rorty holds that "relativist" is an epithet usually attributed to philosophers who "do not accept the Greek distinction ['Platonism' in Rorty's vocabulary] between the way things are in themselves and the relation which they have to other things, and in particular to human needs and interests" *applied by those* committed to the "Greek distinction."[37] Since Rorty himself "eschew[s] the distinction," he insists that, though he has been called a relativist, he is not one (nor, on the same argument, is Dewey): "we pragmatists," he says, "never call *ourselves* relativists. . . . [W]e define ourselves in negative terms."[38] (But what does that matter if others call "us" relativists or if we "define ourselves in negative terms"? Does "pragmatist" signify a defensible policy?)

I grant Rorty's point: it's entirely harmless. But I cannot see its philosophical payoff, since it appears that Rorty *is* bent on recovering (if he can) a mode of "argument" (other than the "Greek") that would suit his deep opposition to all "dualisms" (which, as he says, he shares with Dewey). *Some* affirmation seems to be forthcoming. What, otherwise, would be the point of *applying his distaste for dualisms to science and morality and art?* He must mean to avoid sheer anarchy and arbitrariness. But if so, then nothing he says in disparaging relativism carries any weight at all.

The ultimate weakness of Rorty's "postmodernism" comes to this: he claims the benefits of "unforced agreement," "consensus," "solidarity"—notably, for instance, for whatever science has accomplished—but he refuses to sketch any grounds at all for thinking that those would-be benefits *are* "unforced" or reasonably defended:

> To say that unforced agreement is enough [for science, for pragmatism, for rationality, for distinguishing between the objective and the subjective] raises the specter of relativism [Rorty admits]. "Unforced agreement among whom? Us? The Nazis? Any arbitrary cohort or group?" The answer, of course, is "us." This necessarily ethnocentric answer simply says that we must work by our own lights. Beliefs suggested by another culture must be tested by trying to weave them together with beliefs we already have. . . . [T]he only sense in which science is exemplary is that it is a model of human solidarity.[39]

In what sense *is* science a "model"? In what sense *is* it the fruit of "unforced agreement"? These questions point to the unearned advantages of Rorty's refusal to explain just *what* it is he is preferring and why. The very success of science is now used as a blackmail argument to distract us from the arbitrariness of his refusal to answer. The fact remains that there *is* no principled demarcation between "us" and "another culture." Quine had already made the point in the strongest terms (in *Word and Object*): there is, he says, no principled distinction between the inter- and the intra-linguistic (or -societal); and, of course, Rorty could not, on his own stand, admit such a division.

By contrast, when he agrees with Putnam's pronouncement—namely, "To say, as [Bernard] Williams sometimes does, that convergence to one big picture of knowledge [absolutism] is required by the very concept of knowledge is sheer dogmatism." *Rorty* exposes not only his own dogmatism (perhaps inadvertently) but the fatal flaw in *Putnam's* internal realism as well.[40] For if, on Putnam's view, "the metaphysical notion of 'all objects' has no sense," then, *in principle,* Putnam can no longer assure us that when we are describing what purports to be "the same situation," our alternative descriptions *of "it"* will or must converge (moderately, without reaching the absolutist goal, perhaps in accord with our trusty *Grenzbegriff*) instead of assuming incommensurable forms *à la* Kuhn and Feyerabend.

If we concede that incommensurabilism, like relativism, can be coherently formulated, then Putnam's internal realism—whether "scientific" or "ethical"—must depend on a (suppressed) absolutist longing that cannot count on more than pluralist approximations:

> In *The Many Faces of Realism* I [that is, Putnam] described in detail [how] . . . "the same situation" can be described as involving entirely different numbers and kinds of objects (colored "atoms" alone, versus colored atoms plus "aggregates" of atoms). . . . How many objects are there "really" . . . ? *[E]ither way of describing [the world] is equally "true."* The idea that "object" has some sense which is independent of how . . . and what we are counting as an "object" in a given situation is an illusion.[41]

Putnam neglects to explain (as we have already seen) just how the "*it,*" "the same situation," is *ever* freed from the same conceptual or theorizing encumbrance that affects the alternative parsings he admits. Without explaining *that,* he cannot distinguish between his pluralism and a relativistic or even incommensurabilist reading of his doctrine. For, to *begin* with "the same situation" is to preclude the deeper question, and to admit the question is to preclude our being able to count *a priori* on the determinateness of "the same situation." Putnam unaccountably ignores the conceptual condition—which, in effect, *he* concedes (the inseparability of the subjective and the objective)—on which it makes sense to *ask:* "Is this 'the same situation' or not?" "How do we know we are describing 'the same situation'?" There is nothing in Rorty's account to show that he either escapes Putnam's difficulty or is able to resolve it satisfactorily. But that is to concede the pertinence of the relativism and incommensurabilism question *and* the severe limitation of Rorty's "high metaphilosophical ground." *That* is indeed the ulterior (and neglected) challenge of Kuhn's presentation of the Priestley/Lavoisier puzzle.

I have allowed these quarrels to fester a little, even at the expense of some repetition and a certain stonewalling against conceptual relief. Because I believe the reader's growing impatience leads to the dawning realization that the underlying question has effectively disappeared from the analysts' concern (or from that of pragmatists who favor analytic practices). But that *is* something of a scandal scanted at the very moment we wonder how to recover the relationship between pragmatism and analytic philosophy, now that the English-language tradition is bent on recovering Hegel and reconciling Hegel and analytic philosophy. That is, all the while we remind ourselves that early twentieth-century analytic philosophy had deliberately drummed the "Hegelians" completely out of play and that late analytic philosophy had completely marginalized the profound questions Kuhn and Feyerabend originally raised—both efforts pointing of course in the same direction.

The truth is that Putnam's pluralism is never more than a "logical" or "terminological" pluralism (that may be interpreted in ontological terms): it never advances epistemic credentials by which it could be contrasted with a coherent relativism or incommensurabilism. Putnam never shows us that alternative "pluralisms" *cannot* be epistemically justified *on* incommensurabilist grounds; he shows us only that *if* we have already determined *what* to count as real in a given context, we can, if we wish, parse *that* part of the world by other ways of counting entities. But that is not the decisive issue. Frankly, Quine's "indeterminacy of translation," the parsing of his holism (or "holophrastic sentences"), is significantly more daring than Putnam's conjecture—and is hardly matched by Putnam's.[42] It is also true that Quine's thesis is ultimately incoherent and arbitrarily resolved.

This explains the sense in which Rorty and Putnam fail to provide any reason for not thinking that pragmatism must, in all likelihood, yield to some benign form of relativism. Dewey need not have resisted any such concession, and its defense would go a great distance toward demonstrating that straightforward philosophical arguments can indeed be recovered without falling back to the dilemma posited by absolutism and postmodernism. That is in fact the minimal mark of the gains that span the work that runs from Descartes to Kant to Hegel to Dewey and beyond.

What it signifies, ultimately, is pragmatism's unfinished business. Through the sheer vitality of their running exchange, Rorty and Putnam rescued pragmatism from near oblivion, almost as a by-product of their quarrels. They invented, perhaps without meaning to, a more fundamental contest between pragmatism and analytic naturalism than could have been drawn from the work of the classic pragmatists alone. But, in the process, they exhausted their own resources, and they now appear to be searching for a defensible perch of their own, without bothering any longer to define what pragmatism should mean.

As it turns out, pragmatism has always had deeper linkages with the post-Kantian tradition than the "analysts" had ever bothered to fathom. In particular, admitting all the stalemates on the realism issue that late twentieth-century American philosophy has spawned, it begins to seem sensible to bring the relativist and historicist "menace" into the open, without prejudice, so as to test the best prospects for a pragmatist recovery of realism. We are now at a point where that very patient and sorely tried conviction—the one that insists that relativism is not incoherent or incompatible with a realism robust enough to accommodate the best work of the sciences—may not be as difficult or as awkward to defend as it once appeared to be.

In any event, we cannot drop the realism question merely because Putnam and Rorty have failed to gain the advantage for themselves. We must appreciate the reason for their being obsessed with the relativist threat, as well as the prospect that, in approaching its resolution, the new century will have made its own efforts to bring contemporary philosophy into accord once again with the most persistent quarrels of the ancient world. The open-ended inquiries of the original pragmatists now signify, as well, the unfinished reconciliation of Anglo-American and continental European philosophical practice. In short, we owe to Putnam and Rorty's quarrels and the palpable failure of their respective projects the strong recovery of an implicit quarrel between pragmatism and analytic philosophy that neither would openly endorse and that now stands before us with a larger run of questions than was possible before. That is itself a piece of Hegelian cunning. But whether we are right to anticipate that Dewey provides a better strategy—a pragmatist strategy—remains to be examined. Let us see.

4

John Dewey: The Metaphysics
of Existence

I

The revival of pragmatism, which caught the philosophical community by surprise, was as improbable as the first efforts to collect the original pragmatists. Yet both took place, both took root, gathered force, prospered, were chronicled, and have baffled every explanation of the movement's acknowledged unity. What unity remains is more convincing in retrospect than in the motivation that first linked and separated Peirce, James, and Dewey or lurks in the dwindling disputes that still link Rorty and Putnam.

Viewed now, pragmatism's supposed unity reflects at least its own efforts to establish the fact. Old and new, the pragmatists never lost their fascination with the defense of realism: with whether Cartesian realism could actually succeed or its Hegelian refutation be finally confirmed.

The question was revived with pragmatism's revival. But Rorty's and Putnam's eclectic interests led to a three-cornered quarrel, never official in any academic sense, but widely observed in that spirit between the important claims of analytic naturalism, postmodernism, and what now counts as pragmatism. It hardly matters how the principal antagonists came to be labeled as they now are. The *agon* was a disaster on all the substantive issues, though, in the twenty-five years the quarrel lasted, we have become clearer in our minds about these strategies, about the answer to the realist puzzle, and about the possible bearing of the "analytic"/"continental" divide on the future of pragmatism and English-language philosophy. That's quite a lot. The fact is that a large part of continental philosophy is committed to some amalgam of the flux, interpretive intermediaries, the historicized and culturally formed nature of human existence, acceptance of some form of post-Kantian resolution of the Cartesian *aporiai*, the rejection of materialist closure and reduction and the adequacy of extensionalist analysis, a strong attraction to existentially grounded questions, a tolerance for the denial of modal invariance and necessity and cognitive privilege. In English-language philosophy, the same notions have been congenially cultivated by the pragmatists. So there have been benefits of a sort—certainly, a better grasp of the deeper unity of the motley world of Western philosophy.

To date, the results of the three-legged *agon* look as if they might have been predicted in advance. Rorty continues to urge the pointlessness of canonical metaphysics and epistemology, often in Dewey's name. Putnam has admitted the collapse of his own try at a pragmatist form of realism and is perhaps in the middle of redefining what may be salvaged in the way of reconciling pragmatism and a realism adequate to the work of the sciences. And Donald Davidson, the third participant, an avowed opponent of pragmatism and the champion of the sparest version of current analytic naturalism, still seems wedded to a pared-down realism that could easily pass for Cartesian and has hobbled his every effort to formulate an account of truth, meaning, and knowledge and confirmation robust enough to meet the usual expectations. The most stunning fact about the entire tale is that the debate took place at all or, having done so, resolved so little.

Dewey was certainly aware of the Hegelian answers to the Cartesian and Kantian paradoxes, but he erased most of the textual signs of their sources in his own metaphysical and epistemological writings; and Peirce was always more explicitly engaged with Kant's version of the realism puzzle than with Hegel's. In fact, Peirce preferred Schelling to Hegel. That aside, classical pragmatism conveys a clearer sense than its "revival" of the historical sources of the originating puzzle and the need for a constructivist answer to Cartesianism. It also appears to be less occupied with the separation of realism and idealism in either the Kantian or post-Kantian sense than our own conceptual tastes seem to require. Unless, that is, you actually bother to read Dewey's metaphysics!

There's very little in Rorty, Putnam, or Davidson that pursues these matters in a textually explicit way. Rorty is so dismissive of metaphysics and epistemology that he hardly hides his penchant for misrepresenting Dewey's obvious conviction that a pragmatic realism was both viable and worth constructing. You cannot really read Rorty for a reliable clue about Dewey's central labors. Putnam nowhere consults Dewey in avoiding the inevitable collapse of his own metaphysics. And Davidson simply defends his "naturalizing" stance without any regard for the post-Kantian treatment of the puzzles realism poses. You must bear in mind that I am speaking of the central issue of nearly the last four hundred years of Western philosophy, which, at the beginning of the twenty-first century, has still not been put to rest.

There is, of course, a general tendency to disparage reliance on the published views of past masters in addressing the now-fashionable problems of the most up-to-date discussants. But the fact remains that our pop champions have disappointed us. Their bafflement turns out to be no more up-to-date than realism's long history has already demonstrated. More to the point, Dewey's *Experience and Nature* may actually provide the quickest and most effective instruction about how to recover Hegel's argumentative focus for our contemporary world. To be sure, any such instruction would be stripped down to meet pragmatism's own requirements and to serve Dewey's ingeniously biologized account of the entire realist issue. But that, I suggest, *is* the best solution that we currently have. You must, in a sense, turn away from Putnam and Rorty to Dewey's own texts. You may regard my saying so as a provocation. I make no apology for Dewey's prose; it's a very small price to pay for a genuinely elegant solution. But there clearly remains a very large gap between the two pragmatisms themselves.

My first suggestion, then, about how best to read Dewey comes to this: Dewey, agreeing with Hegel, replaces the fiction of Kant's transcendental ego with actual human beings; as a result, Dewey reins in his early metaphysics in accord with what he takes to be the non-cognitive animal conditions of his epistemology. That, I would say, was Dewey's most original and far-reaching invention, a discovery rightly recovered through an appreciation of Hegel's and Peirce's—and, of course, Darwin's—influence.[1]

Dewey begins as an eclectic Idealist; but gradually, under a Darwinian reading of his developing psychology, he recasts his post-Kantian themes in the leanest possible way: first, by stripping every teleologized or transcendentalized extravagance from his conceptual arsenal and, second, by inventing a distinctly original alternative to the "panpsychist" treatment of the unavoidable epistemological symbiosis the post-Kantians could not entirely escape. Hegel's *Phenomenology* is the best solution the post-Kantians ever managed to formulate—and yet *we*, today, must learn how to read Hegel, in order to offset any hypostatizing of *Geist*. Hegel needed such an armature, just as Dewey initially needed the implied structure of "experience" in the large, to ensure a match between the intelligibility of the cognized world and the relevance of the intelligibilizing power of human cognition—against the Cartesians. Dewey is very nearly the only English-language philosopher to find a convincing way to match the "symbiosis" both Kant and Hegel knew to be required, without yielding to post-Kantian panpsychism and without falling back to Cartesian solutions. That is the mark of Dewey's conception of the "problematic situation."

Put another way, the category "experience"—in both Dewey and William James—almost always signals a vestigial link to post-Kantian Idealism (whether German or British), because it signals the anti-Cartesian notion of the symbiosis of the subjective and the objective. The Idealists, particularly the British Idealists (T. H. Green, for instance, who greatly influenced the early Dewey), saw no alternative way of ensuring the cognizability of the world. Dewey systematically stripped his developing pragmatism from all of these vestigial traces—slowly and haltingly at times—from the time of his growing interest in experimental and social psychology and his efforts to Darwinize Hegel. It's true that he came to view the title of his metaphysical opus, *Experience and Nature,* as an unfortunate choice (because of the Idealist overtones, the panpsychist associations). But the fact remains that Dewey was breaking through to his final account. He never seriously doubted the philosophical importance of his "metaphysics," only the propriety of any easy use of the label, given its recent history. (Rorty is very sly about the matter—deliberately misleading.)

Here is another clue regarding Dewey's conception of nature. Ever since Kant, ever since philosophy recognized the great importance of resolving the paradoxes of Cartesian realism, it has become increasingly clear that a certain "benign antinomy" plays an ineliminable role in every effective resolution: namely, the seeming paradox that holds that metaphysics and epistemology are so indissolubly linked that neither can take final precedence over the other and that, nevertheless, within their inseparable union, each may be accorded a priority of its own that cannot claim stronger resources than those of the original symbiosis. Dewey's argument concludes, of course, that the paradoxes *can* be resolved.

It is a startling fact, nevertheless, that Cartesianism lives!—handsomely— in late analytic philosophy. You have only to remark the extraordinary confidence of the first three maxims of Michael Devitt's well-known (and well-received) attempt to recover what may be fairly viewed as the leanest version of Cartesian realism in the recent analytic literature. Here they are:

Maxim 1. In considering realism, distinguish the constitutive and evidential issues.

Maxim 2. Distinguish the metaphysical (ontological) issues of realism from any semantic issue.

Maxim 3. Settle the realism issue before any epistemological or semantic issue.[2]

Devitt is admirably explicit and remarkably brief. The only trouble with his proposal is that he offers no reason to believe we could ever follow his instruction. (It's as if Kant and Hegel had never practiced their trade. Or the pragmatists, for that matter.) Devitt is an unrepentant Cartesian—never very far from Davidson's persuasion—and Dewey would have been his instant nemesis. In fact, Dewey had already more than met Devitt's challenge before it was ever formulated.

Dewey was himself directly challenged by theorists as diverse as Arthur Murphy, Bertrand Russell, George Santayana, Hans Reichenbach—on grounds that are also Cartesian—as having produced a terrible muddle by conflating science's knowledge of the independent world and the "merely" instrumentalist conditions by which, occasionally, science might actually succeed.[3] Not surprisingly, those critics' arguments converge on something akin to Devitt's manifesto. Murphy's complaint will have to serve as proxy for the rest:

> We know [Murphy declares] both what the world is like under the conditions of observation and enjoyment and also what, in a much more general and approximate way, the unexperienced environment is by which experience is conditioned. If we could not know this there would be no sense in calling this environment "nature" and regarding experience as our means of finding out about it. . . . But to suppose that the whole meaning of what science tells us about the physical environment is reducible to this instrumental function is to treat one context in which things come to us as ultimate for metaphysics, and this is an irreparable mistake.[4]

I trust it will be enough to say that Murphy's challenge is simply a "Cartesian" rebuff, updated for the times, utterly unresponsive to the novelty of Dewey's conception. Dewey very deftly identifies the anti-Cartesian—in effect, the Darwinian—features of *Experience and Nature* that eluded Murphy. He might have answered Devitt in much the same way. He maintains that "experience" is a real ingredient in the world; that it never constitutes or constructs the "independent world"; that the world, when "known," is known under the condition of the inseparability of the subjective and the objective; that knowledge of the world emerges from some real but noncognitive experience (or "ingredient") of (and in) the world; and that whatever we view as the features of the "independent" world are, epistemically but not ontically, artifacts of our evidentiary sources. (Neither Putnam nor Rorty pursues these themes.)

In this way Dewey closes the gap between science and practical experience and, more pointedly, between experience and the animal sources of practical success bearing on survival, well-being, and the satisfaction of our wants and needs. All inquiry, science included, arises out of what Dewey calls an "indeterminate situation," or is gradually transformed into a "problematic situation." He means, by that, "a non-cognitive situation" that engenders a practical and unavoidable impasse for a human subject, "out of what [as he explains] knowing develops."[5] On Dewey's proposal, the resolution of such a practical impasse yields a viable form of constructivism or constructive realism that outflanks Cartesianism and idealism at a single stroke. That is, inquiry and cognition are, for Dewey, natural processes—actual "parts" of reality itself—emerging out of the non-cognitive conditions of animal survival. Dewey reads all this as a Darwinian, hence as resolving at a stroke the entire Cartesian mystification that the post-Kantians (preeminently, Hegel) defeated and displaced. Construing matters thus, it was, for Dewey, only a question of working out the details of his spare pragmatism that would ultimately count as a convincing escape from the Idealist extravagance.

It is important to remark here that an "indeterminate situation" is, at the outset, "non-cognitive" for Dewey, even where it enmeshes linguistically apt humans. Dewey's intuition is that it has realist and existential standing *and* provides a ground on which we may assume the realist standing of emergent cognition itself. (That is what, in different ways, Putnam and Rorty miss.) The latter, be it noted, would be arbitrary if cognition were treated facultatively, in the Cartesian way. But to see this is to see at once the advantage of Dewey's characterization of knowledge in terms of practical know-how, of *savoir-faire,* rather than of *savoir.* In effect, theoretical knowledge is itself a form of practical knowledge, and its realist standing depends on the continuum that runs, *via* a "problematic situation," from noncognitive impasses engaging our animal existence, the emergence of animal cognition from *that,* and the emergence of linguistically structured cognition (and science) from *that.* In this way, Dewey deftly obviates the entire Cartesian *aporia* (which, in our own time, bedevils the views of Devitt and Putnam).

Of course, Darwin's work was not available to Hegel. Nevertheless, Dewey's evolutionary idiom may be counted as a pragmatist simplification of the anti-Cartesian themes of Hegel's *Phenomenology* and larger visions— not that it was deliberately such, but we know (as already remarked) that Dewey admired Hegel's "actualist" disposition. It would not be too extreme to suggest that Dewey's "problematic situation" enabled him to recover whatever he favored in Hegel's account of historical evolution, in terms (his own) that all but ignored the themes of history.

Relative to a "problematic situation," Dewey reminds Murphy, he distinguishes between "subject-matter, object, and contents," which (roughly) is to say he distinguishes between the initial "situation," what is real in it, and whatever comes to be known of the real world in instrumental terms fitted to the resolution of the initial impasse. In that sense, as he explicitly says, all three terms "designate these different statuses of experienced material."[6]

By this economy, Dewey matches the complex aspects of the real world and the various senses in which he uses the term "experience": "experience" signifies, first, the symbiotized world that the pragmatists develop from Hegelian sources (the gist of one of James's master themes, extended by Dewey to include non-cognitive encounters with the world that ultimately influence cognition itself); second, the determinate things of the real world, which cannot be designated apart from the world's being cognitively experienced, under the first condition (in effect, the basis for the rebuttal of Murphy's—and Devitt's—Cartesian views); and, finally, the subjective side of perception and other emergent experiential modes, relative to which, objectively, "objects" are rightly designated as objects and the content of subjective and reflexive states is accorded realist standing in its own right.

Admittedly, Dewey's idiom is often tiresome, but his proposal is first rate. He captures, in a very spare way, Hegel's general solution of the realist problem, without explicit mention of Hegel's theme of the historicity of thought or, indeed, of any of Hegel's distinctive devices. I add at once an important qualification, the full implication of which I cannot, at this moment, judge.

There is an unpublished draft of an essay by Dewey on Hegel's systematic vision, running more than one hundred pages, that gives ample evidence of Dewey's detailed attention to Hegel's conception of history, which Dewey obviously found both attractive and enormously instructive.[7] It has received almost no attention in the discussion of Dewey's philosophy. I regard the absence of any explicit or sustained account of history (or, better, historicity) a distinct limitation in Dewey's otherwise commanding version of pragmatism. But I must also say that one can already see, given Dewey's detailed review of Hegel and his own pragmatist sympathies for Hegel's analysis, that there is absolutely no conceptual barrier against a strong Deweyan account of history and that there is, in fact, good reason to think there is more than a little evidence in Dewey's texts of Dewey's favoring Hegelian-oriented themes. In any event, pragmatism would be greatly strengthened by the addition of an account of historicity.

There is, of course, a more quarrelsome way of reading Dewey. Rorty insists on Dewey's being a prescient postmodernist who anticipates Rorty himself. This is an extraordinary piece of stage-setting. "It is [Rorty affirms] easier to think of [Dewey's *Experience and Nature*] as an explanation of why nobody needs a metaphysics, rather than as itself a metaphysical system."[8] Whatever does Rorty mean? It cannot be "easier" for anyone who actually reads *Experience and Nature!* The only possible way in which Rorty's reading could be given credence supposes that metaphysics makes no sense if it gives up essences, invariances in nature, natural necessities, transcendental conditions, and the like. But that would entail Rorty's believing that Dewey's advocacy of a world of endless change was metaphysically unacceptable or indefensible *and* that this could actually be demonstrated.

Dewey surely explains in *Experience and Nature* what *he* means by "metaphysics" in the revisionary sense he proposes—against the old hegemonies. "If philosophy be criticism," he asks, "what is to be said of the relation of philosophy to metaphysics?"[9] There cannot be an end to metaphysics there. Dewey's theme, of course, is the unrelieved "contingency" of nature and how its discovery is "the beginning of wisdom."[10] That is what separates Dewey from the classic metaphysicians. There is no postmodernism there, because there are no absolutes to provoke it. Dewey has defined a tenable middle ground, and metaphysics remains in full play.

The only possible path from Dewey to Rorty would require, first, Dewey's repudiation of Cartesianism, Kantian transcendentalism, Aristotelian essentialism, and similar philosophical weeds that count against the deep contingency of nature (all of which he willingly supports); and then, second, and for that reason alone, the conclusion that wherever the first step is taken, we may as well admit that there is no way to recover philosophy's account of the "metaphysics of existence," that is to say, the metaphysics *of* the deep contingency of nature. Dewey certainly champions the first, but he never supports the second: that is a complete fantasy on Rorty's part and a *non sequitur* to boot. For you cannot find in all of Rorty's prose a single argument to support his judgment, unless it rests on the false lead just offered.

We may make the correction easily enough by recalling Dewey's words at the close of *Experience and Nature*, which plainly anticipate, in 1929, the metaphysics he insists on in 1939 against Murphy and the other critics (already mentioned) who are collected in the same volume, in which Murphy's paper appears. What he says there also explains what he means, in the *Logic*, in 1938, by the troublesome but essential expression, a "problematic situation," the single most compact clue to his entire doctrine:

In mind, thought, this situation, this predicament, [that is, this "problematic situation,"] becomes aware of itself. . . . The one cord that is never broken is that between the energies and acts which compose nature. Knowledge modifies the tie. But the idea that knowledge breaks the tie, that it inserts something opaque between the interactions of things, is hardly less than infantile. Knowledge as science modifies the particular interactions that come within its reach, because it *is* itself a modification of [such] interactions. . . . The generic insight into existence which alone can define metaphysics in any empirically intelligible sense is itself an added fact of interaction. . . . The universe is no infinite self-representative series, if only because the addition within it of a representation makes it a different universe.[11]

There is no more perspicuous or timely statement of Dewey's metaphysics than this. It's a compendium of everything already said and a perfectly reasonable specimen of Dewey's distinctly original conception of nature. It is also, I would say, more agile than the realisms recently proposed by John McDowell and Hilary Putnam as successors to Putnam's failed "internal realism."[12] And, of course, it marks (almost as an aside) Dewey's escape from "panpsychist" themes.

II

The skill and grand economy of Dewey's metaphysics may elude you. It obviously eluded the "Cartesian" critics of his own day, and it baffles Rorty still. Moreover, Dewey was nothing if not straightforward. His invention of the "indeterminate situation" was pragmatism at its leanest and existential best. At one stroke, it outflanks the Cartesianism that Peirce had targeted; all the while it confines the analysis of meaning and truth and knowledge within the pragmatist priorities of practical intelligence. Here, it favors James's doctrine over Peirce's notion of the "long run."[13] For, whatever his blundering (in *Pragmatism*) may signify, James's intuition about what a pragmatist theory of truth would require caught Peirce off guard, filled a conceptual gap Peirce had touched on but was temperamentally unlikely to pursue once he became involved with his evolutionary speculations, and thereby prepared the ground for Dewey's very simple but magisterial maneuver. That explains why Dewey treats knowledge as "a modification of [*non-cognitive* interactions]" between organism and world. By that single adjustment, Dewey disables every form of cognitive privilege (*savoir*, in the Cartesian sense) and derives the realist standing of objective knowledge (viewed as a constructed competence) from the prior standing of instrumental intelligence (*savoir-faire*), the pragmatist middle term between science and our animal interactions with the world.

You see the trick of Dewey's strategy: the realist standing of our science is ultimately justified constructively from *within* the realist interactions of a viable life, which, from time to time, trap us in one existential impasse or another requiring improvisations that we eventually judge to be continuous with the regularities of nature. Realism, therefore, is a late artifact of our reflections, *not* a first principle of any kind; hence, never more than provisional, perspectived, "interested," "instrumental" (if you wish), fluxive, constructed, lacking any invariance or necessity or essential *telos* or privilege or unique validity. All of this comes from a single maneuver demonstrably superior to any of the more recent analytic attempts to displace it or entrench Cartesianism—hence, a fair alternative to every earlier realism spanning, say, Aristotle and Hegel. That is pragmatism's most important challenge.

You have only to add that the notion of an "indeterminate situation" signifies that Dewey's realism was a metaphysics of *existence,* which is what ensures the amplitude and plasticity of his entire vision. For Dewey, there are no *a priori* fixities to be drawn from the *natures* of things; "features," kinds, essences cannot be more than what we surmise answer to the piecemeal implications of our animal responses to existential impasses.

There you have the deft reason Dewey discards Aristotle's habit of assigning potency and actuality to fixed "natures" (or essences) or essences to fixed potencies: an existentialized metaphysics precludes the need for and plausibility of any such doctrine, rests finally on one or another version of the flux. Teleology cannot then be more than an idealization of the trajectories of animal intelligence; it cannot impose any normative constraints on human life and conduct; it must follow the open-ended purposiveness and continually adjusted values of human improvisation. Neither Aristotle nor Kant need be entirely discounted, but there is no longer any necessity or near-necessity in what they say about nature or reason. Once privilege is set aside, the defeat of modal necessities follows from the coherence of *any* plausible account of human history. That is an extraordinary gain at absolutely no cost.

No doubt this is, for instance, what has worried conventional moral and political theorists (who find Dewey humane and generous in spirit) but who are aware that there are no normative invariants that Dewey holds in reserve. It is not that Dewey means by this to disjoin the public and the private "parts" of morality and politics (as we have considered, in reviewing Rorty's embroidery). It is simply that Dewey is heroically consistent in his sunny realism. His is not an optimism secretly assured that moral and political freedom will ultimately conform with what we already know to be the good of mankind. It is rather that he trusts the race (as we must) to pursue (what amounts to human rationality) whatever evolving experience persuades us is worth installing as our provisional but well-meant good.

That there are dangers in such a policy goes without saying; but those dangers cannot be more severe or more numerous than whatever a confident scan of the essential norms of "human nature," revelation, or self-evident goods have historically proclaimed them to be.[14] We must count on our animal energies and needs, our prudence, our capacity to correct misjudged opportunities, our reading of our own personal and social history, and, above all, our capacity to learn from the general human career that has brought us this far. Dewey is rather daring in his quiet way.

You see the radical intent of Dewey's metaphysics. It's true that Dewey was unconditionally opposed to ancient, medieval, early modern, and Kantian metaphysics and epistemology (and moral philosophy). But if you accept the pragmatist conception of meaning and truth and refine it in terms of Dewey's notion of an "indeterminate situation," you will find it well-nigh impossible to avoid adopting something akin to his metaphysics of existence. The important lesson is that Dewey's *is* a coherent doctrine that arises in a conceptual space that, already by Hegel's time, had completely transformed the canon in which figures like Aristotle, Descartes, and Kant counted as the exemplars for all admissible metaphysics. I must add, of course, that the meaning of the term "metaphysics" was profoundly altered by Kant. Many would say that it now means "epistemology"; and in a way it does, since Kant uses the term "metaphysics" to name an impossible project: the analysis of the noumenal. But the meaning of the term is more usefully linked with Hegel's critique of Kant. Opposing the bare intelligibility of talking about the noumenal, Hegel's recovery of epistemological questions supports the idea that metaphysics and epistemology are the obverse sides of a single inquiry. Dewey's pragmatism, I suggest, is "Hegelian" in this precise sense.

To defeat Dewey now, you must demonstrate at least that the doctrine of the flux is false (that is, the *faute de mieux* thesis that denies that we can ever demonstrate that there are modal invariances or necessities *de re* or *de cogitatione*). For Dewey's argument is, precisely, set to recover metaphysics and epistemology without the presumptively necessary constraints of privilege, foundations, the *a priori*, and the transcendental.

That is where postmodernism and canonical philosophies converge (without agreement on how to proceed): Davidson, for instance, insists in "A Coherence Theory of Truth and Knowledge" on correspondentist and coherentist constraints on knowledge, although he has now abandoned his former arguments, without it being clear as yet whether he has also abandoned his original commitment. Indeed, to yield on his commitment now would, of course, be to yield fatally in the pragmatist or postmodernist direction; and Rorty believes that only an *a priori* or transcendental or invariantist or privileged epistemology could save traditional philosophy, though he also believes that this is now palpably impossible. Dewey's fluxive strategy concedes the advantage to *savoir-faire* over *savoir*, which, effectively, favors constructivism in epistemology and metaphysics over any and every form of Cartesian realism.

I am concerned here chiefly to identify the nerve and force of Dewey's originality rather than to recover Dewey's entire career and wide ranging interests, or, for that matter, a close analysis of where he agrees and disagrees with Peirce and James. It is Dewey's conceptual turn that holds the key to explaining Putnam's and Rorty's failings *qua* late-wave pragmatists, and it is the same turn that focuses the nature of the essential contest between a revived pragmatism and analytic philosophy at the close of the century.[15]

The postmodernist may still insist on his pointless triumph: for, if the modal argument fails, he says, then all the familiar forms of philosophy must be at an end. Yet Dewey's example belies the verdict. It had, you realize, taken the better part of a century to eliminate the opaque machinery of the Hegelian system to arrive at Dewey's economy; and it has taken the better part of another century to prepare the ground for a dialectically useful contest between Dewey's conception and the forceful claims of late twentieth-century analytic philosophy.

It is now, therefore, nearly two centuries since Hegel's *Phenomenology* appeared. "*Geist*" (or "Absolute Mind") has been abandoned (though Hegel himself was never a proper Schellingian); all traces of teleologism have been put at risk; Hegelian vestiges of Kantian transcendentalism are no longer in vogue; the idea of the historicity of thought, which had flourished until recently, is now neglected by pragmatists, as well as by the champions of nearly every English-language movement (and, increasingly, by their European counterparts). Nevertheless, the most recent pragmatists (Putnam and Rorty) as well as the most influential recent analytic philosophers (notably, Davidson) are still committed to protecting one or another version of the Cartesian paradigm, even if all the while they act to exorcise Cartesian faults in one another. At the very beginning of the twenty-first century, we are, it seems, still heavily engaged in resolving the puzzles that confronted Kant and Hegel in a span of little more than the last quarter of the eighteenth century!

The strength of Dewey's solution, which is much clearer now than it was before analytic philosophy's present dominion, depends on the ingeniously simple union of Peirce's and James's theories of meaning and truth, of Hegel's radical treatment of empirical contingency (shorn of all reference to historicity), and Dewey's biologized or Darwinian conception of the "indeterminate situation." There you have the bare bones of Dewey's metaphysics. Its peculiar resilience is better demonstrated, however, by following the mixed fortunes of the lesser pragmatists of our own day. To make this case is to justify philosophy's interest in pragmatism's revival.

Putnam, even more than Rorty, must be credited with bringing James's and Dewey's conception of realism into line with the strongest pressures of late twentieth-century analytic philosophy. Putnam's variant—"internal realism"—counted on resolving the Cartesian paradoxes by featuring, epistemically, a symbiosis of the subjective and the objective without denying the ontic independence of the physical world and (more notably) without denying the explanatory role of the concept of truth. (That, you may remember, was the sense of the "benign antinomy" mentioned earlier.) The maneuver had already been developed by Dewey, most fully in *Experience and Nature*, but it is also, of course, an essential thread in Hegel's *Phenomenology*. Putnam's argument is best rendered in his *Reason, Truth and History* (1981) and more or less summarized in *The Many Faces of Realism* (1987). You have only to compare the prefaces of both books to see that Putnam remained committed to opposing "the dichotomy between 'objective' and 'subjective' views of truth and reason."[16] His constant target remained Cartesian realism, which he labeled "metaphysical realism," a doctrine committed to there being "One True Theory" in accordance with which the mind "copies" the world.

You have, here, also, a hint of the fatal equivocation affecting Putnam's realism. For Putnam never satisfactorily explained the potential importance of the difference between there being many partial descriptions compatible with some single, ideally neutral and comprehensive description of the world in accordance with the "One True Theory" and a plurality of partial or fragmented descriptions first generated by our diverse and changing existential interests—always, in some measure, epistemically blind (according to Dewey)—that, in Putnam's account, are somehow known (if known at all) to converge compatibly with whatever a proper realism would require. *If* Putnam had been faithful to his internalism, he would not have advanced his objective pluralism without an epistemological rationale—or he would not have distinguished it (as he confidently does) from a relativistic alternative. There's a lacuna there: an unanswered question about two very different kinds of pluralism. On the evidence, Putnam cannot escape the charge of relativism Rorty brings against him.[17] The problem is a variant of the problem that dogs Peirce's "long run": neither defends convergence convincingly.

Two observations are worth adding here. For one, Putnam goes to great lengths to demonstrate that there is no single, uniquely valid description of the world; that, relative to our interests, we may always individuate the things of the world (*we know*) in very different ways that (*for that reason*) will not generate paradox or incompatibilities regarding truth. This is as far as Putnam ventures as a pluralist, as if that were enough to capture what is implicit in the pluralism of James and Dewey: you must think of relativism and incommensurabilism *as* alternative realist possibilities to pluralism, that pragmatism has not ruled out.

Putnam puts his own thesis rather neatly: "realism [by which he means, interchangeably, 'internal realism' or 'pragmatic realism'] is *not* incompatible with conceptual relativity."[18] That's fair enough. We may always, he explains, invoke something akin to the play between, say, Carnap's standard view of individuation and some Polish logician's mereological alternative, so as to *arrive at* plural ontologies that are compatible with one another (in the relevant sense) and consistent with a strong view of the independent world.

But how, *on* the symbiotizing thesis, could we ever *show that* all such seemingly divergent descriptions *were* no more than alternative ways of describing *one and the same part of the same world?* There seems to be no viable answer. *That* is the point of relativism's "menace." For, it is against this worry (my second observation) that Putnam invents out of whole cloth his notorious *Grenzbegriff* of truth and rationality—that is, to offset the threat of relativism. But, on the constructivist thesis itself, the *Grenzbegriff* cannot possibly serve any epistemological or methodological function. It cannot show that all responsible epistemologies must converge or prove commensurable in any given period of inquiry. For, if it could, it would have to draw on "externalist" (say, Cartesian) sources, which would violate the constraints of "internal realism."

I mention these difficulties, again, to confirm that Putnam was driven to rather desperate devices (the *Grenzbegriff,* the avoidance of the obvious epistemological threats to his own pluralism) because he was trapped without any conceptual resources but the Cartesian ones. He *had* to secure the realist theme in some explicit way—and he was unable to do so. Dewey meets the need in a trice by the device of the "problematic situation": because it ensures the realist standing of our cognitive efforts by an account of animal origins, *not* by any criterial treatment of our particular claims. That is an extraordinary economy—possibly the slimmest viable resolution of the Cartesian paradox that history affords.

Dewey takes human experience to be part of the real world in a continuum that runs from the non-cognitive to the cognitive; but it is also, for that same reason, a sufficient condition for judging what, relative to our perceived practical impasses, we should take to be our best account of the real world. To admit all that *is,* ineluctably, to treat the theory of truth as explanatory—for constructivist reasons.

In effect, Dewey solves the problem of the realist standing of our inquiries in a way that frees us (*via savoir-faire*) to construct our best account of reality. But to proceed thus is, plainly, to admit all the questions of construction, history, divergent interests, plural and relativist conceptions of the real world, and incommensurable epistemologies that the analytic tradition has effectively suppressed. Putnam obviously saw the danger and dug his heels in.

Putnam has abandoned (with qualifications) his internal realism (or what he had come to count as internal realism[19]). But the reason has nothing to do with the difficulties mentioned. It seems that, having been seduced much earlier (as he admits) by James's attraction to a form of representationalism (on the strength of which James built an idealist picture of reality, which Putnam now rejects[20]), Putnam belatedly discovered that his own version of representationalism was always hostage to the same Cartesian paradoxes he labored to expose. (All this has been said before.)

But it is now not clear whether, in rejecting (quite correctly) "Cartesian" representationalism, Putnam also means to abandon all that he includes under the label "internal realism."[21] It hardly matters, except to get clear about his own intention. Since, for one thing, the doctrine of the symbiosis of the subjective and the objective *is* independent of representationalism and, on the evidence, affords the only viable way to overcome the paradoxes; and, for a second, given the argument of the flux—in particular, given the rejection of cognitive privilege—"internalism" plainly puts Putnam at risk of yielding to one or another form of relativism.

I would say, therefore, that Putnam unqualifiedly fails in his realist undertaking. He also fails to justify his pluralism. (I return to Putnam's pluralism in the final chapter.) You must remember that the whole purpose of the Paul Carus Lectures (*The Many Faces of Realism*)—and much the same is true of the older *Reason, Truth and History*—was, in Putnam's own words, "to further specify the alternative that I see to metaphysical realist [that is, Cartesian] views of reality and truth, on the one hand, and to cultural relativist ones, on the other [by which Putnam means to include at least Rorty's postmodernism]."[22]

I emphasize the outcome, because Putnam's is surely the most sustained— very nearly the only—effort in late twentieth-century American philosophy to recover the pragmatist strategy on realism (Dewey's strategy, I would say, though Putnam seems unfamiliar with it) in a way meant to match the best rigor of analytic philosophy. Putnam meant to show (as I interpret matters) that the penchant for "metaphysical realism" he discerned in the unity of science movement and such affiliated undertakings as Donald Davidson's was indeed something of a return to Cartesian realism. Putnam, of course, believed (still believes) that relativism is as incoherent as Cartesianism. But that hardly shows that Dewey's realist strategy fails, even if it should favor or yield to relativism. The plain fact is that Putnam, divided between his loyalty to Dewey and his older loyalty to science's knowledge of the "independent world," could not quite fathom how a thoroughgoing constructivism imposed on the flux could possibly yield a realism worthy of the natural sciences.

Dewey's own strategy *is* "internalist" (in the sense at stake). Or, better, symbiotized, in a sense that accords with a "problematic situation." It is also hospitable to relativism, though that is never spelled out. Apart from the interpretation I am now suggesting, I am aware of very little more (in the critical literature) than the briefest mention of the essential connection (in Dewey's doctrine) between relativism and realism. Arthur Murphy, who adopts a Cartesian stance against Dewey (as we have seen), remarks in passing that the dependence of realism on the peculiarities of the "indeterminate situation" does indeed introduce in Dewey's account an ineliminable touch of relativism.[23] He means this as a polite objection, but the charge *is* valid and (I think) entirely acceptable. It may be read as the barest trace of the original Hegelian doctrine, which both Murphy and John Herman Randall conventionally label "objective relativism," that is, the upshot of admitting the contemporaneously impenetrable horizon of our or any other form of historical existence.[24] It is, in fact, the same point I've brought against Putnam's pluralism.

Dewey escapes all the conceptual traps, *if* (as I believe) relativism and incommensurabilism *are* coherent. Ralph Sleeper has ventured the single line, bearing on Dewey's metaphysics of existence, that Dewey's ontology "is pluralistic and relativistic, of course, since Dewey accepts no eternal objects or permanent kinds."[25] Sleeper means his claim to rely on the import of the original "indeterminate situation," which, as I say, confounds Putnam's own version of realism. Dewey's master stroke rests with the double fact (1) that our animal interactions with the real world (which are themselves parts of reality) are more fundamental than, and not reducible to, our *cognitive* connections with the world, and (2) that our cognitive connections are entitled to a realist reading for that same reason, that is, are not merely "representational" in any Cartesian or mentalist sense.[26] If you hold all this together, you see the stunning simplicity of Dewey's metaphysics. But you also see the unexamined relevance of the challenge posed by relativism, which neither Putnam nor Rorty satisfactorily addresses.

III

I should say that, ultimately, Dewey's theory favors two strategies: one, to begin with existence rather than essence, which (let me assure you) is not to prioritize "existence" over "nature"; the other, to relativize all metaphysical and epistemological questions (which, though distinct, are not separable) to the precognitive and fluxive "indeterminacies" of existential impasses. I regard this formula as the key to any acceptable summary of Dewey's grand labor. I also believe it must yield in the direction of relativism and even incommensurabilism. I find that entirely acceptable. It catches up in a coherent and balanced way all of Dewey's speculations about metaphysics, epistemology, logic, and practical norms and values.

But I must collect the true fire of the argument.

Dewey, as I say, prefers a metaphysics of existence over essences. He draws his account of nature, therefore, from the fluxive condition of reality, which, in effect, "bets" that no one will be able to demonstrate that there are any modally necessary invariances *de re* or *de cogitatione.* The sheer coherence and wide range of application of Dewey's metaphysics constitute a proof that the ancient canon of the Parmenidean clan (if I may name an honorable history thus) has led the entire company astray, because their arguments rest on the assumption that the denial of reality's invariant structure must yield to paradox or contradiction "somewhere" (as Aristotle pointedly says). But if you cannot show the incoherence of Dewey's alternative—defended, mind you, as an analysis of the human condition—you must consider yielding in favor of Dewey's economies. The argument is "naturalistic" of course, in the sense the classic pragmatists preferred; that is, the argument eschews all conceptual resources that, by its own lights, would count as "supernatural" (or even fictional) and it prefers to be guided by (though not to submit to) the authority of the sciences.[27]

Dewey's metaphysics, however, is not of the "naturalizing" kind so strenuously espoused by Davidson and Rorty or, more equivocally, by Quine, a naturalizing that insists beyond the mild policy mentioned that all explanation is ultimately causal, disallowing all epistemic or legitimative (or normative) discourse, and favoring physicalism and extensionalism over all other options.[28] The extreme doctrine—"naturalizing," in Davidson's idiom—depends, as far as I can see, on the more than doubtful dictum of "the causal closure of the physical world."[29]

I say "more than doubtful," because, of course, if flux holds, then the would-be exceptionless laws of nature must be contingent idealizations of the observed or conjectured regularities of the experienced world; and because "causal closure" begs the question of the reducibility of cultural and historical forces that are inseparable from the physical or biological. (There is good reason to think that necessary laws *are* idealizations anyway.) In short, the status of nomological universals is not a different issue from that of validating something like Dewey's metaphysics of existence or, more specifically, the irreducibility or ineliminability of the symbiotizing claim. The Deweyan maxim might then be put this way: "Natural but not naturalizable."[30]

If you grant all this, then, if you recall the sense in which Putnam's realism fails to escape the charge of relativism—in effect, if we prioritize Dewey's existential indeterminacies, so that Putnam's *Grenzbegriff* is shown to be completely arbitrary—you begin to see the deeper thrust of Dewey's daring. Dewey obliges us at every turn to explain precisely why we think ourselves entitled to fall back to one or another form of the canon that spans, say, Aristotle and Kant.

As early as 1891, reflecting on the instruction of children regarding the difference between percepts and concepts, Dewey already realized that, taken in strictly pragmatist terms, a concept (think of a triangle constructed in imagination) is "'ideal' not sensual . . . it is a mode or *way of mental action*, it cannot be felt or seen or heard. *It can be grasped only in and through the activity which constitutes it*. . . . The concept, in short, is knowledge of what the real object is—the object taken with reference to its principle of construction, while the percept, so called, is knowledge of the object in a more or less accidental or limited way."[31] This has a decidedly Hegelian ring to it. Furthermore, if you favor its constructivist bent, you see at once why Rorty's throwing in with Davidson's naturalizing is completely arbitrary. *Davidson's* commitment is not arbitrary, merely undefended; but Rorty, as a postmodernist, could not possibly have any reason to prefer naturalizing to Deweyan naturalism. Furthermore, you begin to see, by that, the sense in which Rorty is really a "Parmenidean" *manqué*. For what Rorty finally seems to believe is that standard philosophy cannot proceed at all except through invariances and necessities, though it remains impossible to legitimate any inquiry along such lines.

Concepts, then, are modes of active intervention, constructions under our control; percepts are not. There can be little doubt that this is, in essence, the import of Dewey's biologized account of resolving an existential impasse. It shows the near necessity of preferring flux over invariance and practical know-how over theoretical knowledge. Concepts arise at all only as a result of the evolving animal and human activity of attempting to resolve "a problematic situation." You may see in this Dewey's Darwinizing the constructivist themes of Hegel's *Phenomenology*. That is a bit of a leap, but not an unreasonable one.

The idea of an indeterminate situation is a remarkably spare conceptual device that ensures the symbiosis of the subjective and the objective at an existential level well below any cognitive presumption, though compatibly with realism and the acceptance of the flux—*and* potential epistemic incommensurabilities. It obliges us to explain the emergent powers of cognition (in action as well as language) and of theoretical reason in terms that acknowledge the biological continuity of resolving practical impasses and our non-cognitive and animal competences. It affords a very slim strategy. Thus, count—in the pragmatist sense of meaning and truth—all invariances, necessities, essences, universals, natural kinds, fixed concepts, meanings as no more than instrumental constructions or improvisations or gropings (or gradually developing know-how), until we have (equally pragmatized) evidence to the contrary. It turns the tables on all the pieties of standard epistemology.

That is what may have misled Rorty so disastrously: Dewey does not reject epistemology; he merely refuses to countenance its usual circular and self-serving assurances. Rorty believes that a viable metaphysics must rely on privilege and invariance despite the fact that this is impossible! Oddly, he makes no provision for a temperate reappraisal of our cognitive powers: evidently, it must be postmodernism or nothing.

Therefore, Dewey's pragmatism is committed to a kind of holism, but it saves itself from vacuity by nesting science and practical success (*savoir* and *savoir-faire*, let us say) uncompromisingly in the resolution of "problematic situations" and by adhering to the leanest pragmatist reading of Peirce's and James's original guesses regarding meaning and truth.

I emphasize Dewey's holism, because it suggests a telling comparison with Quine's more baffling holism, which Quine thinks is required if we are to ensure the spare physicalism and extensionalism of the best of analytic philosophy. Quine introduces ad hoc a doctrine favoring original "holophrastic sentences"—never properly analyzed, possibly impenetrable to analysis—that nevertheless claims the obvious advantage of possessing realist import, functioning empirically in a quasi-foundational way, and altogether free of "ontic commitment" (in Quine's familiar sense).[32]

Although Quine is often said (with some justice) to be a pragmatist, his holophrastic doctrine—which, mind you, cleverly permits him to advance a more moderate "naturalizing" stance than Davidson's (a fortiori, than Rorty's)—secures his physicalist and extensionalist commitment without ever having to meet anything like Dewey's pragmatist scruple.[33] Dewey and Quine are, in effect, vying to define a suitable form of realism free of any charge of idealism. But they proceed by irreconcilable means.

You see the superiority of Dewey's strategy if you bear in mind that Dewey's originating holism (the "indeterminate situation") is initially cast entirely in non-cognitive terms; whereas Quine's originating holism (the experiences that answer to his "holophrastic" sentences) is outfitted from the start with the strongest possible cognitive advantages, without yet violating (because it is always prior to) the constraints he imposes by way of the "indeterminacy of translation" doctrine and the exposé of the analytic/synthetic "dogma." But if you concede all that, you cannot fail to see that Davidson's recovery of realism (without risking any epistemology), Putnam's appeal to his *Grenzbegriff,* Rorty's "ethnocentric solidarity," and now Quine's holophrastic sentences are all failed vestiges of Cartesian realism that ignore (or violate) the pragmatist scruple. (It is barely possible that Putnam's *Grenzbegriff* presupposes something close to Quine's dubious version of holism, which may itself be a peculiarly cryptic extension of Pierre Duhem's more plausibly situated, though actually problematic, holism.)

The right way to read Dewey, then, is to hold, without compromise, to the pragmatist account of meaning and truth. In a fair sense, the whole of the texts of *Logic* and *Experience and Nature* is occupied with explaining what Dewey intends by his "indeterminate situation." But you cannot read his formula without featuring flux over fixity, know-how over knowledge, adequacy of directed action here and now over correspondentist and neutral truth, and endless instrumentalities over changeless final ends.

Let me offer, in closing, then, two small textual clues to fix the lesson of the entire argument. First, in *Experience and Nature,* Dewey identifies Aristotle as the metonymic bearer of the doctrine he utterly opposes. In effect, he says, Aristotle "bequeathed to the modern world through Latin Christianity . . . the consequences of taking the universal which is instrumental, as if it were final."[34] I cannot imagine a more succinct indictment of one and an affirmation of the other of the two completely opposed systems of thought I have been tracking: Dewey's and what is now called Cartesianism in deference to pragmatism's animus.

But the deeper explanation of Dewey's doctrine (the second clue) is focused more memorably in the following well-known formula:

> Inquiry is the controlled or directed transformation of a indeterminate situation into one that is so determinate in its constituent distinctions and relations as to convert the elements of the original situation into a unified whole.[35]

The decisive lesson is this: in the symbiotized, pre-cognitive, but real situation in which effective cognition first arises, all the "objects" that are marked off as real are provisionally constituted and reconstituted *as* the human agent works deliberately to capture whatever begins to dawn as an acceptable resolution of his impasse. It is the "situation" and *its* "objects" that are transformed, *not* any supposedly independent objects by way of the power of mere thought; Dewey is no idealist here. The evolving "situation" is both part of reality and the medium through which the most stable features of what we take the independent world to be (its "contents," in Dewey's idiom) are gradually mapped and continually revised.[36] Dewey's thesis is that there is no end to the process, no privileged or total picture of reality, no final or essential *telos* in anything, and no need for same. *Nature,* on Dewey's argument, is whatever answers to that. That's all!

"[K]nowledge of nature, but not nature itself[Dewey says] 'emanates' from immediate experience." He is, in speaking thus, paraphrasing and parodying George Santayana's criticism of his doctrine. He permits the rest of Santayana's well-known objection—"everything remote emanates from something immediate"—to count as acceptable. Santayana means (by it) that "everything immediate emanates from something biological." Except for the questionable "aura" of the term "emanate," Dewey advises, he agrees completely that "the view stated in the last sentence is also mine."[37] ("Emanate," you realize, has oblique affinities with Schelling's vision, hence with the panpsychism of the Idealists.)

Santayana's criticism is one of the best remembered indictments of Dewey's naturalism, but it also inadvertently explains the decisive advantage of Dewey's conception over Santayana's complaint. Here is what Santayana says:

> This question, which is the crux of the whole system, may be answered, I think, in a single phrase: *The dominance of the foreground.*

In nature there is no foreground or background, no here, no now, no moral cathedra, no center so really central as to reduce all other things to mere margins and mere perspectives. A foreground is by definition relative to some chosen point of view, to the station assumed in the midst of nature by some creature tethered by fortune to a particular time and place. If such a foreground becomes dominant in a philosophy naturalism is abandoned.[38]

Dewey's answer is utterly compelling. First of all, he shows that Santayana is himself forced to concede *some* "foreground" of his own in order to justify speaking of nature at all. In effect, Santayana concedes the need for *some* "interplay" between ourselves and nature, which term Dewey takes (incorrectly, I would say) to be "synonymous" with his own term "interaction."[39] Second, the implied concession opens the door to subverting every form of the ancient invariances or the more recent Cartesianism that pragmatists were bound to oppose from the vantage of their own attenuated Hegelian origins. And, third, Dewey explains the benignly equivocal sense (against Santayana again) in which *he* starts "with experience as the manifestation of interactions of organism and environment" (that is, the post-Kantian precognitive symbiosis, which James also calls "experience"). So that what comes to be distinguished as real or merely imagined is itself marked off by "different modes of interaction" (or "experience," within the larger space of what is also called "experience").[40]

Once you realize that Dewey's "indeterminate situation" is a much-reduced version of the Hegelian critique of both Kant and Descartes, biologized in the pragmatist manner, you have in hand Dewey's entire fluxive account of nature. The only conception that's missing in Dewey, as far as I can see, is an up-to-date paraphrase of Hegel's notion of historicity. But I am certain that this can be restored, now that the pragmatist advantage has been made clear. (I also believe it is needed.) Dewey was perhaps too sanguine about the equivalence of Santayana's term "interplay" and his own "interaction": for the first is meant to be relational *at* the cognitive level (which is a Cartesian notion), whereas the relationship marked by the second is entirely benign epistemically, since it is first cast in biological and non-cognitive terms.

What Dewey offers in the way of a disciplined realism is, therefore, ampler than, for instance, John McDowell's instructive exposé of a would-be relational "interface" between belief and world (which Putnam now endorses in place of his earlier internal realism).[41] McDowell's demonstration of how to avoid the paradoxes of Cartesian realism is probably the most promising slim recovery of realism the analytic tradition has yet produced. But, you must remember, it is two hundred years too late! Moreover, Mc-Dowell is, by his own admission, a kind of "natural Platonist," whereas Dewey is a constructivist. The distinction is of the greatest importance to realism's best prospects.

Dewey forces the implied contrast on our attention in a number of compelling papers that explain why "natures," "kinds," and similar distinctions are rightly cast in terms of the similarity of *pragmatist interventions* rather than in terms of the sameness or similarity of *perceived qualities:*

> No amount of direct inspection and comparison of [the] qualities [of two *browns,* he says] will yield the needed conception or definition [of *brown*]. What is common and constant is not the quality as quality but the logical function assigned it as an evidentiary sign of something else. Instead of being directly given for comparison and abstraction, the commonness in question is the *product* of operations that depend upon a universal or conception being already at [one's] command [that is, common operations deliberately fitted to collected instances].[42]

This is as clear a formulation of the pragmatist conception of nature as any I know. I think it can be said to justify, by its originality and power, all of Peirce's and James's more "primitive" intuitions about meaning and truth. Certainly, the entire dispute about universals (or "real generals," which occupied Peirce a great deal) is ingeniously blunted by the maneuver Dewey favors here. Dewey's principal discovery is simply this: that if knowledge is originally biologized, it must favor practical know-how over facultative expertise; and if that is so, then all invariances will be judged to be the artifacts of flux.

5

Relativism, Pragmatism, and Realism

Unexpectedly, pragmatism proves to be an unfamiliar country. It's the best-known American philosophy, of course, but it is hard to produce a single tenet that the classic pragmatists support that also sets them apart from other movements in a clear way. Opposition to Cartesianism, loyalty to a certain post-Kantian heritage, the acceptance of one or another form of constructivism will not be enough. I don't deny that these are all defining traits, but they are very widely shared in twentieth-century philosophy and take many different forms. Nearly every Eurocentric movement that can claim legitimate descent from Hegelian and post-Hegelian sources would meet these conditions; for instance, the movements we know as the Frankfurt Critical school, post-Heideggerean hermeneutics, notably the version championed by Hans-Georg Gadamer, Nietzschean-tinged genealogies best represented in the work of Michel Foucault, perhaps even in a pinch the extremely informal, unsystematized conception of societal life collected as the "later Wittgenstein."

Part of the difficulty, as I've tried to explain, is that whatever thesis might be advanced as common ground, it's very likely that a consensus among the classic figures would still seem contrived. Political liberalism, for instance, was never a part of Peirce's principal concerns, nor was evolutionism a part of Dewey's. Even fallibilism meant very different things to Peirce and Dewey and to many who were obviously not pragmatists at all. Karl Popper, for instance, embraced a form of fallibilism.[1] James's theory of truth was certainly not uncongenial to Dewey, but it was unsympathetically received by Peirce; Peirce's theory of meaning and his semiotics had no significant reception at Dewey's or James's hand; and Mead's very limited investigation of history was almost entirely neglected, even by Dewey.

Furthermore, if we must extend pragmatism, as we now plainly must, to include the themes and problems of the recent "revival" effected by Rorty and Putnam, it becomes doubly difficult to find common ground between those two or between either of them and the classic figures. As far as I can see, Putnam and Rorty agree on very little beyond a profound distaste for relativisms of any kind, an opposition to cognitive privilege, a strong but somewhat inchoate attraction to liberalism in practical affairs, and an agreement about the philosophical importance of deciding what to understand by realism and associated notions like truth and knowledge. But even in these regards, Putnam and Rorty share very little and, in spite of their claiming a pragmatist pedigree, there's precious little that either has featured that could be closely linked with the work of the original figures. Putnam has repudiated much of what he once found congenial in James, and Rorty quite deliberately distorts Dewey's philosophical convictions for short-term ("post-philosophical") gains. That is precisely why I treat pragmatism's second life as a "reinvention" more than an actual revival. It accounts for its curiously obscure but very palpable "presence."

I have been suggesting we consider a "third" way of viewing pragmatism. Because the difficulty of fixing the doctrinal distinction of its first phase has made the invention of its second so instantly successful, and because the second has so obviously failed without diminishing any of our awakened interest in the movement's continuation. What, we ask ourselves, is the magnetic connection between pragmatism's two phases? I have been sketching a possible answer, but I admit it increases the estrangement of this most familiar of American philosophies.

Retrospectively, pragmatism's strength and widest influence lie with the spreading forms of fallibilism and whatever concepts fallibilism illuminatingly transforms: notably, the theory of truth that James and Dewey more or less agree on, that James effectively invented, that was never ardently adopted but now seems so much more promising than it ever was in the best days of the pragmatist protectorate.

To be entirely candid, fallibilism failed on Peirce's side and was never rightly understood by Dewey's readers. Yet, it has drawn attention in a fresh way to the puzzles of knowledge, truth, and objectivity—now viewed under the conditions of a radical constructivism. I don't believe the novelty and daring of the pragmatist undertaking has quite struck home. I don't believe the original pragmatists were fully aware of its most heterodox possibilities. Those possibilities were "there" all the time, of course. They were explicitly "there" in the disputes between Rorty and Putnam, for instance. But the recent philosophical turns that Rorty and Putnam have favored—Putnam by abandoning his "internal realism," Rorty by dividing his loyalties between postmodernism and naturalism—confirm a general failure to grasp the point of continuing with "fallibilism's" project under the conditions of pragmatism's reinvention. Everything points to bolder possibilities than the classic pragmatists ever considered, or Putnam and Rorty ever allowed. That, I believe, begins to explain why pragmatism continues to attract adherents beyond the perceived failure of Putnam's and Rorty's deliberate revival.

My own suggestion is, I admit, a little opportunistic—but no more so than Rorty's or Putnam's reinvention. I seize the advantage from the general weakness of their own treatments of realism and truth and from their near obsession with the threat of relativism. They have surely glimpsed the deeper possibilities but have turned their back on them. Once you realize that pragmatism's strength lies with its unrelenting opposition to Cartesianism and that late twentieth-century analytic philosophy is largely Cartesian, you cannot fail to be drawn to realisms of a heterodox sort. The possibility has never been widely pursued in the analytic world. It was aborted only a short while ago after the considerable flurry of interest in the "deviant" inquiries of Thomas Kuhn and Paul Feyerabend, the Edinburgh sociologists of knowledge and science, and the more extreme forms of "social constructionism."[2]

My suggestion is that pragmatism, now reinvented but hardly stable or compelling, must run through the more radical possibilities that its own recovery invites us to consider, in order precisely to determine just what its prospects really are. Rorty and Putnam, I would say, have led us to the question—have, by a great rambling detour—led us to the neglected puzzle at the heart of Western philosophy. We owe it all, as you perhaps now see, to the confrontation between pragmatism and analytic philosophy that Putnam and Rorty first explored, which has now cunningly eluded the deeper conservative purpose of their own intended daring. Each favored flux in his own way, but neither could cap in time what flux made possible; and so each accused the other of being a relativist and hurried to disclaim any sympathies for relativism himself. Too late!

In *that* spirit, the future of "pragmatism" lies with the contest between the potentially irreconcilable forces of naturalism and pragmatism that I've been tracking, particularly those involved in reconstituting what to understand by realism and fallibilism. That strikes me as a natural use of pragmatism's best energies, one that might in fact recover an unforced sense of the continuity between the original and revived phases of the movement and even a sense of the unmarked convergence between Anglo-American and continental philosophy. I doubt there is another possibility of equal promise, unless it is the one that features the recovery of something closer to Deweyan liberalism, which, for my part, seems to have been substantially eclipsed by the tides of political history.

If you agree, then you are not likely to fail to see: first, that the pursuit of fallibilism and the resolution of the pragmatism/naturalism controversy are one and the same, perhaps even a local version of a more general Eurocentric contest; and, second, that this undertaking must eventually come to terms with all the ways a thoroughgoing constructivism might claim to detect, isolate, oppose, and defeat every vestige of what may be collected as "Cartesian realism."

The irony, already acknowledged, is that Cartesianism has made enormous gains among new champions, partly as a result of pragmatism's second life. For Putnam and Rorty are opposed to relativism and incommensurabilism, and, in their ardor to avoid the stigma of relativism's being applied to themselves, have either fallen back to Cartesian themes (Putnam) or tried to opt out of the entire quarrel (Rorty). Putnam also opposes historicism, though he has said very little about it; and Rorty, who professes an interest in historicism, cannot bring himself to defend it in any explicit way.

These doctrines exert a nagging presence in pragmatist and analytic circles, and have been more hospitably received in Europe than in America. Indeed, their dismissal at home has been noticeably blunt—I would say, perfunctory. The reason points to a subterranean commitment to an attenuated Cartesianism that has gripped nearly the whole of the American academy. Hence, just as the disputes between Rorty and Putnam move us beyond the inquiries of the original pragmatists, their own puzzles lead us beyond the pale they would themselves enforce. This suggests the sense in which I mean to pursue relativism's prospects: not primarily to vindicate relativism itself, though I would support it on another occasion; but because it turns out to be the best stalking horse for getting clear about the deficiencies of Putnam's and Rorty's professed pragmatist commitments and about pragmatism's own unexamined promise.

I must ask you, therefore, to allow the strategy to run its course. Pragmatism *should*, I think, *be* hospitable to heterodox possibilities it may not actually favor. Putnam and Rorty go to enormous lengths to disallow them. That seems to give a false impression of pragmatism's open-ended vision. For, after all, Peirce and Dewey opposed *de re* necessities in nature and favored some version of the theory of the flux.

Still, even Peircean fallibilism, certainly its modified adoption by figures like Karl Popper and Imre Lakatos,[3] confirms the temptation of a more than residual commitment to the underlying invariances Cartesianism prefers. In any case, it is hard to see how pragmatism's odyssey will go if we do not ask ourselves whether there are unacknowledged, even insurmountable, coherence constraints affecting every form of constructivism that would disallow (without ceremony) the outlaw experiments of relativism and incommensurabilism. If there are, we need to know them: for then, constructivism and pragmatism would have to yield *somewhere* to Cartesianism; and then Putnam and Rorty would have been in the right all along!

The point is this: the analysis of fallibilism confirms that pragmatism (perhaps any viable epistemology) needs *some* account of the conceptual link between Peirce's "long run" and James's and Dewey's preference for the short runs of practical life. The only plausible replacement for Peirce's intuition seems to be that of an open-ended series of constructivist projections proceeding *seriatim* (partly blindly) on the strength of episodic successes and continually evolving experience. If any such replacement is unable to call on Cartesian or transcendental constraints, then, at the very least, there will be no way to ensure in principal any unique or uniquely convergent line of objective discovery that could preclude the compatibility of relativism and one or another form of constructive realism. That is precisely what Putnam and Rorty fear.

As I say, fallibilism takes two entirely different forms in Peirce and Dewey. In Peirce it signifies the perpetual postponement of inquiry's ever arriving at the "truth about reality" under the condition that the apparent progress of the sciences in that direction is, however rational (or reasonable), no more than the posit of a kind of transcendental Hope (in something like Kant's sense of the free play of Reason without the evidentiary grounds essential to the work of the understanding). In Dewey it signifies the restriction of all cognitive claims within a thoroughly fluxive world, by means of practical skills (on which science itself depends) that first emerge from certain non-cognitive animal powers implicated in our survival and viability.[4]

Hence, both in Peirce and Dewey (though for very different reasons), "truth" and "reality" are no more than constructive posits thought to be apt enough for a realist account of science but utterly opposed to any form of Cartesian realism. There is no rational *telos* in science, and there is no way to overtake the provisional standing of any "pragmatic realism" (Putnam's preferred term for what he officially called "internal realism").

The point of greatest relevance here is simply that pragmatism provides no local or prior grounds for disallowing its compatibility with one or another form of relativism—*if* relativism can be shown to be formally coherent. You see, of course, the obvious motivation for Putnam's and Rorty's insistence on the incoherence of relativism. You may also see the extraordinary (even improbable) aptness of James's misreading of Peirce in that way that prepared the ground (against the naturalizers) for Dewey's treatment of truth as serving an explanatory function—without yet assigning science any rationally accessible realist *telos*. In fact, the plausibility of Peirce's "long run" fallibilism requires his relying on a mass of short-run episodes of beliefs being "made true" in James's sense of "true." It's the concatenation of such bits of history that ensures pragmatism's openness to the radical possibilities of relativism.

II

The defense of relativism is, admittedly, an endless project, but not because of the unlikelihood of ever reaching a plausible argument in its favor. Certainly, there are no knockdown arguments that disallow it, though it has had a remarkably bad press. Claims of self-evidence and indubitability, by which it has been traditionally defeated, are noticeably on the wane; and the incoherence of certain notorious versions of relativism hardly entails the incoherence of every pertinent reading of its classic challenge. It now seems hopeless to suppose that, after two and a half millennia, the standard quarrels about self-evidence could possibly yield a neglected truth about Reason that might still decide the issue crisply. Relativism's standing is, *now,* more likely to be regarded as a question of conceptual proposal and counter-proposal than an inflexible discovery about "the way the world is." If so, it would be prejudicial in the extreme to refuse to countenance any self-consistent recommendation from its vantage by objecting, "But that's not what relativism is!" The fact is, many suppose that *whatever* relativism "is," it is a paradoxical and self-defeating thesis!

That prejudice agrees, of course, with the verdict of Plato's *Theaetetus* and Aristotle's *Metaphysics* Gamma. Protagoras, whom Plato and Aristotle handily "defeat," had a stronger reputation in the ancient world than their easy victories would seem to support. And yet, in spite of the avoidable arbitrariness of Socrates' best shot and the obvious circularity of Aristotle's complaint, the basic arguments against relativism (as against Protagoras) have hardly changed since their first pronouncement. Myles Burnyeat, for instance, an authority on the *Theaetetus,* adopts Socrates' conjecture whole cloth. He sees no other possibility after reviewing more than two thousand years of debate; he believes that, for Protagoras, "true" *must* (cannot but) mean "true-for-x," where "true" is relationally defined—"x" being some would-be cognitive agent or cognitional site that altogether precludes the bare possibility of referring to public evidence or criteria shared with others. Burnyeat does not mean this in a merely textual way.[5]

Of course, the *explication* produces an instant self-referential paradox, makes it impossible for any two cognizers (or even the same agent at different moments) to share the same sense of "true." Nothing, it seems, is ever "true" *sans phrase:* it can only be "true-for-me." Even if it is "true-for-thee," it can only be "'true-for-thee'-*for-me*"! In that sense, apart from its formal incoherence, relativism is inseparable from solipsism. Yet even Protagoras' doctrine, "man is the measure," *can* be read as a relativist dictum that, by escaping solipsism, escapes the paradox. Protagoras' doctrine may even be viable. Why, then, should we refuse to consider a generous reading when the other is so "silly"? (The epithet is Putnam's, which he finds in James and which he applies in charging Rorty with being an out-and-out relativist.)

It would be shocking to find that anyone did seriously subscribe to what Burnyeat offers as the meaning of Protagoras' formula: Protagoras himself, for instance. Yet it is commonly claimed that relativists flaunt the view Burnyeat defines. Even fashionable philosophers like Putnam and Rorty claim that this is precisely what exemplary relativists believe—a doctrine they gleefully impute to one another. Putnam goes Burnyeat one better. He observes, first, that "first-person relativism [implicitly, the doctrine Burnyeat assigns Protagoras] sounds like thinly disguised solipsism"; he then pertinently adds and asks: "But it is hard to see why cultural relativism is any better off, in this respect. Is solipsism with a 'we' any better than solipsism with an 'I'?"[6] That is nearly the whole of Putnam's pronouncement on relativism. Rorty has, if anything, even less to say. Shocking!

The fact is, both devote an inordinate amount of space to the "refutation" of relativism. I can only suppose that each is anxious to disabuse us of the idea that *he* might be at once a pragmatist *and* a relativist. Putnam makes the effort, it seems, because he might not be able to admit he was a pragmatist if pragmatism entailed relativism or was even hospitable to it; and Rorty (I conjecture) makes the effort because the defense of relativism would demonstrate that his own attack on the canonical philosophies of "universality" and "essences" could hardly be the whole of the philosophical story *or* even the point of a defense of pragmatism.

You see how slippery the relativism puzzle is. It is altogether too easy to be caught up in its concatenating snares. I shall not resist those snares, but I don't want us to be carried away without a glance at the philosophical shore. I need to draw your attention straight away to the fairly obvious fact that a viable relativism would not be congruent, ultimately, with a general Cartesian or naturalizing program of analysis. So it is not at all odd that someone like Davidson should oppose admitting relativism as a viable option or, indeed, as rightly favored for this sector of inquiry or for that (for instance, along the lines of Feyerabend's incommensurabilism in the context of explanation in the natural sciences).[7]

But Putnam (also, Rorty) counts himself a pragmatist and, as we have seen, Putnam has played a very strong role in reviving and redefining pragmatism. So it is hardly unimportant to remark that in doing this, Putnam (but also Rorty) takes care to repudiate relativism as utterly incoherent. Still, you cannot find a single argument against relativism that Putnam advances anywhere in his published work that is more than a brief gloss on the tired arguments Plato and Aristotle first fashioned. Rorty is, if possible, even more casual in his dismissal.

I cannot support Putnam's reasoning here. More than that, the contest between pragmatism and naturalism would remain muddled if we could not reach a clear finding about the coherence or incoherence of relativism *and* about the compatibility or incompatibility of relativism and either naturalism or pragmatism. For if relativism were compatible with pragmatism but not with naturalism, even if the classic pragmatists did not pursue the matter (Peirce, of course, *did* have an ingenious account of predicative indeterminacy that was incipiently hospitable to relativism[8]), the demonstrated fact would bear decisively on the contest between pragmatism and naturalizing *and*, conceivably, on Putnam's and Rorty's deeper motivation. In fact, the inquiry about relativism's prospects shows in a particularly clear way certain unsuspected weaknesses in Putnam's and Rorty's preference for "pluralism" (I shall come back to that).

I take it to be a tell-tale sign—I don't say it is an argument as yet—that Putnam (also, Rorty), being a completely unyielding opponent of relativism, signals a deeper (if vestigial) commitment to Cartesianism; for, for one thing, Putnam offers nothing stronger than a potted argument against relativism; and, for another, the dialectical options available to a revived pragmatism (attentive to its post-Kantian sources) would have suggested the grand advantage of an openness toward relativistic and related possibilities. It is, in fact, very hard to see how to reconcile the conceptual amplitude Putnam, but also Rorty. claims to find in pragmatism—for instance his "internalism" and pluralism (and Rorty's "ethnocentricism")—*and* their uncompromising opposition to relativism and incommensurabilism. That will need to be clarified.

Putnam's question (about solipsism with a "we") is, of course, meant to be a rhetorical maneuver. It cannot be entirely apt, because a solipsism with a "we" is not a solipsism at all. *If*, indeed, "we" share a sense of "true," then if we do so in the manner of a "cultural relativist" (whatever that may mean), the counter-argument could not proceed by way of exposing a paradox analogous to the one Burnyeat attributes to Protagoras—though it would still be a mistake.

It's perfectly fair to ask what solipsism-with-a-"we" entails, or whether it is a form of relativism at all, or whether it is illicit in any discernible sense, or simply an empirical blunder. In any case, its complications are gratuitous and hardly worth the bother. For consider that even *if* some "other" society (the Azande, say), marked off in the usual anthropological way (without regard to the puzzle just proposed), *could* converse with us, though, on the evidence, they seemed (to us) to advance an alternative conception of "true" (a form of "cultural solipsism"), and *if* in spite of that *we* claimed that we did share or could share with them conceptual resources in virtue of which we and they *could* recognize together the difficulty we allege, we could never *then* establish that they did in fact hold fast to a notion of "true" that could be paraphrased as "true-for-us" (true-for-the-Azande" but necessarily not for "us" who are not Azande—necessarily not even penetrable by us who are not Azande). Imagine that! We could certainly agree that we did not share certain evidentiary criteria or beliefs, but that would not capture Putnam's trial balloon. *Nothing would!* (You must bear in mind that every known language has its bilinguals.)

I cannot of course prove that absolutely no one would ever champion the preposterous idea that a particular society, which, given the nature of human existence would likely have to communicate and trade with other societies, holds that no one but the members of that society could share the conception of truth they do. But, certainly, it would be a waste of time. Societies are, I concede, forever startled to discover that the members of other societies don't happen to share their most treasured beliefs. But that is a matter of "cultural relativ*ity*," not of "cultural relativ*ism*." The society's mistake would be a matter of first-order belief: it would be a factual mistake, a misunderstanding of their own practice. Putnam may be having us on here: you must pay attention to the fact that he never presents us with a more reasonable version of relativism.

He seems to have conflated quite unacceptably what Burnyeat identifies as Protagoras' "solipsism" with what Donald Davidson identifies as Kuhn's incoherent conceptual incommensurabilism.[9] In fact, on the strength of Davidson's own argument against Kuhn (which is not textually accurate in the least[10]), Davidson would be bound to say that what Putnam is examining is a "limit-condition" under which one society must fail to understand another—earthlings meeting Martians perhaps, or talking trees.

I shall turn to the question of cultural relativism directly. But for the moment I am interested in the extravagance of Putnam's characterization of relativism. Certainly, he agrees with Plato and Aristotle (for much the same reasons the *Theaetetus* offers): that is, that any bona fide relativism is either incoherent or self-defeating. In his Gifford Lectures, which are occupied with different versions of relativism—from which the remark cited above is drawn—Putnam actually confirms the fairness of my charge against him:

he says that he can find no other form of relativism worth the name besides the self-defeating maneuver already mentioned (augmented by what he offers on the matter of a "solipsism with a 'we' as opposed to an 'I'").

Here is his considered view:

> As soon as one tries to state relativism as a *position* it collapses into inconsistency or into solipsism (or perhaps solipsism with a "we" instead of an "I"). The thought that everything we believe is, at best, only "true in our language game" isn't even a coherent thought: is the very existence of our language then only "true in our language game"?[11]

I disagree with most of what Putnam says here, as well as with its philosophical motivation. Certainly, to admit that we can make a truth-claim only if we have "an appropriate language" (as Putnam goes on to say) is not tantamount to claiming that "true" means "true-in-L" (our language). But if this warning is allowed, then why should Putnam ever have supposed that the fact that we can make a relativistic claim only if we have "an appropriate language" would entail that "true" means "true-for *x*" (in the relationalist sense Burnyeat and the *Theaetetus* favor)? The cases seem very similar to me. Let me concede, therefore, the argument against "solipsism-with-a-'we'" and invite Putnam to move on. (You see the narrow gauge of his complaint.)

I dismiss Burnyeat's model therefore, if not the textual accuracy of his reading of *Theaetetus*. (I cannot judge the accuracy of his rendering, though I am inclined to doubt its inescapability, knowing the way ordinary texts may be read.) I admit the validity of the exposé Burnyeat lays out, but I doubt it captures Protagoras' thesis or that a better reading cannot be found. Neither Burnyeat nor Putnam demonstrates that a better reading is impossible. Putnam adds a compensating distinction, drawing on Wittgenstein (in a way meant to show that Wittgenstein himself was not a relativist): "to say that it is true in my language game that you are reading this book is not to say that you are reading this book. . . . To say something is true in a language game is to stand outside of that language game and make a comment; that is not what it is to play a language game."[12] Well, yes and no. If to "stand outside a language *game*" is to stand outside *all* the resources of a particular *language*, then that would be equivalent to Davidson's notion of "complete" conceptual incommensurability (which, I am bound to say, neither Kuhn nor Feyerabend—whom Davidson excoriates—ever urged). But, of course, one couldn't *then* make a "comment" on the language game being played:

not because it would entail a form of relativism but because we simply wouldn't understand the *language!*

Still, if a "language game" may be a fragment of a practice *within* an encompassing language, then we might indeed be able to "comment" on that language game within the resources of a shared language; and then a form of cultural relativism might well be possible and viable: for instance, we might judge that the language game of attributing "beauty" and "charm" invites the use of "beautiful" in a relationalist (or better, a subjectivist) sense (as "beautiful-for-x"), a sense that might conceivably approach Putnam's "cultural relativism." I would not recommend it. There are obviously more important forms of relativism to defend. But it would not produce an insuperable paradox. ("Beautiful-for-x" is fully compatible with rejecting "true-for-x.") Even on his own grounds, Putnam has hardly shown that Wittgenstein was not a relativist, or not even open to a relativistic reading.

The point to bear in mind is this: *if* Putnam really means to treat relativism in terms of a policy regarding the use and meaning and choice of truth-like values, then it is preposterous to suppose that relativists are forever forced to choose a self-defeating policy; and *if* he means, by equating relativism with solipsism, to treat relativism in terms of a certain deep habit (or disorder) of belief—one in which, say, the relativist actually believes he (or "everyone") must judge matters in some methodologically solipsistic way, then I for one recommend forgetting about defending such disordered souls and getting on with other more interesting possibilities.

I see no reason to think that serious relativists must be deprived of the possibility of conjecturing about the logic of public and publicly appraised assertions: certainly, the relativist need not stand completely outside any language. Furthermore, refusing the option before us does not ensure that our "public" language enjoys any privileged neutrality or even that every realism must hold fast to an exceptionless bivalence regarding truth-claims. To insist otherwise is no more than an attenuated Cartesianism.

I trust it will be clear that the defense of relativism is *not* equivalent to a defense of pragmatism but *is* indeed a challenge to the philosophical adequacy of naturalizing—hence, it can be made to play a dialectically important role in assessing the contest between pragmatism and naturalism. Because, oddly enough, the newer pragmatists (Putnam), the newer naturalists (Davidson), and those who profess to be both pragmatists and naturalists (Rorty) all agree—in the most ardent way—that relativism *is* unqualifiedly incompatible with their doctrines (as well as incoherent in its own right). I suggest that, assuming relativism's coherence (which *can* be shown), any "pragmatism" that cannot or will not admit the compatibility or congeniality of (a self-consistent) relativism risks verging on naturalism (in Davidson's sense), as is true of both Rorty's and Putnam's demurrers. It would abandon pragmatism's attractive philosophical openness.

Putnam is explicit about "what" our language games ultimately rely on. Returning to one of Wittgenstein's well-known instructions, he says they rest "not on proof or on Reason but *trust*."[13] Not even *Hope*, in the sense Peirce borrows from Kant (without borrowing Kant's transcendental machinery). But if you take Putnam at his word, then he will have left himself no conceptual ground on which to disallow relativism (or relativism's compatibility with pragmatism)—or indeed the compatibility of (a coherent) relativism and his own doctrine. Nothing in Putnam's argument actually shows that Wittgenstein's claim (in the *Investigations*) could not be reconciled with some admissible form of relativism, incommensurabilism, historicism, or related options—for essentially the same fluxist reasons that apply to pragmatism. (That neither Wittgenstein nor Putnam would be pleased by such a demonstration is neither here nor there.)

III

At about the time of the publication of Putnam's *Reason, Truth and History* (1981)—well, two years later—Richard Rorty, still subscribing, in his Howison Lecture (1983), to something akin to Putnam's "internalism" (which both have of course discarded), explicitly mentions, in advancing an account of relativism that is fairly close to Putnam's, the familiar charge (made by "holists") that pragmatists are relativists; but then, Rorty simply rejects the equation. None of this quite holds up, as can be surmised from the following in which Rorty says:

> "Relativism" is the traditional epithet applied to pragmatism by realism. Three different views are commonly referred to by this name. The first is the ["self-refuting"] view that every belief is as good as every other. The second is the ["eccentric"] view that "true" is an equivocal term, having as many meanings as there are procedures of justification. The third is the ["ethnocentric"] view that there is nothing to be said about either truth or rationality apart from descriptions of the familiar procedures of justification which a given society—*ours*—uses in one or another area of inquiry. The pragmatist holds [that] third view. But . . . it is not clear why "relativist" should be thought an appropriate term for [that].[14]

Rorty's refutation of Putnam is already implicit here, though he forbears. Possibly because his unstable postmodernism is also implicit and, on its own constraints, he is not entitled to raise philosophical objections. But recall Putnam's own jibe at Rorty's relativism, the remark that appears on the final page of *Reason, Truth and History,* the one that mentions the *Grenzbegriff.*[15] There, in a few short strokes, you have the compressed record of the self-inflicted refutation of both Putnam and Rorty, a clue to the viability of cultural relativism, and the sense in which Putnam's internalism and Rorty's ethnocentrism *are,* indeed, relativisms in spite of what they say. You see, of course, that if we read Putnam in the light of what he (now) says about Wittgenstein (and what applies to both Peirce's and Dewey's versions of fallibilism), then he cannot hold the line against mingling pragmatism and relativism: in giving up the *Grenzbegriff,* which Rorty challenges, Putnam will have confirmed Rorty's deeper charge.

Rorty begins his attack on Putnam (about 1985) this way: "I do not see the point of this question," Putnam's question about whether Rorty's remark that "there is only the dialogue" "differs from [a] self-refuting relativism."[16] Putnam has a point. But, surely, Rorty has Putnam on the ropes here.[17] Beyond that, why shouldn't they both accept the relativist's option?

I don't insist that pragmatism is a form of relativism. But it cannot deny an affinity for relativism; the two doctrines cannot be disjoined in either Putnam's or Rorty's account. Putnam is caught in a dilemma: if he gives up Cartesian realism altogether (the *Grenzbegriff*), then he cannot show that pragmatism and relativism are incompatible; and if he insists that they are, then he must be appealing to some ulterior Cartesian or similar reservation, something that would commit him to an "externalist" form of realism. Rorty holds a rather uncompelling "better" position, because, in advocating pragmatism, he does not mean to defend a specific form of realism; he claims to be speaking only as a postmodernist, which is to say, a pragmatist! You will certainly insist on a better answer.

Rorty obliges: "I have been arguing that we pragmatists should grasp the ethnocentric horn of the dilemma [between what amounts to 'objectivism' (Putnam's reading of objectivity in the 'realist' sense) and what Rorty claims is miscast as relativism]. We should say that we must, in practice, privilege our own group, even though there can be no noncircular justification for doing so. . . . [T]he pragmatist, dominated by the desire for solidarity [the ethnocentric option], can only be criticized for taking his own community *too* seriously. He can be criticized for ethnocentrism, not for relativism."[18] This is, of course, no more than word-mongering.

Rorty fails to remark that the expression "his own community" can only be a *construction* having transient standing within some viable population of apt speakers. There is no single or unique "community" that Rorty could possibly name that could be fixed as "his own community." Elsewhere, Rorty takes advantage of the artifactual nature of a "community" to choose as he pleases.[19] He cannot have it both ways: to avoid relativism (*his* brand of relativism), Rorty must opt for the "realist's" reading of "objectivity" (an objectively determined community)—which is precisely what he faults in Putnam's appeal to the *Grenzbegriff.* In that case, he cannot, on his own say-so, *be* a pragmatist. If he insists on the ethnocentric doctrine, on the reading of "community" as a variably constructed artifact *affecting* the very processing of truth-claims, then he cannot avoid the charge of relativism (possibly, Putnam's charge of a "solipsism-with-a-'we'"). This might conceivably have been defended as a coherent option but for the fact that Rorty takes relativism to be as incoherent as Putnam does.

For his part, Putnam cannot be an "internalist," if there is a *realist* "limit-concept of the ideal truth." Putnam is an epistemological optimist, possibly a Peircean fallibilist (as Rorty suggests), possibly even a Kantian transcendentalist, except for the fact that he opposes the idea that "the notion of knowledge entails . . . convergence to a single result."[20] Here, Putnam distances himself from Peirce—in Quine's direction. I do not deny that one may invoke a regulative ideal without assigning it realist standing (an ideal of beauty, say); but it is not possible to do so in the context of making cognitive claims. (That, in effect, is Kant's original discovery.) Therefore Putnam's *Grenzbegriff* is arbitrary, if not completely paradoxical. If so, then Putnam *is* a cultural relativist in spite of himself—or, better, because he is a pragmatist!

The quick solution to all these puzzles is to admit straight out that we cannot fail to favor "our own group, even though there can be no particular justification for doing so." Rorty says we must "privilege our own group." That may be no more than an expression of solidarity. But if Rorty means to say that we first identify a determinate group and then privilege that group, he has made himself the natural target of Putnam's "solipsism-with-a-'we.'" We cannot *privilege* any such group, because wherever (for competent bilinguals, a provision notoriously neglected by Quine) an evidentiary challenge arises, we instantly *include its author within our community!* In the sense in which what Rorty says proves true, it is trivially true: it cuts no ice at all. But then, it cuts no ice against relativism either. The truth is plain enough: in the sense in which we maintain our "solidarity," relativism is as good as its rival.

IV

There are other loose ends to collect. For instance, if the real world must, in being real, possess invariant structures or properties, or if knowledge must rest on indubitable or indefeasible truths, or if we must assume that our knowledge of the world is not distorted (even if it cannot escape adhering to the perspective of one or another of our conceptual schemes), or is such that we cannot deny that our knowledge is a knowledge of a "mind-independent" world, or converges toward a uniquely valid account, then no robust form of relativism *or* pragmatism will ever be defended. On this matter, Rorty is entirely explicit about his position and Putnam's: "Both of us think [he says] that getting rid of the idea of 'the view from nowhere' [Thomas Nagel's and Bernard Williams' view: the phrase is introduced by Nagel]—the idea of a sort of knowing that has nothing to do with agency, values, or interests—might have considerable cultural importance."[21]

That is indeed an essential pragmatist conviction, which both Rorty and Putnam profess. But with it goes the dismissal of any "externalist perspective" or "God's Eye point of view,"[22] which means, of course, that neither Rorty's "community" nor Putnam's *Grenzbegriff* could possibly help either elude the other's unwelcome charge. Along related lines, if there were necessities *de re* or *de cogitatione,* like those that Aristotle and Frege champion, then relativism would be ruled out once again. But so would pragmatism. Certainly, no one has ever demonstrated that would-be ontic or epistemic necessities cannot be coherently denied.

We may add a second tier of conditional arguments that strengthen the prospects of pragmatism and relativism together, without entailing either. These involve the well-known puzzles of confirming referential and predicative success. Put in the simplest terms: there is no criterion on which referential or predicative success is *known* (or can be shown) to obtain.[23] It's true that it would make no sense to deny that we do succeed in an evidentiary way; all truth-bearing discourse would be adversely threatened. But any attempt to establish the fact of such success *in* an evidentiary way would be hopelessly circular. That, mind you, is also the fate of Rorty's recommendation regarding "privileging our own community" and, I may as well add, the burden of Putnam's appeal to Wittgenstein's notion of "trust." It proves to be easier to concede that we literally cannot define the outer limits of "our own community" than that we "privilege" it in epistemic ways; for, whatever it is we do thus privilege, we can never, in advance, define the living community that will remain thus privileged. Hence, ethnocentrism fails, though opportunism need not.

Strategically, the signs are favorable for cultural relativism, in spite of what Putnam says. There are no demonstrable invariances or modal necessities regarding knowledge or reality. If there were, pragmatism would be defeated by a single stroke. We cannot, for instance, demonstrate that a bivalent logic is unconditionally necessary for all truth-bearing discourse; it would never match the vagaries of actual predicative practice, except by fiat. That is, by a kind of retroactive normalizing (say, by "ethnocentric solidarity" or "trust," as Rorty and Putnam prefer). We can always sanitize whatever we thus produce, in perfectly standard bivalent terms. That is as true of epistemic incommensurabilities as of predicative consensus. The sheer fluency of our ordinary "procedures" erases doubts (even memories) about the informalities of our reported rigor. That alone explains the pragmatist penchant (particularly Dewey's) for speaking of the work of practical intelligence in place of the "spectatorial" powers of reason and perception.

In fact, there are many well-known philosophical maneuvers that obscure one or another implicit relativism: for example, Quine's "truth-value gaps," "holisms" regarding the parsing of which "there is no fact of the matter" (according to the "indeterminacy of translation" thesis);[24] truth as the "idealization of warranted assertibility," incapable of ensuring a telic convergence on what is uniquely true (as conceded in Putnam's internalism);[25] large conceptual incommensurabilities well within the bounds of intelligibility (as in Kuhn's theory of paradigm shifts);[26] historically recovered discontinuities of *epistemes* (in the sense Foucault claims to confirm);[27] divergent language games (in Wittgenstein's sense);[28] the multiple and changing "fusion of horizons" that Gadamer makes central to his hermeneutics.[29] Such options have often been thought to have strong affinities for pragmatism, in much the same sense in which Rorty judges Heidegger and Wittgenstein to be pragmatists of sorts. (These options are also, of course, often judged to be actual forms of relativism.) They have their problematic side, no doubt. But we are not obliged to read them in the self-defeating relationalist way that Putnam (for one) recommends.

The fact is that they are all called into question in analytic philosophy (even Quine's holism) because their admission would threaten the hegemony of an extensionalist logic. They signify one or another form of awkward human intervention—of what, in a dismissive sense, Rorty calls interpretive *tertia*[30]—in effect, the epistemic inseparability of our sciences from the linguistic competences our cultural world makes possible. Bear in mind that Rorty construes such mediation as instantly relativistic, which of course he opposes along Davidson's lines. That may indeed strengthen Rorty's own "relativism" (that is, his ethnocentrism). But since it is also incompatible with the non-reductive anti-dualisms of the pragmatists, Rorty must be a double agent.

Relativism may be saved by simpler means. For it is child's play to recover a self-consistent reading of Protagoras that would ensure the acceptable use of the non-canonical accounts of the human world just collected: that is, if we were prepared to compromise with extensionalism. To give up extensionalism is not, however, to abandon bivalence, only to give up its absolute hegemony. But then, by a very small stroke, we would have marked off a space for the play of a relativistic logic, the use of which, carefully constrained, would remain fully compatible with the use of bivalence.

The rest of the argument is easy sledding. We have only to show that relativism may take a coherent form that, arguably, could prove advantageous (more useful, say, than its refusal) in this particular sector of inquiry or that. For it is certainly not necessary that in championing relativism we need to hold that it cannot be defended in any sector if it cannot be defended in every inquiry—or, in every sector equally advantageously. Arguments to the effect, for instance, that it cannot work in arithmetic would have nothing to do with its working in moral and historical and art-critical contexts, or in contexts concerned with fixing the meaning of words, or in processing philosophical claims or even high-level explanations in the physical sciences.

No one actually denies that *if* relativism were genuinely coherent, it could be made to serve a useful function in all sorts of inquiries; for, by an embarrassment of riches, we often find that we can interpret artworks, human actions, histories, the meanings of segments of conversation, conceptual arguments, and causal explanations in ways that are plainly incompatible with one another (that is, incapable of being included in a single inclusive interpretation); and where such descriptions and interpretations cannot be jointly true but are too compelling to be disallowed for reason of an unchallenged scruple about the scope of bivalence, it might prove best to introduce (even ad hoc) a many-valued logic according to which judgments that on a bivalent logic (but not now) would have been incompatible in realist terms.

Such an adjustment need not be construed merely in terms of evidentiary difficulties: they may, in a constructivist sense, be deemed, rather, to reflect the actual ontic structure of one or another sector of inquiry. This might be due, for instance, to the intentional complexities of human culture. Such complexities might obtain in history and the art world, but they might also obtain among competing epistemological conceptions of how to characterize what is being perceived in high-level physics or how to weigh the comparative power of explanatory theories. In terms of a constructive realism, there may be no assured, no uniquely valid resolutions to be had, and those that are favored may well be incompatible (in bivalent terms) or even conceptually incommensurable. Pragmatism has no need to avoid such complications, and there is no obvious way to assure us that they never arise.

Please allow me an aside here. Davidson's well-known diatribe against

Kuhn's and Feyerabend's incommensurabilism (which I've already indicated gets Kuhn's and Feyerabend's actual texts completely wrong) is really meant to defeat all forms of the empiricist doctrine of the "given," which Davidson fears has probably infected Quine's account of "the indeterminacy of translation" (possibly *per* C. I. Lewis's view, which is thought to be a form of pragmatism). The reason for the diatribe, I surmise, is to permit Davidson to characterize his own theory of "radical interpretation" as an improvement on Quine's doctrine of "radical translation" without yielding at all in the relativist's direction. But the fact remains that Davidson's attack on the incoherence of the so-called "scheme/content" dogma (the "third dogma" of empiricism) never gets off the ground, never touches Kuhn and Feyerabend's thesis, which is certainly not a form of empiricism. The idea of an uninterpreted but empirical "given" that could play an evidentiary role in science or practical life *is* indeed a muddle, but it has no bearing on the validity of relativism or incommensurabilism, even if it's true (which I very much doubt) that Quine was committed to such a thesis.[31]

If you allow the argument, you cannot fail to see that by construing the physical sciences as themselves cultural undertakings—by acknowledging the historical drift of scientific theories, by repudiating cognitive privilege, by admitting the work of interpretive schemes—you will no longer be able to disallow a robust relativism from infecting the objective standing of the sciences themselves. But these are, of course, precisely the conditions on which Kuhn's and Feyerabend's epistemological incommensurabilities first threatened the new naturalisms and colored the prospects of a suppler pragmatism.

If you admit this much, you have nearly everything that must be said in order to legitimate relativism or a relativistic version of pragmatism or, for that matter, "cultural relativism" (which, you remember, Putnam dubbed a "solipsism with a 'we'"). *If*, in particular, "neutrality," which Kuhn convincingly shows is "hopeless" (whether we accept his account of "paradigm shifts" or not), there cannot be any uniquely correct catalogue of "what there is" in the way of entities or essential attributes.[32]

Remember: there is no specifically perceptual or other cognitive solution to the question of referential and predicative success. There isn't even a need (*pace* Davidson) to avoid the conceptual incommensurabilities which that very fact makes possible—conceding (with Kuhn) that Galileo (for one) did, indeed, understand and compare the different "paradigms" of Aristotelian and late medieval physics in his analysis of the pendulum. And if contextless neutrality is denied (again with Kuhn), then (*pace* Putnam) no one can actually demonstrate by any supposed Cartesian or objectivist evidence *that*"the same [intended] reality" *is* indeed represented by our diverse conceptual schemes.

Broadly speaking, referential success—the repeated identification of one and the same thing through time and change—*is* the very paradigm of the Principle of Charity, *is* insuperably "constructive" and consensually managed. Both referential and predicative "success" implicate a reliance on social practices akin to what Putnam, drawing on Wittgenstein, calls "trust," that is, consensus lacking criterial force, which subverts the vestigial Cartesianism (or transcendentalism) that lurks beneath Putnam's appeal to his own *Grenzbegriff*. Pragmatists need not be relativists, but they *can* be, consistently. Putnam and Rorty fail us here.

v

The rest of the story calls for a few more steps: one to show the formal coherence and consistency of a relativistic treatment of truth-values; a second to distinguish an innocuous and a problematic sense of "cultural" or "conceptual relativity"; and a third to defend the viability and advantage of "cultural relativism" itself. It is Putnam, of course, who has entrenched these terminological distinctions. But you must bear in mind that neither he nor Rorty *ever* suggests the form a viable relativism might take, or, for that matter, the possible linkage between relativity and relativism. We must rely on our own devices.

The formal condition is entirely straightforward. A coherent relativism responsive to Protagoras' original puzzle must hold that judgments that would be contradictory, logically incompatible, or contrary (on a bivalent logic, but not on the relativist's alternative) need not be so construed. For example, interpretations of artworks or histories that could not (bivalently) be jointly true of the same referent may, on a suitable many valued logic, be jointly valid (objectively valid) when ascribed to the same referent. They may remain "incompatible"—I would rather say that they may be logically "incongruent"—in a sense similar to that in which incongruent interpretations would not be able to be incorporated into a single self-consistent interpretation, or, by a lesser analogy, in the sense in which different but equally valid or acceptable performances of Beethoven's *Third Symphony* could not be combined in a single valid performance. If you grant the point—and why would you not?—you will have effectively admitted the formal coherence of a pertinent form of relativism. The claim's force depends on an analysis of the metaphysics and epistemology of some particular domain of inquiry: it cannot be a merely formal claim if it is to have realist import.

The conception may, however, *be* formalized along the following lines: admit "true" in its bivalent sense; restrict its application by admitting a range of play (possibly ad hoc) for a set of many valued truth-values or truth-like values logically weaker than bivalent values ("reasonable," "apt," "plausible," "acceptable," or the like), marked off by relevance constraints, so that bivalent and relativistic values may be used together without paradox; give up the use of "true" *in* the restricted space in which incongruent judgments are admitted; keep "false"; and substitute for "true" any of the set of many valued values applied to the space in question, so that denying the truth of a judgment entails its falsity (the claim that it is true) but denying its falsity entails affirming one or another of the replacing many valued values but not "true." That's all.

The puzzle about relativism comes to rest on answers to two inseparable questions: one, why we continue to adhere to an exceptionless bivalence if we are prepared to abandon Cartesianism in all its forms; the other, what purposes and interests might relativism felicitously serve. It's hard to believe that the doctrine should have been (and still is) so strenuously opposed on purely formal grounds. I cannot explain it, unless there is something primordially fearsome about the flux and the loss of fixity. But of course there is no pragmatism in the classic sense that is not committed to the flux and the loss of fixity.

However that may be, the fears in question are not meant to be abetted by the formal policy I have just sketched. In any case, our gain hardly counts for much, since relativism's advantage concerns its application. Part of what is needed may be gained merely by distinguishing carefully between "relativism" and "relativity," as Putnam asks us to do, that is, by distinguishing between certain easily confused second-order and first-order considerations. For example, a reasoned choice between bivalence and the carpentered many valued logic just sketched bears on the defense of relativism, not on establishing the facts about cultural relativity (even where the effects of the first are felt in the second).

Now, it is incontestable that different populations may differ in interests, objectives, beliefs, values, norms, penalties, explanations, theories, convictions, taboos, and so on. These differences may be incompatible, but, normally, they will be readily discerned by the members of the different societies involved. They are also likely to be philosophically innocuous in the same sense in which one says that two people belong to opposed political parties. Affirming such differences will normally not entail or presuppose any second-order differences regarding how we should understand the concepts of "truth" and "knowledge" and "confirmation" and the like. Nor will they signify that there must be a neutral or invariant sense of objective truth that societies differing in first-order beliefs and values must share if they can agree in characterizing their first-order differences as they separately do. There is nothing more to mere cultural relativity than that.

If, further, second-order judgments are grounded in the same consensual way that first-order judgments are—and are, therefore, artifactual posits tolerated within consensual limits—then the same kinds of epistemic informality are bound to appear in second-order discourse as in first-order discourse.[33] So the distinction in question, important as it may be to philosophers, will hardly affect the fluency of natural language discourse itself. Nevertheless, I may seem to be neglecting a subtle, essential distinction that Putnam clearly neglects.

Putnam *is* quite careful in distinguishing between "relativism" and "relativity" in the innocuous sense I have just sketched. But he does not seem terribly interested in the plain fact that no analysis of mere cultural *relativity* could ever decide the question whether cultural *relativism* was coherent or viable or not! He makes a splendid effort to show that it would be a mistake to treat certain specimens of conceptual relativity as if they were bona fide specimens of relativism. Fine. But then, in correcting the confusion—which, if I understand him rightly, he locates in a particularly egregious form in Nelson Goodman's defense of "worldmaking," viewed by Goodman as a form of relativism—Putnam *never* considers the question of relativism's own defense (where relativism is not already introduced as absurdly paradoxical).[34]

The confusion Putnam has in mind begins innocently enough. "It is a fact about our present culture [he observes] that there is no philosophical unanimity in it: we do not all accept any one philosophy, and certainly we are not all relativists."[35] Of course. But some of us *are*. What is the difference, and why do philosophers confuse the two, and can it be shown that all apparent attempts to defend relativism as a coherent option rest on the confusion Putnam exposes (in Goodman, for instance)? I very much doubt it.

Putnam explains that "'Internal realism' ('I should have called it pragmatic realism!' [he says]) is, at bottom, just the insistence that realism is *not* incompatible with conceptual relativity." He then proceeds to show how, in terms of "conceptual relativity," we could individuate and count the "particulars" found in the "same states of affairs" in very different ways.[36] This is meant to prepare the ground for resolving the confusion he finds in Goodman. (I must come back to that.) But it also shows that for his own part Putnam restricts the scope of "conceptual relativity" in a way that amounts to a *petitio*: for, surely, *relativism could, if it were viable or defensible, actually be a form of relativity*—for instance, *a "relativity" of epistemic orientation.* Why not?

In this sense, Putnam confounds two very different versions of "cultural relativity" but discusses only one. The restricted version he has in mind we may label "translational," since it treats relativity and relativism disjunctively, though they are not always separable, as I have just noted. Putnam offers the following schema and explanation:

> If the sentence, "points are mere limits," is a contrary of the sentence, "points are not limits but parts of space," even when the first sentence occurs in a systematic scheme for describing physical reality and the second occurs in another systematic scheme for describing physical reality[,] *even though the two schemes are in practice thoroughly equivalent,* then we are in trouble indeed. But the whole point of saying that the two schemes are in practice thoroughly equivalent is that, far from leading us to incompatible predictions or incompatible actions, it makes no difference to our predictions or actions which of the two schemes we use. Nor are the two schemes "equivalent" only in the weak sense of what is sometimes called "empirical equivalence" (that is, leading to the same prediction); rather, each sentence in one of them, say the scheme in which points are concrete particulars, can be correlated in an effective way, with a "translation" in the other scheme, and the sentence and its translation will be used to describe the same states of affairs.[37]

I dub this the "translational" sense, because on Putnam's account the schemes in question are, however different in "meaning" above all, equivalent in that their member sentences are paired (*by* "translation") so that they are *meant* to "describe the same states of affairs" (*salve veritate*).

On Putnam's proposal, they *will* identify the same "objects," though they employ "different conceptual schemes," and they *will* predicate of them the same attributes or at least not incompatible attributes, which may be coordinately translated by reference to the different schemes in play.[38] But Putnam will have avoided, ignored, or simply misconstrued relativistic alternatives *within* the scope of relativity. It may even be true that *Goodman* reads what Putnam treats as a "translational" matter *as* a form of relativism instead. In fact, *Putnam* never examines any relativistic alternatives that might arise as a viable practice—for instance, problematic cases like those posed by Quine's holism or Kuhn's and Feyerabend's incommensurabilism, or, indeed, by more modest garden varieties. If so, then Goodman is entitled to another inning.

Putnam's conceptual relativity proves to be a form of conceptual pluralism tethered to some inchoate version of a "mind-independent" realism that Putnam nowhere secures, strong enough to ensure that *all* objective efforts at identifying the "objects" of our world will conform to the constraints of the "translational" sort of relativity. Putnam's clinching argument might have been the supposed necessity of the *Grenzbegriff*. But we have already seen that the *Grenzbegriff* is an arbitrary machine wheeled out to disallow the threat of relativism, which Putnam's "pragmatic realism" cannot actually support. In short, Putnam excludes the possibility he claims to be exploring: relativity, yes; but relativism, no.

Here, then, is the knock down objection. If, on Putnam's denial of a principled demarcation between the "subjective" and the "objective," the individuation and reidentification of real "objects" cannot be conceptually disjoined from the exercise of what we take our cognitive abilities to be, then, for one thing, cultural relativity may well include instances of diverging epistemologies (or of the epistemic practices they map), and, for a second, those divergences may harbor epistemic incommensurabilities *that could not be expected to conform to the terms of Putnam's translational pluralism.* I see no way in which Putnam's version of pragmatism could effectuate the hoped for exclusion. But if not, then Putnam's campaign against the coherence of relativism and the compatibility of relativism and realism (and of relativism and pragmatism) collapses—conditionally, on the assumption that relativism and incommensurabilism can be coherently formulated.

In any case, there is a noticeable weakness in the epistemological claims of all recent analytic forms of realism that bear on the fortunes of relativism. You will find it, for instance, in Quine's mysterious notion of "holophrastic sentences" (and the "holist" experiences of the world they presumably describe)—which (according to Quine) may then be parsed in plural ways as equivalent *sets* of sentences answering to the truth of the same holophrastic sentences, but *not* the member sentences of any two such sets taken pairwise.[39] You will also find the unanswered challenge posed by the incommensurabilist threat in the work of theorists like Kuhn and Feyerabend, who claim that the very characterization of, say, chemical experiments (those made by Priestley and Lavoisier for instance) are conceptually inseparable from the epistemologies they employ (or the cognitive practices such theories try to describe).[40] But if that were conceded (Putnam's pragmatism and sympathy for Wittgenstein seem to be open to that much), then *if,* in addition, our epistemologies *were* actually incommensurable (within the bounds of "cultural relativity"), it would be apparent at once that Putnam had failed to address the relativist's option he himself dismisses.

It is even possible that Goodman wished to defend his "many worlds" thesis along similar lines. He may have chosen his examples badly (if even that is true). Putnam reports Goodman as affirming that "logic does indeed tell us that [two] incompatible statements cannot both be true *of the same world*, but, in his view, the equal 'rightness' of both of those incompatible versions shows that they are true *of different worlds*." Putnam then demonstrates, in effect, that Goodman victimizes himself by accepting "the idea that statements which appear to be incompatible, taken according to their surface grammar, really are incompatible."[41]

Putnam is surely justified in mentioning the possibility: it is precisely what he explains by his "translational" version of conceptual relativity. But he can't suppose (or can he?) that every seemingly valid contrary (of Goodman's sort) is never an actual incompatible. You must bear in mind that Putnam reports Goodman as rejecting "the claim"—it certainly looks as if Putnam denies, with Goodman—"that our conceptual schemes *are* just different 'descriptions' of what are in some sense 'the same facts.'" But that, you see, is very close to conceding the incommensurabilist's proposal. So that when Putnam affirms that "Goodman would say (and I [Putnam] would agree) that [no would-be description of the world] can claim to be 'the way things are independent of experience' [since there] is no one uniquely true description of reality,"[42] he *must* realize that he has simply left the gate open to the relativist he hoped to defeat. I see no difference between the weakness of his reasoning here and his prioritizing the *Grenzbegriff*. Putnam nowhere satisfies us on the fixed determinacy of reference and denotation. But if not, then how can he possibly show that his "translational" reading of pluralism covers all the conceptual options that are viable?

I regard Goodman's proposal as a completely unwieldy extravagance, though not for Putnam's reasons. Quine and Davidson oppose Goodman, largely it seems because they resist the splitting of the actual world.[43] But more to the point, Goodman's and Putnam's maneuvers count as different ways of stonewalling on the relativism issue. Goodman could have dropped the plural "irrealist" worlds if he had only adopted something like the relativistic "logic" sketched above, which fits "one world." Although it is entirely true that he concedes the "literal relativism of *Ways of Worldmaking*."

He says little more than this: "My sort of relativism holds that there are many right world-versions, some of them conflicting with each other, but insists on the distinction between right and wrong versions."[44] He also says "there is . . . no such thing as the real world, no unique, ready-made absolute reality apart from and independent of all versions and visions. . . . A version is not so much made right by a world as a world is made by a right version."[45] Some profess to find in this Goodman's reading of William James's pragmatism or his radical empiricism. Perhaps it *is* meant to be a form of pragmatism. It is certainly directed against the same target Putnam tags as "metaphysical realism," though it holds the line on bivalence. I see its formal charm but find it epistemically and methodologically opaque.

There is no account in Goodman as to how we are to proceed in any epistemically rigorous way—how, in effect, we are to determine what to count as a "right version." Clearly, if deciding *that* is an evidentiary matter of any kind, then judging "right versions" (but not the "worlds" we decide to "make") seems palpably committed to "one actual world"—in the benign sense in which whatever we consider must (as we say) belong (in a trivial sense) to the same universe of discourse as does "everything else." Many will wonder whether Goodman's thesis may not be incoherent after all. Also, the defense of a robust form of relativism will restrict its own puzzle cases to one and the same actual world, whether or not it admits Goodman's interesting conceit of "many actual worlds." (I confess I find it unworkable.)

Quine, discussing "the indeterminacy of translation" (in the one actual world) gives us to understand that there is "no fact of the matter" in initially parsing the "indeterminacy" (in effect, the "structure" of the holist experience with which he begins[46]); but, if so, then how does he know which predications rightly go with which parsings, or whether the parsings offered can be shown to be the parsings *of one and the same or a different part of experience?* Nowhere does he provide an answer.

Quine's maneuver affords a way, of course, of avoiding the direct challenge of a relativistic logic, one that he finesses by admitting truth-value gaps at the critical point in his argument. Alternatively put: there *is* no way to admit the truth of his so-called "holophrastic sentences" *and then parse them, and then* refuse to endorse a form of relativism while falling back to truth-value gaps, when truth-gaps must be overcome somewhere.[47] It looks as if Quine actually introduces the idea of "holophrastic sentences" (and the holistic experiences they are said to answer to) in order to gain the advantage of the truth-gap doctrine; for, if you drop the holophrastic thesis, Quine's argument appears to devolve into the incommensurabilist's! (That is perhaps what Davidson feared.)

It is an unexpected gain to find that Putnam's "translational" account of the "same" objects (viewed from the vantage of different "schemes"), Goodman's avoidance of incompatible truths (apparently assigned to the same

objects but to "different worlds"), and Quine's "indeterminacy of translation" in parsing a common "holist" or "holophrastic" body of experience,
should each register the same (or very similar) worries about the threat of
one or another form of relativism that would otherwise confront a realism
cast in pragmatist terms. All three, I would say, invoke inexplicit epistemic
"intermediaries" completely at variance with Davidson's and Rorty's naturalizing veto.

VI

You must remember that, on the argument being offered, both referential
and predicative success inherently lack sufficient evidentiary or criterial
confirmation, except constructively, *on* the sufferance of some form of consensual tolerance within our acknowledged practice or "language game"—
that is, on the resources of what I have been calling *savoir-faire* rather than
savoir. Furthermore, you must bear in mind that agreement about referential identity is entirely compatible with admitting divergent predicative
schemes that might generate either incommensurabilities or incompatible
predications about the same *denotata;* and that there is no way to ensure our
grasp of a neutral reality which our referential and predicative policies may
count on securing in the "translational" manner.[48] That is part of the price
of abandoning Cartesianism.

So we are confronted by the prospect of a robust and coherent relativism.
To avoid misunderstanding and certain formal paradoxes like those of
relationalism (which Burnyeat attributes to Protagoras), I add a further constraint, namely, that the *theory* of truth (for instance, coherence, correspondence, the pragmatist sense of what is good in the way of belief and practice)
has absolutely no epistemic or criterial force at all, only an explanatory and
systematizing role within an epistemology joined to a constructive realism.

The irony is that against theorists like Rorty who are self-styled pragmatists or postmodernists, and despite the fact that they are really covert Cartesians of the naturalizing sort, the theory of truth (notably, the pragmatist
theory) does *have* explanatory power precisely because it *does not* have evidentiary power; for it is by way of our theory of truth (for instance, by invoking something in accord with the spirit of James's account) that we are
able to explain why we take our local epistemic practices to answer to what
objective truth requires.[49] The question cannot fail to be a normative matter (as Putnam notes). But that alone would not have been enough to justify
invoking "Reason" criterially (as Putnam once believed, but now does not[50]).
Bear in mind that what we normally do when we actually appraise truth-
claims is shift from theories that link truth to our accounts of knowledge

and reality to the practices in accord with which we assign particular truth-values or truth-like values to particular claims. There, it is a foregone conclusion that, in a constructivist setting, we must be able to provide an explanation of pertinent assignments. (So much the worse for Davidson's and Rorty's versions of naturalizing.)

In any case, *if* relativism were vindicated, it would be completely unconvincing to argue along with Davidson and Rorty that our theory of truth had no explanatory role to play. At the very least, we would expect it to explain why we are prepared to countenance truth-like claims weaker than bivalent ones; and, of course, if that were so, then, by parity of reasoning, supporting bivalence without exception would itself invite a comparable rationale. There would then be nothing left of Rorty's naturalized (or postmodernist) account of truth, and not much more of Davidson's.

That is the promised "second step" of my argument. The third is simplicity itself: *any* coherent rationale that legitimates the practice of using epistemic incommensurabilities and contrarieties encountered (or capable of being encountered) in the first-order space of "cultural relativity" *is, ipso facto, a viable form of "cultural relativism"*! There is no self-defeating paradox there, no "solipsism with a 'we,'" nothing of the sort. On its face, the third step provides a complete *reductio* of both Rorty's and Putnam's counterclaims. More than that, since, if it has any distinction at all, pragmatism is an unyielding opponent of all forms of Cartesianism, no one can reasonably define as genuinely pragmatist any theory of knowledge that would rule out a priori relativism's relevance or eligibility.

Pragmatism need not, I say again, be an explicit relativism; nor need it be an explicit historicism. But, *pace* Putnam and Rorty, there is no prospect of reviving pragmatism without reviving the fortunes of both relativism and historicism. Putnam and Rorty fail to secure their respective brands of pragmatism, not because they attack relativism's viability, but because they attack it *because* it is incompatible with the vestigial Cartesianism each covertly supports: Putnam, by adhering to his *Grenzbegriff* and the presumed sufficiency of the "translational" treatment of relativity (or pluralism); Rorty, by adhering to his strong reading of Davidson's naturalism.[51]

Cultural plurality, then, corresponds to cultural relativity. But pluralism, as opposed to relativism, apparently holds (as in Putnam, Rorty, Richard Bernstein, and others) that cultural relativity need never concede, and can never be made to admit, evidence of coherent relativistic practices within its own space.[52] That, I would say, is a supremely Cartesian claim whose compelling argument I have never seen and doubt could ever be supplied. I have in fact just demonstrated how to draw a relativism or an incommensurabilism from the admitted space of cultural relativity: the point is, there seems to be no way of admitting the latter (relativity) without conceding that the former (relativism) may be lurking there!

The reclamation of relativism, therefore, is likely to proceed persuasively if it begins with evidence drawn from the facts about relativity: to the effect that relativistic practices are not infrequently discovered *in* actual historical life, though usually they are quickly reinterpreted along bivalent lines, once the consensual pressures become sufficiently regular (as they do in making "paradigm shifts" in the sciences and in entrenching critical practices in the arts). Still, from time to time, we hear and glimpse the whirring machinery and we realize that, in just this way, relativism wins by "losing" and pragmatism accommodates whatever heterodox practices it finds congenial.

There is always room enough for pragmatism to demur on the matter of actually embracing relativism. But it cannot then disallow its challenge. And if it must eventually yield, then it must. Putnam, Rorty, Goodman, and Quine are figures of whom one is inclined to say: they are all pragmatists of a sort, but they are analytic philosophers as well. Either they deny that they are relativists (like Putnam and Rorty) or they confine their accommodation of relativistic possibilities in such a way that bivalence remains supreme (Goodman and Quine). But, of course, to honor ingenuity that way is to make room as well for relativism's inning.

That *is* pragmatism's glory. Best, therefore, to resist the naturalizer's tricks and treats. If we mean to revive or reinvent pragmatism, we may as well endow it with as free a sense of conceptual possibility as can be defended against the entrenched canons. That, after all, was its original charge.

Last Word: A Touch of Prophecy

There you have the tale and the argument. But what does it mean? I find a peripety of sorts, the perceived exhaustion of rhetorical forces, the late correction of an unacknowledged wrong, confusion in high places yielding a measure of good sense that might never have been perceived, a minor skirmish expanding to include the entire trajectory of Western philosophy, an omen of a change resisting change, upstart energies that have misjudged their apparent triumph: all the ingredients of a regular Greek tragedy—or comedy.

There's a danger, of course, in trying to be too prophetic. But if you grasp the lesson for what it is, you have no choice but to understand it! Well then, let me start again. We are witnessing flux beginning to dominate over fixity, logical informality over false precision, animal sensibility over reasoned principle, contingent histories over necessary truths, make-shift conjecture over First Philosophy, concatenated bits of insight over cosmic order, encountered heterogeneity over *a priori* unity, horizoned speculation over reality's Plan, possibly penance over *hubris*.

The master thread is the contest between pragmatism and naturalizing, largely spent in grappling with what realism should now mean at the start of the new century. It's clear enough that the realism question was inherited from post-Kantian sources that were never rightly applied in their most effective form. To grasp the original lesson is to realize how little has changed over a span of nearly four hundred years. An appalling admission!

The naturalizers have come to sense, if not to admit, the misplaced daring of their original zeal. Their vision of a closed physics of the whole of nature, for instance, was stalemated even before it began its work. All their rationales have unraveled under the relentless but hardly perceived recovery of the Hegelian correction. The revivifying pragmatists learned that they had to be pirates, the brashest of opportunists, if ever they hoped to peddle their best themes under the banner of uniting the classic movement with the naturalizers. Of course, they failed; that is, they failed to mark the difference between analytic rigor and naturalizing dogma. Still others, the postmodernists, spying sham all around, made a marvelous show of philosophical virtue by mastering all the contending techniques without risking a single commitment of their own; they claimed (and still claim) to have swept the stables clean as well as bare. But, you may ask, to what end? None that has shown its hand as yet.

The pragmatists, I would say, have by far the most inventive prospects in the tradition of the English language. But they must complete the recovery of the post-Kantian correction to claim their title. Viewed in the slimmest way, they will find that there is no essential difference between the recovery of history (the historicity of thought) and the exposé of the failed promises of reductionism. What remains is the master question we have all but lost: the analysis of the human condition itself, the meaning (in every sector of inquiry) of the relationship between nature and culture.

At the beginning of the new century, it is still true that the pragmatists are floundering. The naturalizers are still very much on the offensive. I foresee that a good part of our century will spend itself in the old *agon*, though among new champions. Three converging programs seem likely to dominate: neo-Darwinism viewed as the best reductive model of the cultural world; extreme Chomskyan economies of linguistic competence alleged to yield the sparest model of human rationality; and the presumably adequate computational analysis of every form of human perception and intelligence. The pragmatists have little more than their original intuition to rely on, namely, that whatever is paradigmatic of the human in thought and action remains *sui generis*, however continuous it must be with the biological world from which (we concede) it must have emerged.

That is still the deepest meaning of the original *agon*—weakly noted, let it be said—that arose between Descartes and the "mechanists" of his day and, in an opposed direction, between Descartes and Montaigne. But to see the point of these continuities is to see in addition that the pragmatists must still make common cause with those forces of analytic philosophy that require the naturalizers to make their case explicit, as well as with the forces of continental philosophy closest to the post-Kantian temperament. Only if such a union is effected can we rightly expect, however late in the new century, to have changed philosophy's direction in a fresh and productive way. But that would mean, perhaps reasonably enough, that a muddle almost four hundred years in the making would have been resolved in a period of less than three centuries. Platonism, of course, has already taken longer.

Notes

Prologue

1. Morris Dickstein, "Introduction: Pragmatism Then and Now," in *The Revival of Pragmatism: New Essays on Social Thought, Law, and Culture* (Durham: Duke University Press, 1998), p. 11.

2. Stanley Cavell, "What's the Use of Calling Emerson a Pragmatist?" in *The Revival of Pragmatism: New Essays on Social Thought, Law, and Culture,* ed. Morris Dickstein (Durham: Duke University Press, 1998), p. 72.

3 "Naturalizing" is a term of art drawn from Quine's and Davidson's usage, as in Quine's influential paper "Epistemology Naturalized," which I adopt in this chapter and in the rest of the book. I contrast the sense of "naturalism" favored by the classic pragmatists and that of "naturalizing" more or less shared by Quine, Davidson, and Rorty.

4. See, for instance, Robert B. Brandom, *Articulating Reasons: An Introduction to Inferentialism* (Cambridge: Harvard University Press, 2000). Brandom's entire effort, which pauses to acknowledge "my teacher, Richard Rorty" (p. 32), is an attempt to reclaim an "inferentialist" account of semantics (read: semantics-*cum*-epistemology) that begins with Gottlob Frege (as something of a pragmatist) and, on Brandom's account, threads its way through Wilfrid Sellars (also a pragmatist) and Rorty, to recover "a *hegelian*" approach to "the realm of culture" (pp. 32–33) said to yield "a kind of conceptual [or linguistic] pragmatism" (p. 4), according to the following formula: "Cultural products and activities become explicit as such [inferentially] only by the use of normative vocabulary that is in principle not reducible to the vocabulary of the natural sciences (though of course the same phenomena under other descriptions are available in that vocabulary). Indeed the deployment of the vocabulary of the natural sciences (like that of any other vocabulary) is itself a cultural phenomenon, something that becomes intelligible only within the conceptual horizon provided by the *Geisteswissenschaften*. The study of natures itself has a history, and its own nature, if any, must be approached through the study of that history. This is a picture and an aspiration that we owe to Hegel" (p. 33). Without attempting an assessment of Brandom's arguments, this is a thesis, offered in the name of Rorty's innovations, of a transformed pragmatism. But it hardly suits Rorty's own postmodernism. See the exchange between Brandom and Rorty in *Rorty and His Critics,* ed. Robert B. Brandom (Oxford: Blackwell Publishers, 2000). Indeed, Brandom turns the tables on Rorty's endorsement of Davidson's "naturalizing" by reinterpreting Davidson's naturalism as fully in accord with the "hegelian" reversal just remarked. (Notice Brandom's emphasis on the normative.) I leave the assessment of these gymnastic adjustments to the reader. See Donald Davidson, "A Coherence Theory of Truth and Knowledge," in *Truth and Interpretation: Perspectives on the Philosophy of Donald Davidson,* ed. Ernest Lapore (Oxford: Basil Blackwell, 1986); also, Richard Rorty, "Pragmatism, Davidson and Truth," in the same volume.

5. Hilary Putnam, *Reason, Truth, and History* (Cambridge: Cambridge University Press, 1980), p. 216.

6. See Richard Rorty, "Solidarity or Objectivity?" in *Post-Analytic Philosophy,* ed. John Rajchman and Cornel West (New York: Columbia University Press, 1985); reprint-

ed in Richard Rorty, *Philosophical Papers*, vol. 1 (Cambridge: Cambridge University Press, 1991).

7. I must enter an important caveat here, though I am not prepared to bank on it without more explicit evidence. Dewey wrote a lengthy analysis (in 1897) of Hegel's entire system, with a temperate sense of Hegel's view of history, which he reads in the spirit of his own evolving vision. The essay is unpublished and Dewey never put his hand to writing a pragmatist recovery of Hegel's theory. But he treats Hegel as the "great actualist," which is to emphasize (against the usual readings) that Hegel always featured effective history in a manner pragmatism might have championed; he opposes (in Hegel's favor) any reading of "absolute" history that would assign history a closed and inclusive *telos* of its own or a finished *geistlich* or horizonal structure of any kind; and he opposes any reading of Hegel that would have supported later attempts to interpret Hegel's political and historical writings as the work of a nationalist ideologue.

These latter concerns may explain in some measure Dewey's otherwise curious avoidance of any sustained analysis of the problem of history. But the existence of the essay lends support to efforts to reconstruct (from Dewey's voluminous writings) what might accord with his mature pragmatism. There is no question that he had made a start on what, later, would be reasonably viewed as a pragmatist reading of Hegel. See, further, chapter 4, below, note 7. I am indebted here to a chance conversation with James Allan Good, who allowed me to see his recent Ph.D. dissertation, "A Search for Unity in Diversity: The 'Permanent Hegelian Deposit' in the Philosophy of John Dewey" (Rice University, 2000). There is, currently, a great deal of interest in recovering Dewey's early reading of Hegel and post-Kantian German philosophy and (so-called) British Idealism. Good actually favors the view that Dewey became "the consummate historicist" (p. 142), after separating his historicist reading of Hegel from his own earlier ("Hegelian") belief (so characterized) in the inseparability of the "individual self" from "the absolute self . . . an ahistorical reality": on this reading, time and history are themselves internal to "absolute self-consciousness," which must be "atemporal." These extravagances confirm the marvel of Dewey's having extricated himself from the wild speculations of the "Idealists," both German and British. But there remains, of course, a deeper and more sober sense in which the overcoming of the *aporiai* of Kantian and pre-Kantian philosophy required Dewey to salvage what could not be responsibly ignored in the best work of the German and British traditions. Good's account proceeds, to a large extent, by interpreting Dewey as salvaging Hegel (against the "Hegelians") by pragmatist means, as by offering a "functionalist" theory of the self against all "transcendental absolutes." That is a question contemporary analytic philosophy has not adequately addressed. But see, further, John McDowell, *Mind and World* (Cambridge: Harvard University Press, 1996). When, as we proceed, I take it for granted that Dewey is a "Hegelian" of sorts, I mean it in the spirit of the themes just mentioned. But I think it is overly sanguine to call Dewey a "historicist."

8. Putnam, *Reason, Truth, and History*, p. 49.

9. See W. V. Quine, "Epistemology Naturalized," in *Ontological Relativity and Other Essays* (New York: Columbia University Press, 1969). The book includes Quine's John Dewey Lectures. See, also, Barry Stroud, "The Significance of Naturalized Epistemology," *Midwest Studies in Philosophy* 6 (1981).

10. See Rorty, "Pragmatism, Davidson, and Truth."

11. I believe this is a fair account of the unity of Rorty's *philosophical* work. The single most important paper in this regard remains his "Pragmatism, Davidson and Truth."

12. See, particularly, Jaegwon Kim, *Supervenience and Mind: Selected Philosophical Essays* (Cambridge: Cambridge University Press, 1993).

13. See Donald Davidson, "Mental Events," in *Essays on Actions and Events* (Oxford: Clarendon, 1980).

14. See John Dewey, *Reconstruction in Philosophy*, rev. and enl. ed. (Boston: Beacon Press, 1957); and *Quest for Certainty* (New York: Minton, Balch, 1929). See also Richard Rorty, *Consequences of Pragmatism* (*Essays 1972–1980*) (Minneapolis: University of Minnesota Press, 1982).

15. See, for Rorty's most recent reckoning, Richard Rorty, "On Heidegger's Nazism," in *Philosophy and Social Hope* (Harmondsworth: Penguin Books, 1999).

16. For some specimen views, see Alvin I. Goldman, *Liaisons: Philosophy Meets the Cognitive and Social Sciences* (Cambridge: MIT Press, 1992); and *Naturalizing Epistemology*, ed. Hilary Kornblith, 2d ed. (Cambridge: MIT Press, 1994).

17. See Charles Morris, chap. 2 in *The Pragmatic Movement in American Philosophy* (New York: George Braziller, 1970); Israel Scheffler, chap. 7 in *Four Pragmatists: A Critical Introduction to Peirce, James, Mead, and Dewey* (London: Routledge and Kegan Paul, 1974); John E. Smith, chap. 2 in *Purpose and Thought: The Meaning of Pragmatism* (New Haven: Yale University Press, 1978); H. S. Thayer, *Meaning and Action: A Critical History of Pragmatism* (Indianapolis: Bobbs-Merrill, 1968); R. W. Sleeper, chap. 3 in *The Necessity of Pragmatism: John Dewey's Conception of Philosophy* (New Haven: Yale University Press, 1986); Carl Hausman, chap. 1 in *Charles S. Peirce's Evolutionary Philosophy* (Cambridge: Cambridge University Press, 1993); Murray C. Murphey, *The Development of Peirce's Philosophy* (Indianapolis: Hackett Publishing Co., 1991); Gerald E. Myers, chap. 10 in *William James, His Life and Thought* (New Haven: Yale University Press, 1986); John P. Murphy, *Pragmatism: From Peirce to Davidson* (Boulder: Westview Press, 1990); H. O. Mounce, chap. 2 and 3 in *The Two Pragmatisms: From Peirce to Rorty* (London: Routledge, 1997).

18. See sec. 5.196 in *Collected Papers of Charles Sanders Peirce*, ed. Charles Hartshorne and Paul Weiss (Cambridge: Harvard University Press, 1935). The passage belongs to the "Lectures on Pragmatism," which dates from 1903. The dating is of some importance, since it appears to catch up Peirce's rejection of Kant's transcendentalism (or "intuition," as Peirce flags it): see "Questions Concerning Certain Faculties Claimed for Man," sections 5.213–263 that had already appeared in 1868. This fits very well with Dewey's reformulation of pragmatism, despite divergences from Peirce. See, particularly, John Dewey, "The Superstition of Necessity," reprinted in Jo Ann Boydston, ed., *John Dewey: The Early Works, 1882–1898*, vol. 4 (Cambridge: Southern Illinois University Press, 1971). The essay first appeared in 1893.

19. See Peter Hylton, *Russell, Idealism, and the Emergence of Analytic Philosophy* (Oxford: Clarendon, 1990).

20. See William James, chap. 28 in *The Principles of Psychology* (Cambridge: Harvard University Press, 1981). James appears as a nativist here, also as a thinker whom Edmund Husserl took to be more than sympathetic with phenomenology, but above all as a naturalist.

21. See Hilary Putnam, lecture 1 of "Sense, Nonsense, and the Senses: An Inquiry into the Powers of the Human Mind" (The John Dewey Lectures, 1994), *Journal of Philosophy* 91 (1994), particularly notes 8, 10. On James's uncertain account of "sensation," see Myers, chap. 3 in *William James: His Life and Thought*, particularly pp. 85–89.

22. See McDowell, *Mind and World*.

23. See Hilary Putnam, *The Many Faces of Realism* (LaSalle: Open Court, 1987), pp. 26–28, 70–71.

24. See Dewey, *The Quest for Certainty*; and *Essays in Experimental Logic* (New York: Dover, n.d.).

25. Putnam, *The Many Faces of Realism*, pp. 20–21.

26. Rorty, "Pragmatism, Davidson and Truth," p. 333. Also see Davidson, "A Coherence Theory of Truth and Knowledge."

27. Rorty, "Pragmatism, Davidson and Truth," p. 333.

28. In Davidson's hands, in his influential paper "On the Very Idea of a Conceptual Scheme," the question of "interpretive intermediaries"—*tertia*, in Rorty's idiom, though the restriction of "tertia" is misleading—is applied most famously to Thomas Kuhn and Paul Feyerabend, though it makes perfect sense to claim that Quine's penchant for "analytical hypotheses" in resolving the "indeterminacy of translation" puzzle makes Quine Davidson's most important target. I shall return to the issue, lightly. See Donald Davidson, "On the Very Idea of a Conceptual Scheme," in *Inquiries into Truth and Interpretation* (Oxford: Clarendon, 1984).

29. See Rorty, "Pragmatism, Davidson, and Truth," p. 333.

30. Rorty, "Pragmatism, Davidson, and Truth," p. 346.

31. Rorty, "Pragmatism, Davidson and Truth," p. 345–346. See also Hilary Putnam, *Realism and Reason* (Cambridge: Cambridge University Press, 1983), p. xv (which Rorty cites).

32. Putnam, "Sense, Nonsense, and the Senses," p. 454.

33. Compare Donald Davidson, "The Folly of Trying to Define Truth," *Journal of Philosophy* 93 (1996).

34. Putnam, *Reason, Truth, and History*, pp. 49–50.

35. See Rorty, "Pragmatism, Davidson, and Truth," p. 335.

36. Davidson, "A Coherence Theory of Truth and Knowledge," p. 313. The point of Davidson's remark is to take advantage of the fact that Putnam had himself explored the possibility of a brain kept alive in a vat, receiving stimuli but completely unable to explore the "external world" in any familiar way. Putnam, it should be said, did not find the speculation coherent.

37. Ibid., p. 312. Also see Donald Davidson, "Afterthoughts," in *Reading Rorty: Critical Responses to Philosophy and the Mirror of Nature (and Beyond)*, ed. Alan R. Malachowski (Oxford: Basil Blackwell, 1990), pp. 134–137.

38. See Michael Devitt, *Realism and Truth*, 2d ed. (Princeton: Princeton University Press, 1991).

39. See W. V. Quine, "Postscript on Metaphor," in *Theories and Things* (Cambridge: Harvard University Press, 1981).

Chapter 1. Cartesian Realism and the Revival of Pragmatism

1. See Richard Rorty, "Private Irony and Liberal Hope," in *Contingency, Irony, and Solidarity* (Cambridge: Cambridge University Press, 1989).

2. See Richard Rorty, "Overcoming the Tradition: Heidegger and Dewey," in *Consequences of Pragmatism (Essays: 1972–1980)* (Minneapolis: University of Minnesota Press, 1982). When I say that Rorty deforms both Dewey and Heidegger, I have in mind Rorty's neglecting, in *Being and Time*, Heidegger's use of what he calls *existentialia* in our understanding of *Dasein*. The important point is that *existentialia* are not "natural" or "naturalistic" categories; hence, that all of Heidegger's allusions to the "instrumental" role of theory in practice (Rorty mentions paragraphs 31–33 of *Being and Time*, which Mark Okrent has relied on) *are not pragmatist in any sense but* are quasi-transcendental in the precise sense in which *existentialia* replace or supersede Kantian transcendental categories. I'm afraid it's not unusual for Rorty to isolate a sentence or two from its obvious context, and then make a plausible comparison with sentences that, in *their* context, would have an entirely different significance than what we are encouraged to think is their proper sense. I resist attributing the practice directly to postmodernism. But I must admit that by the end of chapter 2 it may seem quite reasonable to accept the judgment. See, further, Mark Okrent, *Heidegger's Pragmatism* (Ithaca: Cornell University Press, 1988).

3. Rorty, introduction to *Consequences of Pragmatism*, p. xiii.

4. Richard Rorty, "Pragmatism, Davidson and Truth," in *Truth and Interpretation: Perspectives on Donald Davidson's Philosophy*, ed. Ernest Lepore (Oxford: Basil Blackwell, 1986).

5. Donald Davidson, "The Structure and Content of Truth," *Journal of Philosophy* 87 (1990). This comprises Davidson's John Dewey Lectures.

6. Richard Rorty, "Is Truth a Goal of Inquiry? Donald Davidson versus Crispin Wright," in *Philosophical Papers* (Cambridge: Cambridge University Press, 1998), 3: 21–22.

7. See Davidson, "The Structure and Content of Truth," p. 332.

8. Rorty, "Is Truth a Goal of Inquiry?" p. 23.

9. Davidson, "The Structure and Content of Truth," p. 309; cited by Rorty.

10. This is indeed the source of an incautious impression conveyed in Robert B. Brandom, *Articulating Reasons: An Introduction in Inferentialism* (Cambridge: Harvard Uni-

versity Press, 2000). See, particularly, the introduction and chapter 1, for Brandom's handling of Frege as a kind of pragmatist. The ironies are palpable. For Brandom is himself relying on Rorty's extreme revision of what pragmatism means in order to reintroduce the validity of epistemological inquiry (under the label of "inferentialism"), against Rorty's own postmodernism. The application of the Peircean and Jamesian constraints would have put an instant stop to the "pragmatist" recovery of Frege. Brandom himself says, in passing, "The later Wittgenstein, Quine, and Sellars (as well as Dummett and Davidson) are linguistic pragmatists, whose strategy of coming at the meaning of expressions by considering their use provides a counterbalance to the Frege-Russell-Carnap-Tarski platonistic model-theoretic approach to meaning" (pp. 6–7). At the very least, this is to contort the obvious meaning of "pragmatist" so that the word has no philosophical spine; though to say that is not to oppose the interesting contrast Brandom puts before us. Yet, in saying all that, Brandom does not wish to deny that Frege *is* a "pragmatist"— though, as you see, he is apparently also a "platonist" (that is, *not* a pragmatist). This reading of Frege is very much of a piece with Rorty's reading of Heidegger.

11. See Alfred Tarski, "The Concept of Truth in Formalized Languages," in *Logic, Semantics, Metamathematics,* trans. J. H. Woodger, ed. John Corcoran, 2d ed. (Indianapolis: Hackett, 1983). See the "Postscript" (sec. 7).

12. See Donald Davidson, "The Folly of Trying to Define Truth," *Journal of Philosophy* 93 (1996).

13. Richard Rorty, *Philosophy and Social Hope* (Harmondsworth: Penguin, 1999), p. 24.

14. See Hilary Putnam, "Sense, Nonsense, and the Senses: An Inquiry into the Powers of the Human Mind," *Journal of Philosophy* 91 (1994). (This comprises Putnam's John Dewey Lectures of 1994.)

15. Hilary Putnam, "Values, Facts and Cognition," in *Reason, Truth and History* (Cambridge: Cambridge University Press, 1981), p. 216.

16. For a very brief sense of this, see Hilary Putnam and Ruth Anna Putnam, "William James's Ideas" (1989), in *Realism with a Human Face,* ed. James Conant (Cambridge: Harvard University Press, 1990), pp. 225, 226.

17. See, further, Hilary Putnam, "Bernard Williams and the Absolute Conception of the World," in *Renewing Philosophy* (Cambridge: Harvard University Press, 1992). I find this paper particularly revealing about Putnam's dialectical strategy.

18. Putnam, "Values, Facts, and Cognition," p. 216. See, further, chap. 5.

19. Richard Rorty, "Solidarity or Objectivity?" (1985), in *Post-Analytic Philosophy,* ed. John Rajchman and Cornel West (New York: Columbia University Press, 1985), p. 10.

20. Davidson, "A Coherence Theory of Truth and Knowledge," p. 308. Compare Donald Davidson, "What Is Present to the Mind?" in *Subjective, Intersubjective, Objective* (Oxford: Clarendon, 2001), which betrays the slippage between first-order and second-order claims.

21. See Donald Davidson, "A Coherence Theory of Truth and Knowledge."

22. Hilary Putnam, "Two Conceptions of Rationality," in *Reason, Truth, and History,* p. 126.

23. See, for a sense of Putnam's reasoning, "Objectivity and the Science/Ethics Distinction," in *Realism with a Human Face,* which seems to be the original from which "Bernard Williams and the Absolute Conception of the World" is a spin-off. The larger paper also appears in *The Quality of Life,* ed. Martha Nussbaum and Amartya Sen (Oxford: Clarendon, 1993), which helps to confirm (though there is additional evidence) that Nussbaum's recent invocation of Aristotelian essentialism—"pragmatized," in effect— owes a great deal to the convergence of Putnam and Habermas. See Martha C. Nussbaum, "Human Capabilities, Female Human Beings," in *Women, Culture, and Development: A Study of Human Capabilities,* ed. Martha Nussbaum and Jonathan Glover (Oxford: Clarendon, 1995). I believe the project fails, for essentially the same reason Putnam's and Habermas's versions fail. See, also, Jürgen Habermas, "Discourse Ethics: Notes on a Program of Philosophical Justification," in *Moral Consciousness and Communicative Action,* trans. Christian Lenhardt and Shierry Weber Nicholsen (Cambridge: MIT Press,

1990). For a close reading of Habermas and Karl-Otto Apel's treatment of criteria of "rationality," see Joseph Margolis, "Vicissitudes of Transcendental Reason," in *Habermas and Pragmatism,* ed. Mitchell Aboulafia, Myra Bookman, and Cathy Kemp (London: Routledge, 2002). On Habermas's view of rational consensus, see Nicholas Rescher, *Pluralism: Against the Demand of Consensus* (Oxford: Clarendon, 1993). I note here as well that Putnam, who was, by his own admission, very much attracted to William James's philosophical intuitions, found a version of the *Grenzbegriff* theme (and the actual use of the term) in James's famous essay, "The Will to Believe" in *The Will to Believe* (New York: Longman's, 1897). James is actually more plausible than Putnam, since he speaks of "a mere aspiration or *Grenzbegriff,* marking the infinitely remote ideal of our thinking life"—which has obvious affinities with Charles Peirce's notion of the infinite "long run" (itself a formula regarding rational hope rather than any rational norms constraining the truth of actual beliefs).

24. I provide the evidence in "Vicissitudes of Transcendental Reason."

25. See John McDowell, *Mind and World* (Cambridge: Harvard University Press, 1996).

26. Davidson, "A Coherence Theory of Truth and Knowledge," p. 309.

27. Hilary Putnam, *Pragmatism: An Open Question* (Oxford: Blackwell, 1995), pp. 64–65. I have paraphrased (possibly emended) Putnam's first two points, though they seem in accord with what he says here.

28. Davidson, "The Structure and Content of Truth," pp. 279–282. See, also, John Dewey, *Reconstruction in Philosophy* (New York: Holt, 1920), p. 156 (cited by Davidson). Dewey's book has been re-issued in an enlarged edition by Beacon Press, 1957; see prologue above, n. 14.

29. Davidson, "The Structure and Content of Truth," pp. 304–305.

30. The essential texts for their respective views in this regard appear in Davidson, "A Coherence Theory of Truth and Knowledge," and Rorty, "Pragmatism, Davidson and Truth."

31. Davidson, "A Coherence Theory of Truth and Knowledge," p. 312.

32. Ibid., p. 314. The line from Wittgenstein appears in Ludwig Wittgenstein, *Philosophical Investigations,* trans. G. E. M. Anscombe (New York: Macmillan, 1953), at I, paragraph 242.

33. Rorty, "Pragmatism, Davidson and Truth," p. 335.

34. Hilary Putnam, *The Many Faces of Realism* (La Salle: Open Court, 1987), p. 28.

35. See Putnam, "Sense, Nonsense, and the Senses," lecture 1.

36. I daresay this is the common thread that joins the very different (even opposed) philosophies of Brandom and McDowell: the one, "Hegelian" in a way that does not seem to challenge the epistemological confidence of the "Cartesians" at all, unless at some extremely abstract utopian level never brought to bear on the processing of truth-claims; the other, "Kantian" (with a very much dampened "Hegelian" modification) that is entirely satisfied with a purely formal (not epistemological) resolution of the Cartesian paradox. Brandom and McDowell are worth bearing in mind in this regard, because— for reasons that have more to do with the alignment of competing forces in the American academy at the present time than with the obvious options that spring from the post-Kantians and the classic pragmatists themselves (not to mention the largely neglected options offered by the entire modern European tradition)—the alternatives Brandom and MacDowell feature are at least specimens of the principal directions American philosophy (epistemology-*cum*-metaphysics-*cum*-semantics-*cum*-philosophy-of-mind) are bound to take if not forcefully confronted by stronger lines of reasoning. See McDowell, *Mind and World;* and Brandom, *Articulating Reasons.*

37. See Michael de Montaigne, "The Apology of Raymond Sebond," in *The Complete Essays,* trans. M. A. Screech (London: Penguin Books, 1993).

38. Here I agree with John Searle's finding, but not with his reasoning, which favors the reverse of Hegel's thinking. See John R. Searle, *The Construction of Social Reality* (New York: Free Press, 1985). I explore the case for cultural realism (that is, a realism that cannot be reduced to the realism of physical nature but is implicated in the admission of the

latter) in *Selves and Other Texts: The Case for Cultural Realism* (University Park: Pennsylvania State University Press, 2001). The point of entry there—by way of artworks, selves, and history—is only obliquely linked with the arguments being advanced here.

39. See Michael Devitt, introduction to *Realism and Truth,* 2d ed. (Princeton: Princeton University Press, 1997).

40. G. W. F. Hegel, introduction to *Phenomenology of Spirit,* trans. A. V. Miller (Oxford: Oxford University Press, 1977), p. 46.

41. See Richard Rorty, *Philosophy and the Mirror of Nature* (Princeton: Princeton University Press, 1979).

42. For a sense of Davidson's difficulties, see Donald Davidson, "Afterthoughts, 1987," in *Reading Rorty: Critical Responses to Philosophy and the Mirror of Nature (and Beyond),* ed. Alan R. Malachowski (Oxford: Basil Blackwell, 1990).

43. Devitt, *Realism and Truth,* p. vii.

44. Michael Dummett, *The Logical Basis of Metaphysics* (Cambridge: Harvard University Press, 1991), pp. 1–2.

45. Ibid., pp. 198–199.

46. See ibid., pp. 9–15.

47. See "Sense, Nonsense, and the Senses," pp. 445–447; and Hilary Putnam, "Pragmatism and the Contemporary Debate," in *Pragmatism,* pp. 64–68.

48. McDowell, *Mind and World,* pp. 1–7, 85–86.

49. Ibid., p. 26.

50. See John McDowell, "Having the World in View: Sellars, Kant, and Intentionality," *The Journal of Philosophy* 95 (1998); and *Mind, Value, and Reality,* pt. 3 (Cambridge: Harvard University Press, 1998).

51. McDowell, "Having the World in View," p. 490.

52. McDowell, *Mind and World,* pp. 41–44.

53. Ibid., pp. 83–84.

54. Ibid., p. 92.

55. Ibid., p. 163.

56. See Putnam, "Sense, Nonsense, and the Senses," pp. 461–464.

57. McDowell, *Mind and World,* pp. 3, 5.

58. Ibid., p. 124; also see pp. 87–90.

59. Ibid., p. 54. See the rest of lecture 3 and chap. 5–9 in Gareth Evans, *The Varieties of Reference,* ed. John McDowell (Oxford: Clarendon, 1982).

Chapter 2. Richard Rorty: Philosophy by Other Means

1. W. V. Quine, *From a Logical Point of View* (Cambridge: Harvard University Press, 1953); *Word and Object* (Cambridge: MIT Press, 1960).

2. Nelson Goodman, *The Structure of Appearance,* 2d ed. (Indianapolis: Bobbs-Merrill, 1966); *Fact, Fiction, and Forecast,* 2d ed. (Indianapolis: Bobbs-Merrill, 1965); and *Ways of Worldmaking* (Indianapolis: Hackett, 1978).

3. Donald Davidson, *Essays on Actions and Events* (Oxford: Clarendon, 1980); *Inquiries into Truth and Interpretation* (Oxford: Clarendon, 1984).

4. It is difficult not to see in the recent reprinting (as a separate book) of Sellars's essay, "Empiricism and the Philosophy of Mind" (by Harvard University Press, 1997)—introduced by Rorty and bound together with a study guide provided by Robert Brandom—a deliberate bid to install Sellars as an assured bridge figure between pragmatism and analytic philosophy, by which to facilitate the deformation of pragmatism itself in the general direction of Davidson's naturalism. At the same time, it is meant to draw the new union in the direction of Rorty's postmodernism. (The re-issue, by the way, uses as its title the title of the original essay.) This is quite a complicated affair. If that is what its purpose was, then things did not go quite as planned, though one hears Sellars dutifully named a pragmatist. For Rorty's "postmodernism" or "post-philosophy" has not really gained adherents among the strongest analysts, though Rorty's ingenuity continues to attract debaters; for his part, Brandom seems to have struck out along more conventional analytic lines, content to take advantage of Rorty's free play with the use of the epithet

"pragmatist," though without yielding in the postmodernist direction. See, particularly, Robert B. Brandom, *Articulating Reasons: An Introduction to Inferentialism* (Cambridge: Harvard University Press, 2000), and *Making It Explicit: Reason, Representing, and Discursive Commitment* (Cambridge: Harvard University Press, 1994), which features the "pragmatist" Sellars (without any trace of eliminativism), which the *Articulating Reasons* book helps to make accessible. (It may be of some interest to note that the latter book is dedicated to Sellars and Rorty.) See, also, Rorty's response to Brandom, in *Rorty and His Critics*, ed. Robert B. Brandom (Oxford: Blackwell, 2000). I see in this the beginning of Rorty's eclipse *and* the continuation, along more unlikely lines, of the general cobbling of pragmatism and the views of its natural opponents. Whether Sellars is really central to either Rorty's or Brandom's maneuver is by no means certain.

5. Quine's essay appears in *Ontological Relativity and Other Essays* (New York: Columbia University Press, 1969). Davidson's essay appears in *Truth and Interpretation: Perspectives on the Philosophy of Donald Davidson*, ed. Ernest Lepore (Oxford: Basil Blackwell, 1986).

6. Quine, sec. 15–16 in *Word and Object*.

7. For a critique of Quine's "meaning holism," see Jerry Fodor and Ernest Lepore, *Holism: A Shopper's Guide* (Oxford: Blackwell, 1992), particularly chap. 2; see, also, Hilary Putnam, "Meaning Holism" (and Quine's reply), both in *The Philosophy of W. V. Quine*, ed. Lewis Edwin Hahn and Paul Arthur Schilpp (La Salle: Open Court, 1986).

8. "The Structure and Content of Truth," *Journal of Philosophy* 87 (1990).

9. In the "Coherence" paper.

10. See Richard Rorty, "Pragmatism, Davidson and Truth," in *Truth and Interpretation*; also, Richard Rorty, "Is Truth a Goal of Inquiry? Donald Davidson versus Crispin Wright," in *Philosophical Papers*, vol. 3 (Cambridge: Cambridge University Press, 1998).

11. In *Reading Rorty: Critical Responses to Philosophy and the Mirror of Nature (and Beyond)*, ed. Alan R. Malachowski (Oxford: Basil Blackwell, 1990), pp. 134–137, Davidson views the upshot of his exchange with Rorty as something of a bargain: Rorty "now explicitly rejects James and Peirce on truth" (in effect, "the pragmatist theory of truth"), and, for his part, Davidson concedes the indefensibility (which Rorty correctly noted) of regarding his own remarks about the coherence and correspondence features of truth as a "theory" of truth. (Rorty's treatment of truth, it should be noted, keeps shifting.)

12. Rorty, introduction to *Philosophical Papers*, 3: 8.

13. Both appear in Wilfrid Sellars, *Science, Perception and Reality* (New York: Routledge & Kegan Paul, 1963). For a survey of current forms of scientific and pragmatic realisms, see Sami Pihlstrom, "Structuring the World: The Issue of Realism and the Nature of Ontological Problems in Classical and Contemporary Pragmatism," chap. 4 in *Acta Philosophica Fennica* (Helsinki) 59 (1996).

14. See Rorty, "Pragmatism, Davidson and Truth."

15. See the list of doctrines Rorty takes to be definitive of both pragmatism and naturalizing, in "Pragmatism, Davidson and Truth," p. 335. What may be the latest evidence of a decided difference of opinion between Davidson and Rorty appears in Donald Davidson, "Truth Rehabilitated" and Richard Rorty, "Response to Donald Davidson," both included in *Rorty and His Critics*. Here, Davidson makes abundantly clear why he is not a "deflationist" about truth: "Almost everyone agrees [he says] that some sentences, at least, have the value true or false, and that for such sentences, we may speak of truth conditions" (p. 70). Rorty cites another of Davidson's sentences (from the same paper) that advances the same message, about which he says, "This sentence troubles people like me" (p. 74). He prefers "uses" to "truth-conditions," by which (in effect) he means to signify his preference for Wittgenstein *and* James (as he reads them) over Davidson—as if (once again) James really did mean to subscribe to Rorty's post-philosophical recommendations. Here, Rorty's entire argument begins to unravel.

16. Richard Rorty, "Introduction" in Wilfrid Sellars, *Empiricism and the Philosophy of Mind* (Cambridge: Harvard University Press, 1997), p. 7.

17. Sellars, *Science, Perception and Reality*, p. 126.

18. Richard Rorty, "Charles Taylor on Truth," in *Philosophical Papers* (Cambridge: Cambridge University Press, 1998), 3:89n10, 93.

19. Rorty, "Charles Taylor on Truth," p. 93.

20. Richard Rorty, *Philosophy and the Mirror of Nature* (Princeton: Princeton University Press, 1979), p. 199 (in the context of pp. 192–215).

21. W. V. Quine, "Let Me Accentuate the Positive," in *Reading Rorty*, p. 117.

22. See Hilary Putnam, *Reason, Truth and History* (Cambridge: Cambridge University Press, 1981), p. 216.

23. See Richard Rorty, "Pragmatism, Relativism and Irrationality," *Proceedings and Addresses of the American Philosophical Association* (August 1980).

24. Richard Rorty, "Antirepresentationalism, Ethnocentrism, and Liberalism," in *Philosophical Papers,* 1:7, 12.

25. Reprinted in Richard Rorty, *Philosophical Papers,* vol. 3.

26. See Richard Rorty, *Philosophy and Social Hope* (London: Penguin, 1999), pp. xviii–xix.

27. Richard Rorty's paper, "Feminism and Pragmatism," was given as a Tanner Lecture (1991). Nancy Fraser served as a respondent on that occasion. Rorty's paper, originally published in the same number of the *Michigan Quarterly Review* as Fraser's response, has now been reprinted in *Philosophical Papers,* vol. 3. For Fraser's paper, see Nancy Fraser, "From Irony to Prophecy to Politics," *Michigan Quarterly Review* 30 (1991).

28. Fraser, "From Irony to Prophecy to Politics," p. 259.

29. Rorty, "Feminism and Pragmatism," p. 206.

30. See John Dewey, *Human Nature and Conduct: An Introduction to Social Psychology* (New York: Modern Library, 1936), p. 278.

31. Rorty, "Feminism and Pragmatism," p. 207.

32. Fraser, "From Irony to Prophecy to Politics," pp. 263–264.

33. See Richard Rorty, "The Contingency of a Liberal Community" and "Private Irony and Liberal Hope," both in *Contingency, Irony, and Solidarity* (Cambridge: Cambridge University Press, 1989); and Nancy Fraser, "Solidarity or Singularity? Richard Rorty between Romanticism and Technology," in *Reading Rorty.*

34. Reprinted (with altered title) in *Philosophical Papers,* vol. 3.

35. For a sense of Dennett's treatment, see Daniel C. Dennett, *Consciousness Explained* (Boston: Little, Brown and Co., 1990). In particular, see chaps. 5 and 12–14.

36. Dennett, *Consciousness Explained,* pp. 106, 107.

37. Ibid., p. 16.

38. Rorty's paper on Dennett appeared (under another title) in *Dennett and His Critics: Demystifying Mind,* ed. Bo Dahlbom (Oxford: Basil Blackwell, 1993). Dennett responds to his critics in the same volume, in "Back from the Drawing Board." The sentences cited appear on p. 234.

39. Rorty, "Daniel Dennett on Intrinsicality," p. 100.

40. Ibid., pp. 100–101.

41. See Thomas S. Kuhn, sec. 10 in *The Structure of Scientific Revolutions,* rev. and enl. ed. (Chicago: University of Chicago Press, 1970).

42. Rorty, *Philosophy and Social Hope,* p. xii.

43. Richard Rorty, "The Contingency of Language," in *Contingency, Irony, and Solidarity,* p. 6.

44. See P. K. Feyerabend, chap. 6 in *Against Method, Outline of a Anarchistic Theory of Knowledge* (London: NLB, 1975).

45. See Donald Davidson, "On the Very Idea of a Conceptual Scheme," in *Inquiries into Truth and Interpretation.*

46. See W. V. Quine, "Two Dogmas of Empiricism," in *From a Logical Point of View* (Cambridge: Harvard University Press, 1963); *Word and Object,* sec. 15–16.

47. See Davidson, "A Coherence Theory of Truth and Knowledge"; and Rorty, "Pragmatism, Davidson, and Truth."

48. Rorty, "Daniel Dennett on Intrinsicality," p. 118.

49. Ibid., p. 110.

50. Donald Davidson, "The Myth of the Subjective," in *Relativism, Interpretation and Confirmation*, ed. Michael Krausz (Notre Dame: University of Notre Dame Press, 1989), p. 170; cited by Rorty.

51. Rorty, "Daniel Dennett on Intrinsicality," p. 105.

52. Ibid., p. 105. See, also, Richard Rorty, "Inquiry as Recontextualization: An Antidualist Account of Interpretation," in *Philosophical Papers*, (Cambridge: Cambridge University Press, 1991), 1:96–97.

53. Rorty, "Daniel Dennett on Intrinsicality," p. 106.

54. See sec. 82–92 in *The Collected Papers of Charles Sanders Peirce*, vol. 5, ed. Charles Hartshorne and Paul Weiss (Cambridge: Harvard University Press, 1962).

Chapter 3. Anticipating Dewey's Advantage

1. See Richard Rorty, "Feminism and Pragmatism," in *Philosophical Papers* (Cambridge: Cambridge University Press, 1998), 3:207–208. Also see chap. 3.

2. Richard Rorty, "The Contingency of Language," in *Contingency, Irony, and Solidarity* (Cambridge: Cambridge University Press, 1989), p. 1.

3. Rorty, "The Contingency of Language," p. 9.

4. See, for example, Michael Devitt, *Realism and Truth*, 2d ed. (Princeton: Princeton University Press, 1991).

5. See Harold Bloom, chap. 1 in *A Map of Misreading* (Oxford: Oxford University Press, 1975).

6. Richard J. Bernstein, *The New Constellation: The Ethical-Political Horizons of Modernity/Postmodernity* (Cambridge: MIT Press, 1992), pp. 267, 270.

7. See Jean-François Lyotard, *The Postmodern Condition: A Report in Knowledge*, trans. Geoff Bennington and Brian Massumi (Minneapolis: University of Minnesota Press, 1984).

8. Bernstein, *The New Constellation*, p. 324.

9. See, further, Joseph Margolis, *Historied Thought, Constructed World: A Conceptual Primer for the Turn of the Millennium* (Berkeley: University of California Press, 1995).

10. See Richard J. Bernstein, *Beyond Objectivism and Relativism: Science, Hermeneutics, and Praxis* (Philadelphia: University of Pennsylvania Press, 1983).

11. Hilary Putnam, *Reason, Truth and History* (Cambridge: Cambridge University Press, 1981), p. ix.

12. Ibid., pp. 49–50.

13. See, for instance, Hilary Putnam, "Sense, Nonsense, and the Senses: An Inquiry into the Powers of the Human Mind," *Journal of Philosophy* 91 (1994): 182n36, 183n40.

14. See lecture 1 of Putnam, "Sense, Nonsense, and the Senses."

15. See Putnam, *Reason, Truth and History*, pp. 214–216.

16. See Richard Rorty, "Hilary Putnam and the Relativist Menace," in *Philosophical Papers*, vol. 3.

17. See Donald Davidson, "A Coherence Theory of Truth and Knowledge," in *Truth and Interpretation: Perspectives on the Philosophy of Donald Davidson*, ed. Ernest Lepore (Oxford: Basil Blackwell, 1986).

18. See Donald Davidson, "Afterthoughts, 1987," added to a reprinting of "A Coherence Theory of Truth and Knowledge," in *Reading Rorty: Critical Responses to Philosophy and the Mirror of Nature (and Beyond)*, ed. Alan R. Malachowski (Oxford: Basil Blackwell, 1990). On Rorty's reading of Davidson on truth, see Richard Rorty, "Pragmatism, Davidson, and Truth," in *Truth and Interpretation: Perspectives on the Philosophy of Donald Davidson*; and Richard Rorty, "Is Truth a Goal of Inquiry? Donald Davidson versus Crispin Wright," in *Philosophical Papers*, vol. 3.

19. See Rorty, "Pragmatism, Davidson, and Truth"; see also "Hilary Putnam and the Relativist Menace."

20. See W. V. Quine, "Let Me Accentuate the Positive," in *Reading Rorty*.

21. Hilary Putnam, "The Prospects of Artificial Intelligence," in *Renewing Philosophy* (Cambridge: Harvard University Press, 1992), p. 3.

22. Compare Bernstein's *Beyond Objectivism and Relativism* to Putnam's "Sense, Nonsense, and the Senses."

23. See John McDowell, *Mind and World* (Cambridge: Harvard University Press, 1996).

24. See Margolis, *Historied Thought, Constructed World.*

25. See Rorty, "Hilary Putnam and the Relativist Menace."

26. See chapter 4, below, in this book.

27. See, for instance, Hilary Putnam, "Wittgenstein on Reference and Relativism," in *Renewing Philosophy.* See also Myles Burnyeat, "Protagoras and Self-Refutation in Plato's Theaetetus," *Philosophical Review* 85 (1976).

28. Rorty, "Hilary Putnam and the Relativist Menace," p. 52.

29. See Davidson, "A Coherence Theory of Truth and Knowledge," p. 307.

30. See Hilary Putnam, "The Craving for Objectivity," in *Realism with a Human Face,* ed. James Conant (Cambridge: Harvard University Press, 1990).

31. See Richard Rorty, "Solidarity or Objectivity?" in *Philosophical Papers,* vol. 1; see also "Hilary Putnam and the Relativist Menace," p. 51n26.

32. See Karl R. Popper, "Of Clouds and Clocks," in *Objective Knowledge: An Evolutionary Approach* (Oxford: Clarendon, 1972).

33. Richard Rorty, "Relativism: Finding and Making," in *Philosophy and Social Hope* (London: Penguin, 1999), pp. xviii–xix.

34. For a fuller account, see Joseph Margolis, "The Benign Antinomy of a Constructed Realism," presented at the conference, The Future of Realism in the American Tradition of Pragmatic Naturalism, SUNY Buffalo, New York, October 20–22, 2000 (publication pending).

35. See Donald Davidson, "The Very Idea of a Conceptual Scheme," in *Inquiries into Truth and Interpretation* (Oxford: Clarendon, 1984). I have discussed more closely Davidson's attack on conceptual incommensurability, in an as yet unpublished paper, "Incommensurability Modestly Recovered," first presented at the conference, Incommensurability (and Related Matters), University of Hannover, Germany, Spring 1999.

36. See, further, Robert B. Brandom, *Articulating Reasons: An Introduction to Inferentialism* (Cambridge: Harvard University Press, 2000); also, however, see the exchange between Brandom and Rorty, in *Rorty and His Critics,* ed. Robert B. Brandom (Oxford: Blackwell, 2000).

37. Rorty, *Philosophy and Social Hope,* p. xvi.

38. Ibid., p. xvi.

39. Richard Rorty, "Science as Solidarity," in *Philosophical Papers,* 1:38–39.

40. The remark is cited in Rorty, "Hilary Putnam and the Relativist Menace," p. 44. Putnam has made the point in many places. Here it is taken from Hilary Putnam, "Objectivity and the Science/Ethics Distinction," in *Realism with a Human Face,* ed. James Conant (Cambridge: Harvard University Press, 1990), p. 171.

41. Hilary Putnam, "Irrealism and Deconstruction," in *Renewing Philosophy,* p. 120.

42. See W. V. Quine, sec. 15 and 16 in *Word and Object* (Cambridge: MIT Press, 1960); see also chap. 1 in *Pursuit of Truth,* rev. ed. (Cambridge: Harvard University Press, 1992).

Chapter 4. John Dewey: The Metaphysics of Existence

1. Dewey, it is important to note, draws human cognitive powers out of non-cognitive animal sources. (So does Peirce.) But this is *not* to deny that animals are capable of cognition in some sense that cannot be called into question by merely acknowledging that they lack language. The non-discursive is not the same as the non-cognitive. That is either a mistake or, at the very least, a questionable thesis that requires defense. It is worth remarking, therefore, that Brandom, who regards himself as a "linguistic pragmatist" and is now seen to be a sort of successor to Rorty—combining, it is said, pragmatist, analytic, *and* Hegelian credentials—*equates* the non-discursive with the non-cognitive *and* the non-conceptual. This certainly is not in accord with classic pragmatism and, in my opinion, is completely unconvincing. Brandom's argument (which follows Sellars) is meant to restrict the conceptual to the (inferential) processing of the linguistic. Dewey (you will

appreciate) links the inferential to the experiential (as the last citation suggests), which then applies to animals as well as humans. (Darwinians cannot fail to make such a concession.) There are a great many difficulties, therefore, with Brandom's conjecture, the principal clue being that, on a reasonable account, "concepts" are themselves theoretical constructs introduced to facilitate the analysis of cognitive powers of any sort—to include but not to be restricted to the linguistic. In any event, the very claim that the conceptual is inherently linguistic (rather than, say, *modeled* linguistically) is both a step in the Cartesian direction and a step away from any familiar form of pragmatism. Both Dewey and Peirce, remember, account for human cognition by evolutionary means from animal cognition. See Robert B. Brandom, *Articulating Reasons: An Introduction to Inferentialism* (Cambridge: Harvard University Press, 2000), pp. 5–11. This goes some distance toward explaining why Rorty's and/or Brandom's attraction to Sellars, Frege, Davidson, and similar-minded theorists is pragmatist only in the most Pickwickian sense.

2. Michael Devitt, *Realism and Truth,* 2d ed. (Princeton: Princeton University Press, 1991), pp. 3–4.

3. All four are commentators in *The Philosophy of John Dewey,* ed. Paul Arthur Schilpp, 2d ed. (New York: Tudor, 1951).

4. Arthur E. Murphy, "Dewey's Epistemology and Metaphysics," in *The Philosophy of John Dewey,* pp. 223–224. I have reversed the order of the two citations.

5. John Dewey, "Experience, Knowledge, and Value: A Rejoinder," in *The Philosophy of John Dewey,* p. 566. These themes are central to Dewey's *Logic* and *Experience and Nature.* See John Dewey, *Logic: The Theory of Inquiry* (New York: Henry Holt, 1938) and *Experience and Nature,* 2d ed. (New York: Dover, 1958).

6. Dewey, "Experience, Knowledge and Value: A Rejoinder," p. 566.

7. I have read Dewey's unpublished typescript, tagged as "Hegel's Philosophy of Spirit: Lectures by John Dewey" (University of Chicago, 1897), Southern Illinois University, Morris Library, Special Collection, John Dewey Papers, Collection 102. I have also read a very generous review of the essay and a thoughtful reflection on the relationship between Hegel and Dewey in a recent dissertation by James Allan Good, "A Search for Unity in Diversity: The 'Permanent Hegelian Deposit' in the Philosophy of John Dewey" (Rice University, 2001). Good's is the most sustained recent discussion of Dewey's reading of Hegel. The trouble, of course, is that Dewey does not develop his own theory in a way that would invite comparison. There may well have been political reasons, approaching the time of World War I, and after, that account for Dewey's deliberately avoiding the sustained use of the Hegelian materials. One should bear in mind that one cannot tell from Dewey's essay whether Dewey actually worked from Hegel's texts. It does, however, provide a good impression of Dewey's carefully constructed perspective on Hegel himself. See, also, note 5, Prologue, above.

8. Richard Rorty, "Dewey's Metaphysics," in *Consequences of Pragmatism (Essays: 1972–1980)* (Minneapolis: University of Minnesota Press, 1982), p. 72.

9. Dewey, *Experience and Nature,* p. 412.

10. Ibid., p. 413.

11. Ibid., pp. 414–415.

12. See John McDowell, *Mind and World* (Cambridge: Harvard University Press, 1996).

13. See sections 354–357 in *Collected Papers of Charles Sanders Peirce,* vol. 5, ed. Charles Hartshorne and Paul Weiss (Cambridge: Harvard University Press, 1935).

14. See, for instance, John Dewey, *The Quest for Certainty* (New York: Minton, Balch, 1929).

15. On Davidson's change of mind, see Davidson, "Afterthoughts, 1987," which is included together with the text of "A Coherence Theory," in *Reading Rorty: Critical Responses to Philosophy and the Mirror of Nature (and Beyond),* ed. Alan R. Malachowski (Oxford: Blackwell, 1990). For an early criticism of Davidson, see Susan Haack, chap. 3 in *Evidence and Inquiry: Toward Reconstruction in Epistemology* (Oxford: Blackwell, 1993). I am in general accord with Haack in her criticism of Davidson and Rorty (see also chap. 9). I do not, however, share her preferences in classic pragmatism (though I think

I may say I admire Peirce above Dewey, in spite of the fact that I favor Dewey over Peirce for philosophical reasons). The reason is simply that I think truth must be construed in constructivist terms, not primarily in terms of Peirce's long run. I would say that Haack is a realist who, however much a pragmatist, opposes a constructivist reading of truth. I take that to be incompatible with the doctrine of the flux and with the principal advantages of the entire movement. See Haack, pp. 188–194.

16. Hilary Putnam, *The Many Faces of Reason* (La Salle: Open Court, 1987), p. 1. The same phrasing appears in Hilary Putnam, *Reason, Truth and History* (Cambridge: Cambridge University Press, 1981), p. ix.

17. See, for instance, Richard Rorty, "Hilary Putnam and the Relativist Menace," in *Philosophical Papers*, vol. 3 (Cambridge: Cambridge University Press, 1998).

18. Putnam, *The Many Faces of Realism*, p. 17.

19. See, particularly, Hilary Putnam's John Dewey Lectures (1994), published as "Sense, Nonsense, and the Senses: An Inquiry into the Powers of the Human Mind," *Journal of Philosophy* 91 (1994): 461n36, 463n41. The entire text has been included, unaltered, in Hilary Putnam, *The Threefold Cord: Mind, Body, and World* (New York: Columbia University Press, 1999). Putnam has added some essays to this last volume, but they do not appear to alter the position advanced in the Dewey Lectures.

20. See Putnam, "Sense, Nonsense, and the Senses," p. 448 and note 8.

21. The key passage appears in Putnam, "Sense, Nonsense, and the Senses," p. 463n41. I judge that Putnam has not given up the rejection of "a sharp line between properties we 'discover' in the world and properties we 'project' onto the world"; but I cannot be sure that that now entails the symbiosis of the subjective and the objective. If the entailment holds, then Putnam remains "Hegelian" (or at least a somewhat Hegelian reader of Kant); but if it does not, then, I'm afraid, Putnam will have fallen back into Cartesian realism or into a somewhat Kantianized version of the Cartesian position (*sans* representationalism, of course). Putnam's recent book, *The Threefold Cord*, which adds the text of the Josiah Royce Lectures (1997) to the John Dewey Lectures, does not take up the unanswered question. We shall have to wait to see how Putnam plays his new hand.

22. Putnam, *The Many Faces of Realism*, p. 1.

23. Murphy, "Dewey's Epistemology and Metaphysics," pp. 219–221.

24. See John Herman Randall, Jr., "Dewey's Interpretation of the History of Philosophy," in *The Philosophy of John Dewey*.

25. R. W. Sleeper, *The Necessity of Pragmatism: John Dewey's Conception of Philosophy* (New Haven: Yale University Press, 1986), p. 161.

26. See John R. Shook, *Dewey's Empirical Theory of Knowledge and Reality* (Nashville: Vanderbilt University Press, 2000), p. 7. Shook does not pursue the relativistic issue further: it's very likely Dewey did not pursue the matter.

27. See, further, *American Philosophic Naturalism in the Twentieth Century,* ed. John Ryder (Amherst: Prometheus Books, 1994). Note Ryder's introduction.

28. See Donald Davidson, "A Coherence Theory of Truth and Knowledge," and Richard Rorty, "Pragmatism, Davidson and Truth," both in *Truth and Interpretation: Perspectives on the Philosophy of Donald Davidson,* ed. Ernest Lepore (Oxford: Basil Blackwell, 1986). Something of the labile nature of both Rorty's and Davidson's style of argument may be gleaned from W. V. Quine, "Let Me Accentuate the Positive," and Donald Davidson's "Afterthoughts, 1987."

29. See Jaegwon Kim, chap. 6 in *Philosophy of Mind* (Boulder: Westview Press, 1996), particularly pp. 147–148.

30. See my prologue, above, to this book.

31. John Dewey, "How Do Concepts Arise from Percepts?" in *The Early Works, 1882–1898,* ed. Jo Ann Boydston (Carbondale: Southern Illinois University Press, 1969), 3:144–145. This should be compared with Brandom, *Articulating Reasons,* pp. 5–11.

32. See W. V. Quine, *Pursuit of Truth,* rev. ed. (Cambridge: Harvard University Press, 1992). Note chap. 1.

33. See W. V. Quine, "Epistemology Naturalized," in *Ontological Relativity and Other Essays* (New York: Columbia University Press, 1969).

34. Dewey, *Experience and Nature,* p. 116.

35. Dewey, *Logic,* p. 104.

36. See Dewey, chap. 2 in *Experience and Nature,* particularly pp. 67–69.

37. Dewey, "Experience, Knowledge, and Value," pp. 533–534.

38. George Santayana, "Dewey's Naturalistic Metaphysics," in *The Philosophy of John Dewey,* p. 251. The passage cited above, which Dewey straightforwardly co-opts, appears in Santayana's text, p. 258n1.

39. Dewey, "Experience, Knowledge, and Value," p. 330.

40. Ibid., p. 331.

41. See McDowell, *Mind and World;* also, Putnam, "Sense, Nonsense, and the Senses."

42. John Dewey, "What Are Universals?" in *The Later Works, 1935–1937,* ed. Jo Ann Boydston (Carbondale: Southern Illinois University Press, 1987), 11:111; see also "Characteristics and Characters: Kinds and Classes," in vol. 11.

Chapter 5. Relativism, Pragmatism, and Realism

1. See Karl R. Popper, "Of Clouds and Clocks," in *Objective Knowledge: An Evolutionary Approach* (Oxford: Clarendon, 1972).

2. 2 See, for a sample, Ian Hacking, *The Social Construction of What?* (Cambridge: Harvard University Press, 1999), and Bruno Latour, *Pandora's Hope: Essays on the Reality of Science Studies* (Cambridge: Harvard University Press, 1999). In mentioning these accounts, I am not endorsing them or the views they serve. But I take the views they collect to be more serious as options than the analytic philosophy of science would be prepared to concede.

3. See Joseph Margolis, "Peirce's Fallibilism," *Transactions of the Charles S. Peirce Society* 84 (1998).

4. See chapter 4 above.

5. Myles Burnyeat, "Protagoras and Self-Refutation in Plato's Theaetetus," *Philosophical Review* 85 (1976).

6. Hilary Putnam, "Materialism and Relativism," in *Renewing Philosophy* (Cambridge: Harvard University Press, 1992), p. 76.

7. 7 See Paul K. Feyerabend, *Against Method: Outline of a Anarchistic Theory of Knowledge* (London: NLB, 1975).

8. 8 See sec. 5.448 (note 1) and 5.449 in *Collected Papers of Charles Sanders Peirce.*

9. See Donald Davidson, "On the Very Idea of a Conceptual Scheme" (1974), in *Inquiries into Truth and Interpretation* (Oxford: Clarendon, 1984).

10. The evidence is collected in Joseph Margolis, "Incommensurability Modestly Recovered," (paper presented at the conference, Incommensurability (and Related Matters), University of Hannover, Germany, June 9–16, 1999.

11. Hilary Putnam, "Wittgenstein on Reference and Relativism," in *Renewing Philosophy,* p. 177. When Putnam speaks of what "has often been pointed out," he is speaking of his own discussion in *Reason, Truth, and History* (Cambridge: Cambridge University Press, 1981), pp. 119–124, which confirms that his position has not changed and, in effect, supports Plato's attack.

12. Putnam, "Wittgenstein on Reference and Relativism," p. 176.

13. Ibid., p. 177.

14. Richard Rorty, "Solidarity or Objectivity?" in *Post-Analytic Philosophy,* ed. John Rajchman and Cornel West (New York: Columbia University Press, 1985), pp. 5–6; reprinted in Richard Rorty, *Philosophical Papers,* vol. 1 (Cambridge: Cambridge University Press, 1991).

15. Hilary Putnam, "Values, Facts and Cognition," in *Reason, Truth and History,* p. 216.

16. Rorty, "Solidarity or Objectivity?," p. 10.

17. See Richard Rorty, "Hilary Putnam and the Relativist Menace," in *Philosophical Papers,* vol. 3 (Cambridge: Cambridge University Press, 1998).

18. Rorty, "Solidarity or Objectivity?" pp. 12–13.

19. See Richard Rorty, "Self-Creating and Affiliation: Proust, Nietzsche, and Heideg-

ger," in *Contingency, Irony, and Solidarity* (Cambridge: Cambridge University Press, 1989).

20. Rorty, "Hilary Putnam and the Relativist Menace," p. 52.

21. Ibid., p. 45. See also Hilary Putnam, "Bernard Williams and the Absolute Conception of the World," in *Renewing Philosophy*.

22. Hilary Putnam, "Two Philosophical Perspectives," in *Reason, Truth and History*, p. 49.

23. See Joseph Margolis, *Historied Thought, Constructed World: A Conceptual Primer for the Turn of the Millennium* (Berkeley: University of California Press, 1995).

24. W. V. Quine, sec. 15 and 16 in *Word and Object* (Cambridge: MIT Press, 1960).

25. See Putnam, "Values, Facts, and Cognition."

26. Thomas S. Kuhn, sec. 10 in *The Structure of Scientific Revolutions*, rev. and enl. ed. (Chicago: University of Chicago Press, 1970).

27. See Michel Foucault, "Nietzsche, Genealogy, History," in *Language, Counter-Memory, Practice: Selected Essays and Interviews*, ed. Donald F. Bouchard, trans. Donald F. Bouchard and Sherry Simon (Ithaca: Cornell University Press, 1977).

28. Ludwig Wittgenstein, *Philosophical Investigations*, trans. G. E. M. Anscombe (Oxford: Basil Blackwell, 1953).

29. See Hans-Georg Gadamer, pt. 2, sec. 2 of *Truth and Method*, 2d rev. ed., trans. Joel Weinsheimer and Donald G. Marshall (New York: Continuum, 1989).

30. Richard Rorty, "Pragmatism, Davidson, and Truth," in *Truth and Interpretation: Perspectives on the Philosophy of Donald Davidson*, ed. Ernest Lepore (Oxford: Basil Blackwell, 1986), pp. 344–345.

31. To see the motivation of Davidson's argument you must compare three of his papers: "The Myth of the Subjective," in Donald Davidson, *Subjective, Intersubjective, Objective* (Oxford: Clarendon, 2001); "On the Very Idea of a Conceptual Scheme"; and "A Coherence Theory of Truth and Knowledge," in *Truth and Interpretation: Perspectives on the Philosophy of Donald Davidson*, ed. Ernest Lepore (Oxford: Basil Blackwell, 1986). See also C. I. Lewis, *Mind and the World Order* (New York: Scribner's, 1960), p. 38; cited by Davidson. The evidence regarding Davidson's treatment of relativism and incommensurabilism confirms that the principal analytic discussants of the entire realism issue in the interval from about 1970 to the end of the century (Putnam, Rorty, and Davidson) all fail to come to terms with relativism's challenge, in spite of the fact that Quine (and Nelson Goodman) as well as Kuhn and Feyerabend are attracted to one or another form of relativism. The issue of the "myth of the given"—hence, the fate of empiricism—has attracted new interest as a result of Rorty's and Brandom's attempt to recover Wilfrid Sellars as an important pragmatist (a matter touched on earlier in this book). It is worth mentioning that McDowell's recent discussion of the realism issue is motivated in good part by the wish to avoid *both* any empiricism that yields to the myth of the given (without yet abandoning empiricism) *and* any contemporary version of Cartesian realism no matter how attenuated (without yet abandoning realism). That is the lesson intended in John McDowell, *Mind and World* (Cambridge: Harvard University Press, 1996).

32. Kuhn, *Structure of Scientific Revolutions*, p. 126. See also Richard J. Bernstein, *Beyond Objectivism and Relativism: Science, Hermeneutics, and Praxis* (Philadelphia: University of Pennsylvania Press, 1983); and Putnam, "Two Philosophical Perspectives."

33. Views congenial to this notion may be sampled in Peter Galison, introduction to *Image and Logic: A Material Culture of Microphysics* (Chicago: University of Chicago Press, 1997); Ian Hacking, "Language, Truth and Reason," in *Rationality and Relativism*, ed. Martin Hollis and Steven Lukes (Cambridge: MIT Press, 1982); and, of course, Kuhn, sec. 10, *The Structure of Scientific Revolutions*.

34. For Goodman's theory, see Nelson Goodman, *Ways of Worldmaking* (Indianapolis: Hackett, 1978). For an extremely clear exposition of Goodman's thesis and the subsequent quarrels it provoked, see Hilary Putnam, "Irrealism and Deconstruction," in *Renewing Philosophy*.

35. Hilary Putnam, "Materialism and Relativism," in *Renewing Philosophy*, p. 71.

36. Hilary Putnam, *The Many Faces of Realism* (La Salle: Open Court, 1987), pp. 17–18.

37. Hilary Putnam, "Irrealism and Deconstruction," pp. 116–17. I have inserted a comma in square brackets before the clause beginning "even though the two schemes."

38. Ibid., p. 120; see *The Many Faces of Realism*, pp. 16–21.

39. See W. V. Quine, chap. 1 and 2 in *Theory of Truth*, rev. ed. (Cambridge: Harvard University Press, 1990); and sec. 15 and 16 in *Word and Object* (Cambridge: MIT Press, 1960).

40. See Margolis, "Incommensurability Modestly Recovered."

41. Putnam, "Irrealism and Deconstruction," p. 116.

42. Ibid., p. 110.

43. W. V. Quine's review of Goodman's *Ways of Worldmaking*, which presses the point, is not included in *Starmaking: Realism, Anti-Realism, and Irrealism*, ed. Peter J. McCormick (Cambridge: MIT Press, 1996), but it appeared in the *New York Review of Books*, 25 November 1978. I have not been able to find Davidson's comments (perhaps they were oral), but they are reported by Putnam in *Renewing Philosophy*, pp. 115–117. Putnam seems to read Davidson's paper, "On the Very Idea of a Conceptual Scheme" (1974), as if it were (in part) about an early incarnation of Goodman's thesis, though of course it is not mentioned there.

44. Nelson Goodman, *Of Mind and Other Matters* (Cambridge: Harvard University Press, 1984), pp. 52–53.

45. Ibid., p. 127.

46. See W. V. Quine, chap. 1 in *Pursuit of Truth*, rev. ed. (Cambridge: Harvard University Press, 1992).

47. See Quine, *Word and Object*, p. 73.

48. Putnam, "Irrealism and Deconstruction," p. 117.

49. Contrast Rorty, "Pragmatism, Davidson, and Truth."

50. See Putnam, "Wittgenstein on Reference and Relativism," pp. 174–176.

51. See Rorty, "Pragmatism, Davidson, and Truth."

52. See Bernstein, *Beyond Objectivism and Relativism*.

Index

Apel, Karl-Otto, 33

Bernstein, Richard:
  on pluralism and relativism, 90–92
  on Rorty, 89–92
Bloom, Harold, 87, 88
Brandom, Robert, 61, 103
Burnyeat, Miles, 136–138, 140, 156

"Cambridge changes" (Geach), 83
Cartesianism (Cartesian realism), 12–16, 38–
  39, 42
  and anti-Cartesian tradition, 39–42, 52–53
  Hegel on, 38–39, 45–46
Cavell, Stanley, 1–2
constructivism (constructive realism), 41–45

Davidson, Donald:
  as Cartesian, 15
  and causal theory of belief, 26–29, 30–31,
    34
  on Kuhn and Feyerabend, 147–148
  on naturalism (naturalizing), 16–18, 35
  on Putnam, 33–34
  on Quine, 21–22, 55–56
  on realism, 29, 33–34
  Rorty on, 16–18, 21, 25–27, 28, 54–58
  and Tarski, 28
  on truth, 19, 21, 26–30
Dennett, Daniel, 67–72
Derrida, Jacques, 94
Descartes, René, 41
Devitt, Michael, 33, 46, 111–112
Dewey, John, 1–2
  and constructive realism, 97–98, 102, 117
  as Darwinian, 98, 102, 112–114
  diverging from Peirce, 10
  and exchange with Santayana, 128–129
  and "experience" as category, 110–111, 112,
    114, 115–116, 129
  Experience and Nature, 110, 112, 115
  favoring James over Peirce, 116

Hegelian sympathies of, 110, 113–114, 118,
  129
and holism, 126–127
how to read, 110–115
and Idealism, 9–10, 110
and metaphysics of existence, 110–119, 122,
  123–125
and Peirce, on fallibilism, 134–135
on percepts and concepts, 125–126, 130
on "problematic [indeterminate] situation," 102, 110, 112–114, 116, 117
and Quine, on holism, 126–127
and response to Murphy, 112–114, 115–116
Dummett, Michael, 38, 46–47

"ethnocentric solidarity" (Rorty), 4, 100,
  103–104, 144–145

fallibilism, 133–136
Feyerabend, Paul, 78, 102–103, 106, 137, 140,
  147, 148, 152, 153
Fichte, J. G., 39
Fraser, Nancy, 64–67

Galileo, 73, 77, 148
Goodman, Nelson, 54–55, 151–156

Habermas, Jürgen, 3
Hegel, G. W. F.:
  not an idealist, 14, 43, 87
  Phenomenology, 13, 110
historicity:
  and Davidson on Kuhn and Feyerabend,
    102–103
  and incommensurability, 78
  neglected by pragmatists, 112, 122
holism:
  bearing of, on postmodernist strategy, 69–
    72
  Dewey and Quine compared on, 126–127
  Rorty on, 68–71, 76–77, 79–81
  Rorty on, and Secondness, 82–83